THE
GOVERNANCE
DISCOURSE

THE GOVERNANCE DISCOURSE

A Reader

edited by

BIDYUT CHAKRABARTY
and
MOHIT BHATTACHARYA

OXFORD
UNIVERSITY PRESS

OXFORD
UNIVERSITY PRESS

22 Workspace, 2nd Floor, 1/22 Asaf Ali Road, New Delhi 110002

Oxford University Press is a department of the University of Oxford. It furthers the University's objective of excellence in research, scholarship, and education by publishing worldwide in

Oxford   New York

Auckland   Cape Town   Dar es Salaam   Hong Kong   Karachi   Kuala Lumpur
Madrid   Melbourne   Mexico City   Nairobi   New Delhi   Shanghai   Taipei   Toronto

With offices in
Argentina   Austria   Brazil   Chile   Czech Republic   France   Greece   Guatemala
Hungary   Italy   Japan   Poland   Portugal   Singapore   South Korea   Switzerland
Thailand   Turkey   Ukraine   Vietnam

Oxford is a registered trademark of Oxford University Press
in the UK and in certain other countries

Published in India
by Oxford University Press, New Delhi

ISBN-13: 978-019-569664-6
ISBN-10: 019-569664-6

Typeset in Sabon by Le Studio Graphique, Gurgaon 122 001
Printed in India by Repro India Limited
Published by Oxford University Press
YMCA Library Building, Jai Singh Road, New Delhi 110 001

*This volume is dedicated
to our wives, Sanchita and Krishna
who always stood by us.*

Contents

PART I
CONCEPTUAL UNDERPINNING OF GOVERNANCE

Tables and Figures

TABLES

FIGURES

Preface

Governance is a much discussed and also most contentious concept in contemporary academic discourse for a variety of reasons. Given its uncritical endorsement of 'neo-liberal' political thrust, Governance is more than a mere theoretical shift in the domain of Public Administration. Conforming to an ideological agenda of the donors, the practitioners of governance seem to have reinvented the development discourse in an ethnocentric way. This is clearly 'neo-Taylorism' which seeks to provide 'a universal' solution to 'problems' irrespective of the socio-economic contexts. In this sense, Governance model appears to be 'nothing new'; instead, it can be safely defined as 'old wine in a new bottle'. Nonetheless, this has shaken the conceptual foundation of the hierarchical and centralized form of organization which in Weberian judgement was portrayed as the most rational form of public administration.

This compilation would not have been possible without the unstinted support of the contributors who have written for us. We are grateful to them. There are colleagues who have enriched the volume by giving their inputs. We put on record our appreciation for them. We are thankful to the anonymous readers of the manuscript. Their suggestions were very useful while revising the content of the volume. We are indebted to our students for their critical role in making this work seem worthwhile. We also owe a debt of gratitude to the participants of various workshops and seminars where we presented our views on Governance. Their critical intervention helped us unravel the complex dynamics of the phenomenon which is basically the practitioners' contribution to Public Administration. We also express our gratitude to the editors of the Oxford University Press who with their unflinching support made our task easier. Finally, we fondly acknowledge the significant contribution of our families without which it would not have been possible to concentrate on our academic pursuits.

BIDYUT CHAKRABARTY

MOHIT BHATTACHARYA

Publisher's Acknowledgements

The publisher acknowledges the following for permission to include articles/extract in this volume:

Indian Journal of Public Administration for Mohit Bhattacharya, 'Contextualizing Good Governance', XLIV (3), July–September 1998.

Macmillan India Ltd. for Subhash C. Bhatnagar, 'E-Government: Building a SMART Administration for India's States', in Stephen Howes, Ashok K. Lahiri, and Nicholas Stern (eds), *State-level Reforms in India: Towards More Effective Government*, New Delhi, 2003, pp. 256–66.

USAID-India for Vinod B. Annigeri, Lizann Prosser, Jack Reynolds, and Raghu Roy, *An Assessment of Public–Private Partnership Opportunities in India*, New Delhi, 2004.

Abbreviations

ADB	Asian Development Bank
BIFR	Board of Industrial and Financial Reconstruction
BOT	Build, Operate and Transfer
C2C	Citizen to Citizen
C2G	Citizen to Government
CAAI	Civil Aviation Authority of India
CARD	Computer-aided Administration of Registration Department
CBDT	Central Board of Direct Taxes
CCI	Controller of Capital Issues
CCI	Controller of Capital Issues
CDSL	Central Securities Depository Limited
CERC	Central Electricity Regulatory Commission
CONCOR	Container Corporation of India
CRC	Citizen Report Card
CWC	Central Warehousing Corporation
DAC	Development Assistance Committee
DCA	Department of Company Affairs
DFID	Department of Funding International Development
DoT	Department of Telecom
FAST	Fully-automated Services of Transport
GOI	Government of India
IAS	Indian Administrative Service
ICEDIS	Indian Customs Electronic Data Interchange System
ICS	Indian Civil Service
ICT	Information and Communication Technology
IFPS	Innovation in Family Planning Services
IFPS	Innovations in Family Planning Services
IRDA	Insurance Regulatory and Development Authority

IT	Information Technology
MDGs	Millennium Development Goals
MKSS	Mazdoor Kisan Shakti Sangathan
NGOs	Non-Governmental Organizations
NHPC	National Hydroelectric Power Corporation
NPM	New Public Management
NSCCL	National Securities Clearing Corporation of India
NTPC	National Thermal Power Corporation
OECD	Organization of Economic Cooperation and Development
PAC	Public Affairs Centre
PGCIL	Power Grid Corporation of India Limited
PIL	Public Interest Litigation
PMO	Prime Minister's Office
PPP	Public-Private-Partnership
RBI	Reserve Bank of India
RCH	Reproductive and Child Health
RTI	Right to Information
SAIs	Supreme Audit Institutions
SEBI	Securities and Exchange Board of India
SERC	State Electricity Regulatory Commission
SEWA	Society for Education, Welfare and Action
SHCIL	Stock Holding Corporation of India Limited
SMART	Simple, Moral, Accountable, Responsive and Transparent
TAMP	Tariff Authority for Major Ports
TDC	Transnational Discourse Communities
TDSAT	Telecom Dispute Settlement and Appellate Tribunal
TRAI	Telecom Regulatory Authority of India
TWINS	Twin Cities Network Services
UNDP	United Nations Development Programme
USAID	United of States Agency for International Development
VOICE	Vijaywada On-line Centre
WDR	World Development Report
WTO	World Trade Organization

1

Introduction

Bidyut Chakrabarty and Mohit Bhattacharya

Public administration as a discipline has historically been a confluence of many discourses because of the very eclectic nature of its subject of study covering a wide spectrum of organizations, actors, and behaviours. Government as the formally constituted action arm of the state to regulate society is emerging, at best, as a nodal centre in the midst of a host of definite and inchoate regulating agencies in society. The new emphasis in recent times on 'governance' (as against 'government') has thus to be judged in a wider historical-sociological perspective centred around the state-society relationship. Before dwelling on the concept of governance, there are three preliminary points to make: first, governance as a concept and as a paradigm is the practitioners' contribution to public administration in the sense that it can be traced to the World Bank's touting of the concept in the context of Sub-Saharan Africa. Failure to repay the World Bank loans, among other things, led to its formulation; second, the World Bank's definition of governance is very limited and is associated with administrative and managerial arrangements seeking to instill 'efficiency' in public administration; and, third, governance is political as well in the sense that it includes an insistence on 'competitive democracies' of the Western variety. In a way, governance is a well-defined administrative set-up that draws its sustenance from 'participatory democracy'. Its historical roots cannot be ignored, for governance was articulated when the state-led development paradigm, at the behest of the former Soviet Union, collapsed. In this long introduction, our aim is twofold: first, by contextualizing governance, we will trace its roots in the contemporary global socio-economic and political circumstances, especially in the aftermath of the disintegration of the Soviet Union. Second, since the conceptual roots of governance are located in the neo-liberal theoretical discourses, it is incumbent on the analysts to identify the significant intellectual inputs that informed the alternative to the state-directed development paradigm.

GOVERNANCE: DEFINITIONAL DIFFICULTIES[1]

There is no entry in the *International Encyclopedia of the Social Sciences* on 'Governance'. This is a clear evidence of the term's new entry in social scientific discussion. As the neo-liberal view started downplaying the state and overvaluing the 'market', and the trend was set to decentre the state from its monopoly status in social control, the idea of 'governance' gained in prominence, connoting a plurality of rules replacing the state's monopoly. The transition from 'government' theories to 'governance' theories implies a more processual view of politics and the state: the assumption of a hierarchical structure capable of panoptically overviewing society, somewhat implicit in a 'government' perspective, is abandoned. Frederickson thus argues that 'governance is used in place of public administration to distance the writer from the traditions of public administration and from criticism of bureaucracy'.[2] 'Governance'— like new public management (NPM)—defies simple definitions,[3] but indicates the emergence of a more plural political world, a declining role of the nation-state, and a more complex set of societal problems. The growing respectability of governance as a paradigm coincides with those societal changes sometimes theorized as a shift from government to governance in the context of globalization: from coordinated hierarchical structures and processes of societal steering to a network-based process of exchange and negotiation. Society is seen as a network of negotiating units, whose compositions vary, as do their positions in the power structure, over time and across subjects. From a 'government' perspective, a logical structure is presupposed: thus, in this line of thinking, it is possible to identify relatively clear distinctions and connections, implications and derivations between policies and programmes. Seen from a 'governance' point of view, the policy process must constantly negotiate logics and rationalities.

Perhaps the widest definition of governance is given in the Report of the Commission on Global Governance, entitled, *Our Global Neighbourhood*.

Governance is the sum of the many ways individuals and institutions, public and private, manage their common affairs. It is a continuing process through which conflicting or diverse interests may be accommodated and co-operative action may be taken. It includes formal institutions and regimes empowered to enforce compliance, as well as informal arrangements that people and institutions either have agreed to or perceive to be in their interest.

The late Göran Ohlin wrote in the context of international cooperation, 'what some may have in mind is a vague notion of something less than government but more than chaos—regimes of the kind that already exist for many purposes.' But, one could also interpret it as meaning more than government: including not only global, central, provincial, and local government, but also relations with civil society, the private profit-seeking sector, the market, the family, and the individual citizen, insofar as these relations bear on governing a society. That civil society and civic culture (as it has evolved through hundred years) are particularly important for good governance is shown for Italy in Robert D. Putnam's excellent book, *Making Democracy Work*.[4] He shows that what he calls civic 'norms and networks of social engagement' facilitate the working of democracy. The social capital of trust and reciprocity that is invested in norms and networks of civic life is seen as a vital factor of effective government and economic progress.[5] That the market is an important institution of governance does not need stressing nowadays. Cultural factors, too, determine, as well as are determined by, governance.

There are many views of 'good governance',[6] seeking to prove it to be a panacea for 'bad governance' in a changing world demanding more dynamic, result-oriented, transparent, and accountable government, on the one hand, and a networking of formal institutions of government, the market and the private sector, and civil society, on the other. As has been rightly cautioned, good governance has also its pitfalls, as there seems to be a tendency to 'depoliticize' government and bring in more technicism and expertise at the cost of citizens' age-old and hard fought democratic right to govern politically. The concern for good governance in international development arose out of a particular politics at a time when there were major arguments regarding the need to down-size the state. Throughout the 'governance' discourse, references are made to current approaches of improving governance that is calculated to reduce the act of governing to an apolitical and technical exercise. A key issue, however, is that governance is about power and politics. As various forms of confrontations and people's struggles for their 'rights' in various parts of the Third World clearly point out, for democracy to survive, 'governance' has to be seen as a project of continuous struggle for social construction, which includes issues of inclusion, equity, and equality.

Governance is a conceptual riddle. Semantically, it refers to government-run administration. Hence, it should be studied within the format of public administration. However, given its roots in the concern of the World Bank for recovering 'loans' given to the Sub-Saharan African states, it has become integrally linked with the 'neo-liberal' thrust in contemporary global politics. Defined as a specific mode of institutionalized administration, governance is rooted in what is generally known as 'a network society'. Drawn from a serious search for a new theoretical discourse, it also articulates a paradigm seeking to conceptualize 'the global society'. As Manuel Castells succinctly puts it,

[t]oward the end of the second millennium of the Christian era several events of historical significance transformed the social landscape of human life. A technological revolution, centred around information technologies, began to reshape, at accelerated pace, the national basis of society. Economies throughout the world have become globally interdependent, introducing a new form of relationship between economy, state and society, in a system of variable geometry. The collapse of Soviet statism, and the subsequent demise of the international communist movement has undermined for the time being, the historical challenge to capitalism... reduced the risk of nuclear holocaust and fundamentally altered global geopolitics. Capitalism itself has undergone a process of profound restructuring, characterized by greater flexibility in management....As a consequence of this general overhauling of the capitalist system, still underway, we have witnessed global integration of financial markets...the incorporation of valuable segments of economies throughout the world into an interdependent system working as unit in real time.[7]

In an interdependent world, governance is also projected as perhaps the most appropriate device to confront and mitigate the challenges of the network society. It is identified as 'a perception of the good society and the means to attain it: a construction of rationalities and a range of political technologies constantly negotiated among actors in a network'.[8] Governance is thus sought to be universalized as a condition of development. This also implies that failures in development efforts have largely been the result of 'poor governance', explained in 'politics-specific' terms and democratic processes that induce 'inefficiency'. The nature of political authorities in the network societies, however, cannot be taken for granted because of 'the processes and struggles that take place involving attempts at constructing new political authorities'.[9]

Governance generally means 'the act or process of governing, specifically authoritative direction and control'.[10] To be more precise, governance can be further defined as 'the political direction and control exercised over the actions of the members, citizens or inhabitants of communities, societies and states'.[11] While conceptualizing good governance in the context of debt-ridden Sub-Saharan Africa, the World Bank was guided by the awareness that,

efforts to create an enabling environment and to build capacities will be wasted if the political context is not favourable. Ultimately better governance requires political renewal. This means a concerted attack on corruption from the highest to lowest level. This can be done by setting good example, by strengthening accountability, by encouraging public debate, and by maturing a free press. It also means...fostering grassroots and non-governmental organizations such as farmers' associations, cooperatives and women's groups.[12]

Underlining the above goal, the World Bank defined good governance in the following manner:

Good governance is epitomized by predictable, open and enlightened policy making, a bureaucracy imbued with a professional ethos acting in furtherance of the public good, the rule of law, transparent processes and a strong civil society participating in public affairs.[13]

As evident, there are four key elements: (1) public sector management, (2) accountability, (3) legal framework for development, and (4) information and transparency. Improving governance would begin with an assessment of the institutional environment (accountability, rule of law, openness, and transparency) which determines the patrimonial profile of the country. Good governance is also contrasted with 'poor governance' which is held responsible for lack of sound development in Sub-Saharan African nation-states. Poor governance is, according to the World Bank formulation, 'charac- terized by arbitrary policy making, unaccountable bureaucracies, un-enforced or unjust legal systems, the abuse of executive power, a civil society unengaged in public life and widespread corruption'.[14] According to the World Bank, some of the main symptoms of poor governance are as follows:[15]

1. failure to make a clear separation between what is public and what is private, hence, a tendency to divert public resources for private gain;
2. failure to establish a predictable framework of law and government behaviour conducive to development, or arbitrariness in the application of rules and laws;
3. excessive rules, regulations, licensing requirements, and so forth, which impede the functioning of markets and encourage rent-seeking;
4. priorities inconsistent with development, resulting in misallocation of resources; and
5. excessively narrowly based or non-transparent decision making.

Underlying the litany of Africa's development problems is thus 'a crisis of governance'. The World Bank expressed concern for 'the lack of official accountability, the control of information and a failure to respect the rule of law'. Since governance is 'the conscious management of regime structures, with a view to enhancing the public realm' the World Bank thus insists on 'independence for the judiciary, scrupulous respect for the law and human rights at every level of government, transparent accountability of public monies, and independent public auditors responsible to a representative legislature, not to an executive'.[16] Such a distortion in public institutions appears to be unavoidable because they, superimposed 'on political and economic systems in which they had no roots, continued to lack accountability...but were captured by clan pressures, politicized by booty [resembling largely] the kinds of patrimonial states common in early Europe'.[17] The tragedy of 'mismanagement' and 'corruption' seems to have its roots in this colonial imposition of states and bureaucratic institutions, rather than 'their natural evolution through a process of citizen demands for accountability and ruler adjustments'.[18] Driven by the concern for efficient governance, another World Bank document, *Governance and Development* (1992),[19] defines governance as 'the manner in which power is exercised in the management of a country's economic and social resources for development'. That denotes, (1) the form of political regime (parliamentary or presidential, military or civilian, and authoritarian or democratic), (2) the process in which the power is exercised, and (3) the capacity of the government to design, formulate, and implement policies—to discharge the government functions. While the first aspect of governance falls outside the World Bank's ambit, the second and third aspects, as claimed by the World Bank, appear critical to the bank.[20] However on a closer look at the subsequent elaboration of the concept by other international agencies endorsing the World Bank agenda, it is clear that these three aspects remain integral to governance. Absorbing the primary thrust of the World Bank prescriptions, the UNDP, for instance, elaborates the concept by underlining that governance is 'the essence of economic, political and administrative authority to manage a country's affairs at all levels. It comprises mechanisms, processes and institutions through which citizens and groups articulate their interests, exercise their legal rights, meet their local obligations and mediate their differences'.[21] The nature of governance is thus contingent on the historical circumstances in which it is articulated simply because the relations between rulers and ruled differ in every country. As mentioned in a working paper of the World Bank,

history, custom, law, society and political economy affect the way in which the ruled in a country hold rulers to account for their performance, the relative openness of a socio-political system or an economy, and the degree of predictability in government decision-making and interaction with the public.[22]

Governance is also articulated by the UNDP in terms of the following major eight characteristics.[23] It is participatory, consensus oriented, accountable, transparent, responsive, effective and efficient, equitable and inclusive, and follows the rule of law. It assures that corruption is minimized, the views of minorities are taken into account, and that the voices of the most vulnerable in society are heard in decision making. It is also responsive to the present and future needs of society.

Governance is a complex phenomenon underlining the above characteristics which are elaborated as follows:

Participation

Participation by both men and women is the cornerstone of good governance. Participation could be either direct or through legitimate intermediate institutions or representatives. It is important to point out that representative democracy does not necessarily mean that the concerns of the most vulnerable in society would be taken into consideration in decision making. Participation needs to be informed and organized. This means freedom of association and expression, on the one hand, and an organized civil society, on the other hand.

Rule of Law

Good governance requires fair legal frameworks that are enforced impartially. It also requires full protection of human rights, particularly those of minorities. Impartial enforcement of laws requires an independent judiciary and an impartial and incorruptible police force.

Transparency

Transparency means that decisions taken and their enforcement are done in a manner that follows rules and regulations. It also means that information is freely available and directly accessible to those who will be affected by such decisions and their enforcement. It also means that enough information is provided and that it is provided in easily understandable forms and media.

Responsiveness

Good governance requires that institutions and processes try to serve all stakeholders within a reasonable time frame. By being responsive, governmental institutions gain 'legitimacy' in the public realm, which will automatically ensure their wider acceptance and, thus, effectiveness in governance. Apart from well-designed structural devices, responsiveness of public institutions can be meaningfully ascertained only if there is a serious civil society engagement in public affairs.

CONSENSUS ORIENTED

There are several actors and as many viewpoints in a given society. Good governance requires mediation of the different interests in society to reach a broad consensus on what is in the best interest of the whole community and how this can be achieved. It also requires a broad and long-term perspective on what is needed for sustainable human development and how to achieve the goals of such development. This can only result from an understanding of the historical, cultural, and social contexts of a given society or community.

EQUITY AND INCLUSIVENESS

A society's well-being depends on ensuring that all its members feel that they have a stake in it and do not feel excluded from mainstream society. This requires that all groups, but particularly the most vulnerable, have opportunities to improve or maintain their well-being.

EFFECTIVENESS AND EFFICIENCY

Good governance means that processes and institutions produce results that meet the needs of society, while making the best use of resources at their disposal. The concept of efficiency in the context of good governance also covers the sustainable use of natural resources and protection of the environment.

ACCOUNTABILITY

Accountability is a key requirement of good governance. Not only governmental institutions but also the private sector and civil society organizations must be accountable to the public and to their institutional stakeholders. Who is accountable to whom varies depending on whether decisions or actions taken are internal or external to an organization or institution. In general, an organization or an institution is accountable to those who will be affected by its decisions or actions. Accountability cannot be enforced without transparency and the rule of law.[24]

STRATEGIC VISION

Leaders and the public have a broad and long-term perspective on good governance and human development, along with a sense of what is needed for such development. There is also an understanding of the historical, cultural, and social complexities in which that perspective is grounded.[25]

Governance is thus a checklist of criteria of managing public affairs. As Lewis T. Preston, the World Bank President, categorically stated in his foreword to *Governance and Development* (1992),

[g]ood governance is an essential complement to sound economic policies. Efficient and accountable management by the public sector and a predictable and transparent policy framework are critical to the efficiency of markets and governments, and hence to economic development.[26]

Broadly speaking, good governance is conceptually three-dimensional. First, it refers to certain espoused principles of public administration, namely, accountability, transparency, and participation. Second, it dwells also on the processes in which political power is articulated and exercised. The process involves a complex interplay among the prevalent values, policies, and institutions that are critical to making and implementing decisions for the society in question. Governance also recognizes the importance of interactions between state, market, and civil society. Third, successful application of governance, as both principles and processes, is contingent on the regulatory capacity of the state. While control without good governance is oppressive, good governance without the capacity to apply them is an empty slogan. A perusal of these features suggests that governance is not a magical formula. Instead, it seeks to articulate a device to improve governmental functioning in areas where government is apparently minimal and is largely appropriated by 'partisan' interests where it exists. Hence it is stated that,

Governance is a continuum, and not necessarily unidirectional, it does not automatically improve over time. It is a plant that needs constant tending. Citizens need to demand good governance. Their ability to do so is enhanced by literacy, education and employment opportunities. Government needs to prove responsive to those demands....Change occurs sometimes in response to external or internal threats. It also occurs through pressures from different interest groups, some of which may be in the form of populist demands. Although lenders and aid agencies and other outsiders can contribute resources and ideas to improve governance, for change to be effective it must be rooted firmly in the societies concerned and cannot be imposed from outside.[27]

A careful reading of the World Bank formula suggests the following checklist of requirements of the new governance paradigm:

1. a recommended shift in general emphasis from policy to management, with administrators becoming fully cost-conscious in every action they take and before making decisions;
2. clusters rather than pyramids as the preferred model for the design of administrative systems (for example, autonomous agencies form liaison with major ministries as equal partners in various governmental projects);
3. in place of planning and hierarchical execution of decisions, a dichotomy between core policy activities and adaptive operational services;
4. a process-oriented administration gives way to an output-oriented administration (hence the insistence on performance indicators, evaluations, and performance-related pay and quality improvement);
5. flexible provision of individualized products instead of collective provision (the customer replaces the citizen, and 'the production line' of public administration is broken down into individual pieces for contracting-out or privatization);
6. an emphasis on cost-cutting rather than spending (the modern administrator's motto is value for money, that is, to do more and better with less or the same); and
7. the purpose of ownership is seen as efficient management rather than possession (budgeting in terms of simple input/output quantities is replaced by 'accrual' accounting, and all public services are considered for privatization, if their commercial viability may be sustained at less cost in the private sector).[28]

As evident, there is no standard recipe for good governance except (1) respect for rule of law—it is the duty of civil society to ensure that the rule of law is maintained and protected, (2) special care for the disadvantaged and weak, (3) tolerance and broad-mindedness to embrace unity and diversity—values of multiculturalism, and (4) respect for institutions upholding the spirit of democracy, primarily procedural democracy.

To sum up the discussion on the definition of good governance, one can safely make the following points: governance is a conceptual approach (1) concerning 'big questions' of a 'constitutional' nature that establish rules of political conduct; (2) involving creative intervention by political actors to change structures that inhibit expression of human potential; (3) emphasizing the nature of interactions between state and social actors and among social actors themselves; and (4) referring to particular types of relationships among political actors which are socially sanctioned rather than arbitrary.[29] Taking all these features together, governance refers to 'the traditions, institutions and processes that determine how power is exercised, how citizens are given a voice and how decisions are made on issues of public concern'.[30] Governance is thus inherently 'political' since it involves 'bargaining and compromise, winners and losers, among actors with different interests and resources'.[31] Thus, governance is also a platform for interactions between the stakeholders and government, which is always frictional owing to, largely, obvious incompatibility of interests among them. Informed by this concern, governance is also defined as 'engaged governance' whereby engagement between government and civil society is formally recognized. The primary focus is on the policy cycle of the government within a value-driven governance system. Drawn from the UNDP description of governance as 'processes' involving civil society institutions, engaged governance is a serious theoretical formulation underlining how authority is exercised, and what mechanisms and processes are seen to be legitimate from the point of view of the stakeholders. What is striking in this conceptualization is the endeavour to respond to some of the major normative questions that relate to, respectively, questions round the distribution and the exercise of power and the empowerment of citizens, broadly defined as participants in governance lexicon.[32] Governance is, thus, integral to the World Bank rhetoric and lending policies toward the Third World, addressing 'not only issues of political legitimacy and democracy, but also the need for administrative efficiency by means of marketization and competition'.[33] Drawn from the World Bank concern, the Development Assistance Committee (DAC) of the Organization of Economic Cooperation and Development (OECD) thus underlines,

the concept of 'governance' is complex. The term is used...in accordance with a World Bank definition, to denote the use of political authority and exercise of control in society in relation to management of its resources for social and economic development. The broad definition encompasses the role of public authority in establishing the environment in which economic operators function and in determining the distribution of benefits as well as the nature of relationship between the ruler and the ruled.[34]

THE CONTEXT OF 'GOVERNANCE'

'Governance' as a model of public administration cannot be understood without reference to the context in which it has been conceptualized. There is no doubt that 'globalization' provides significant inputs to its epistemological articulation. The phenomenon of 'globalization' is a much talked about theme today. Enthusiasts look on it as creating for humanity an almost borderless human existence with traditional sovereign states melting away in a fast-growing web of interconnectedness. Pessimists perceive the evolving situation as creating a grossly unequal international states system with massive gainers on one side—particularly the Western developed nations—in a historically structured uneven economic playing field, and miserable losers on the other—especially the 'developing countries' (the Third World, so to say), which had embarked upon a long-drawn-out and complex process of nation building and speedy socio-economic reconstruction after coming out of a long era of exploitative colonial rule. Drawing on the bitter experiences of many Third World countries, apprehensions have been expressed in some quarters that 'globalization' would, in reality, mean pernicious control over economy, polity, and culture by powerful multinationals aided and abetted by irresponsible domestic elites—the compradors, so to say. Thus, surrounding 'globalization', the central point that is being raised is: is it going to be an unalloyed promise of prosperity for everybody, or, is it going to bring in its trail a pathological process of 'recolonization' whereby the Third World would again be reverted to the old historical process of subjugation to the 'First World's politico-economic hegemony'.

Against this mixed backdrop of expectations and suspicions, 'globalization' needs to be understood not as much in terms of a dreamy-eyed philosophy as in its being a concrete managerial-administrative issue, with the state being enmeshed willy-nilly in a network of complex relationships. In this connection, the detailed observations of Guido Bertulucci, Director of the Division for Public Economics and Public Administration, DESA (United Nations) are worth quoting:

The functions and role of the State have been transformed substantially. The general configuration of its responsibilities has changed and this has introduced important modifications both in the policy arena and in the State's requirements for high-level skills, qualitatively and quantitatively.... A parallel shift has moved the State's centre of gravity and with it the locus of power. Decentralization, debureaucratization and deregulation are adding to the importance not only of local government, but also of non-state actors on whom significant functions are devolved or outsourced....Increasingly, the State is called upon to act as 'linking pin' of processes of planning, consultation, negotiation and decision-making involving diverse actors, State and non-state, at different levels of governance. The State is the hub of activities connecting multiple partners and stakeholders from very varied fields, regions, cultures, occupations, professions and interests.

Yet, the state is the first casualty. In the 1999 Seattle meeting of the WTO, the state that drew its strength from the 1648 Westphalia Treaty seems to have lost its credibility, because, as Bertulucci argues,

[e]xperience suggests that one of the main causes of the crises plaguing developing countries and the inability of some of them to integrate in the world economy is state capacity deficit. Globalization is certainly presenting many opportunities, including foreign direct investment, trade, access to information technology; however, only countries that have in place an effective public administration, solid political and economic institutions, adequate social policies and a committed leadership can ensure that all sectors of society benefit from greater integration into the world economy.

In order to make full use of the opportunities provided by globalization, as Bertulucci observes, developing countries need, among other things, to reinvest in their public sector and enhance their capacity for policy analysis, formulation, and implementation. Hence, what countries need most in order to enable people to enjoy the benefits of globalization is to focus on strengthening their institutions, developing human resources capacity, and achieving technological adequacy. This alone can enable them to capture the economic gains that participation in globalization may bring and, at the same time, help them to mitigate globalization's social costs.

GOVERNANCE: A NEW PERSPECTIVE IN PUBLIC ADMINISTRATION

As a dynamic discipline responsive to contextual and environmental factors, public administration has been shifting its core concerns in recent times. Shedding the original overreliance of the subject on bureaucratic rationality, with its accompanying syndromes of centrality and virtual eclipse of 'politics', there has been a steady search for innovative architectural designs of government. Decentralization, legislative oversight, privatization, and direct citizens' involvement emerged as alternative ways of managing public affairs. The neo-liberal thrust of the late 1980s posited the market and the private sector as a state-challenging philosophy. This was the moment of the birth of the new public management movement resurrecting, virtually, the old Taylorian private management philosophy as a counterweight to Weberian bureaucracy. Next came in succession the 'governance' paradigm replacing, as it were, the traditional 'government' focus in administering public affairs. Tinged by the self-propagated neo-liberalist ideology, the governance discourse ushered in the concept of plurality of actors solving problems of collective societal living. Other additionalities have been posed as being qualitative aspects of public management such as openness and transparency, responsiveness and accountability, and the rule of law and respect for human rights.

In these 'reinventing government' exercises, the procedural and institutional aspects of government seem to have been subordinated to concerns about 'results' and 'performance' at any cost. There has been, thus, a clear trend toward depoliticization and technicization of public administration. The new public philosophy seems to be unknowingly throwing the baby with the bath water. Productivity, performance, results, efficiency, and effectiveness—these buzzwords were being parroted without much concern for the canons of democratic governance. There has been, thus, a distinct trend toward distancing public management from the public. The reactions to these developments have been many and diverse. One major criticism

has been that the 'publicness' of public administration seems to have
fallen on the wayside. Another allied comment has been that the
anchor concept of 'public accountability' in public management
seems to be in jeopardy. Still another argument has been that the
new management cult has been eroding the legitimacy of the state
by instigating passive client-citizenship and alienating the poor and
marginalized sections of society.

Depending on the specific perspective taken, the theme of
globalization, along with its varied ramifications, has been the subject
of conflicting interpretations. Economists and international trade
experts have been adopting their own disciplinary angles. Political
scientists and sociologists have taken their respective viewpoints.
Public administration has been, basically, an inward looking
discipline concerned with the management of a country's domestic
public affairs. Very recently, it has woken up to the need of focusing
on the pulls and pressures of the on-going processes of globalization
and their impact on domestic administrative management. Since then,
the search has been on to 'reinvent' or 'reposition' the discipline in
the context of a newly emergent world order. Public administration,
thus, now represents 'a decisive move away from direct provision
by government agencies and their employees—the standard "bureau
model" of the past'.[35]

Traditionally, public administration has been concerned with
the policies and actions of a country's formal governmental
machineries, including their organizational structures, decisional
processes and behavioural dimensions. Globalization, as it is being
currently perceived, has considerable implications for the management of a country's public affairs contextually as well as substantively. To revert to Bertulucci's significant comments, globalization
that involves greater integration of a country into the world economy
demands well-designed state capacity building. The state has to
emerge in a new 'linking-pin' role with enhanced capacity to engage
in strategic planning, negotiations, and consultations with varied
actors. To reap the full benefit of economic gains and to reduce the
likely social costs of globalization, there is the urgent need to
strengthen appropriate institutions (for example, the bureaucracy
and especially the policy-level leadership, decentralized local
governance system, etc.), develop human resources, and update

technological capacity. The following table, showing the changing perspectives in public administration, is illustrative here.

TABLE 1.1 Changing Perspectives in Public Administration
(from traditional public administration to governance)

Traditional Public Administration	New Public Management	Governance
Bureaucracy (state-centric)	Neo-liberal, downsizing, state vs. market, productivity vs. efficiency	Multiple actors, ethical concerns, responsiveness, accountability, transparency

The purpose of the present discussion is to clearly bring out these implications by placing public administration within the framework of contemporary globalization process and discourse. There is almost a universal recognition today of the urgent need for a realignment of a country's public administrative system, but the direction and contents of reform are far from clear, as is evident in the following argument, made by the UNDP while specifying the aim of governance:

The pressures of globalization have focused more attention onto the public sector. While globalization could serve to integrate people, it has demonstrated a capacity to marginalize many. To combat this requires governance approaches that embrace transparency, accountability and stakeholder participation in policy debates, as well as a government that uses its resources efficiently to allow its citizens to compete in a global market, and to reduce the gap between the poorest and richest inhabitants of the world. Globalization not only increases the need for strong international and regional venues for dialogue, global policy-making and enforcement of international agreements and regulations, but also enhances the pressures for strong national governments, competent to integrate and negotiate in a global environment, and capable to stand up to global forces that neglect the particular claims and challenges of developing countries, in particular the Least Developed ones.[36]

Special emphasis, thus, needs to be laid on the perceived impact as well as actual consequences of globalization on the public administration system of Third World countries. More precisely, the discussion focuses on five major interconnected aspects of the core theme:

1. Meaning of 'globalization' and the present status of 'globalization' discourse.
2. Implications of 'globalization' for traditional public administration as an operative system in a country situation.
3. Need for repositioning the discipline of public administration in the face of 'globalization' discourse.
4. Exploring the special kind of relationship, if any, between 'globalization' and development administration in view of the fact that the developing countries have been pursuing their 'development' programmes for the last five decades or so.
5. Implications of globalization for administrative 'ethics', in general, and for 'development ethics', in particular.

HISTORICAL ROOTS OF GOVERNANCE

Historical circumstances appear to have favoured the articulation of governance as a mode of public administration. To be precise, governance is conceptualized in a historical context supporting 'the decline, if not end, of authority'. In OECD formulations, four sets of historical developments seem to have influenced these profound shifts in governance: The first is the impact of struggles for 'greater democracy and competitive markets'. The second set is linked with the ways in which 'changes in economic productivity and material wealth alter both the aims and methods of governance'. The third set of forces relate to demands for reforming the well-entrenched and excessively rule-bound system of administration. Finally, the fourth set is about managerial innovations and their application to transform 'the institutional design and organizational structure' of administrative operation.[37] The search for new conceptualization had an antecedent also in the collapse of the Soviet Union where 'alternative management practices', grounded in Marxism-Leninism, were articulated and also successfully executed. Within the developed capitalist countries, almost simultaneously, there was the rise of strong anti-bureaucratic and anti-state criticism directed against what came to be called 'government overload' as a consequence of 'welfare backlash'. The state, it was alleged, has over the years taken upon itself a large array of activities that have inflated its budgetary and financial commitments and that have led to the 'overgrowth' of bureaucracy. The battle cry was to 'downsize' government and allow more free play to the market and civil society—giving rise to the new ideology of 'neo-liberalism'.

Following the onset of globalization, the traditional bureaucratic model appears to have lost its significance, presumably because of growing importance of the non-state actors in administration. The instrumental view of administration does not, therefore, appear to be tenable for reasons connected with 'the pluralization of state'. Given the increasing role of transnational forces even in domestic administration, the state-centred theories of bureaucracy seem to be inadequate in addressing the radical metamorphosis of public administration both in the developed and in the developing countries. One can, thus, safely argue that while the twentieth century was the age of organization where bureaucracy symbolized the core values of public administration, the twenty-first century has ushered in an era of 'network-based organization' drawn from neo-liberal values.

Government is being 'reinvented' not only structurally but also ideologically in an environment where neo-liberal values seem to have triumphed. The state retreats and the government withdraws from areas that traditionally remained their domain. Globalization has led to a 'marriage' between corporate discipline and entrepreneurial spirit, with the government discarding its traditional image of 'a doer'. Seeking to accommodate 'the market impulse', the government has become 'an enabler'. Globalization, thus, restricts the national governments and limits its policy options. A new situation has emerged, and the governmental functions are redefined within the neo-conservative theoretical parameters. The corporate state has become a reality resulting in an obvious shrinkage of the traditional state system. The state is increasingly being guided by neo-liberal values endorsing globalization of capital. Public administration is now 'governance', which is nothing but checklists of certain activities designed both to stabilize and to consolidate neo-liberalism. The distinction between public and private administration is no longer critical in conceptualizing public administration. Citizens are customers, and those involved in public administration are functionaries seeking to approximate the 'corporate' culture.

Accountability in public bureaucracy is ascertained not only internally but also through various external agencies, including citizen's charter.

Riding piggyback on globalization, the structural adjustment programme led to economic reforms in the developing countries that largely 'delegitimized' the role of 'the hegemonic state'. Also, the conditional loans to developing countries by transnational agencies make them dependent on global capital. As was emphasized in the 1989 World Bank report, to be eligible for financial assistance from the World Bank, countries need to recast their socio-economic and political goals in accordance with the World Bank prescriptions. The report thus insists that the countries

that had adopted a sound medium-term economic policy framework would be eligible for Bank support. Support would be decided on a case-to-case basis, taking into account the strength of the medium-term adjustment program (sic) the severity of the debt burden, the scope for voluntary market-based operations, the medium-term financing plan, and the potential benefits from Bank support, particularly for investment and growth.[38]

In return for a new wave of loans from various international agencies, including the World Bank, several postcolonial states adopted structural adjustment programmes that were a package of measures suggested by the World Bank and other donors. The aim of adjustment was to provide an effective alternative to 'the dominant postwar, state-led development paradigm...by promoting open and free competitive market economies, supervised by minimal states'.[39] Two processes seem to work in the structural adjustment programme: on the one hand, the concerned economy is sought to be stabilized by 'immediate devaluation' and 'drastic public expenditure cuts'. This is accompanied, on the other, by a process of adjustment that seeks to 'transform the economic structure and institutions through varying doses of deregulation, privatization, slimming down of allegedly oversized public bureaucracies, reducing subsidies and encouraging realistic prices to emerge as a stimulus to greater efficiency and productivity, especially for export'.[40]

There appears to be a vicious circle from which there is no escape for the developing countries, presumably because the alternative ideological power centres are too weak to be effective partners in sustaining the drive for development. Furthermore, the drive towards 'depoliticizing development' systematically obscures 'power', 'class', and 'politics'. Critical to development are activities around 'civil society'—that, by implication, identifies development as a mere techno-economic effort which takes place outside the political arena. This is an argument that clearly undermines the role of ideology in development, especially in the developing countries where public administration is critically 'partisan' for historical reasons.

THEORETICAL ROOTS OF GOVERNANCE

Conceptually, governance is linked with the ideological triumph of neo-liberalism. The theoretical roots of governance are located in 'neo-liberal' economic theories, especially 'new right ideology'. Government is 'redefined' in market paradigms by redrawing boundaries of public administration. In the new dispensation, governance is an interface between state, market, and civil society. The 'governance' discourse has its origin in, (1) the new thrust toward neo-liberalist restraint on the 'state' along with the positing of 'market' as a competing social authority and bringing in 'civil society' as a provider of local-level social services, (2) the international funding authorities' (particularly, the World Bank) concern for more accountable, transparent, open and participative rule, and (3) the newly emergent 'globalization' trend—a socio-economic integration of the world propelled by economic, technological, and political considerations.

The new right ideology seeks to redefine public administration by championing the cause of the free market and calls for a significant reduction in the size and role of government in society. Although the advocacy has generally been in favour of a greater role for the market and a lesser role for the state, the new right had within it a neo-liberal wing and neo-conservative wing. The former has been primarily concerned with the promotion of individual liberty and the latter with the restoration of traditional values.

Four main schools of new right thought are Chicago, Austrian, public choice, and supply side. The supply side approach needs separate treatment. All that can be noted in our context is that it is based on neo-classical micro-economic theory, and its main perspective for growth is reduction in interest rate.

As the chief critic of Keynesian economic ideas that dominated the postwar era until the mid-1970s, Milton Friedman has been the most prominent of the Chicago school of economists. Their main argument has been that empirical analysis of the consequences of government actions clearly establishes that the market is more effective than government in achieving social goals. That this argument had a major impact can be understood from his conceptualization of the legitimate role of government, which is very much based on the doctrine of 'limited government' propounded in the past by Adam Smith.

Friedman identified four areas of legitimate government activity: protection of individuals from external coercion; administration of justice; provision of public goods and settling of some problems arising from neighbourhood effects; and protection of the innocent such as the insane and children. He was aware of the fact that special interests requiring government intervention in their favour exerted excessive influence on the political process. Money supply which, in his view, was the cause of inflation could be solved by non-discretionary monetary rules. He was attracted to the idea of constitutional reform to provide limited government.

The Austrian school, represented by, among others, Carl Manger, Friedrich Hayek, and Ludurig Von Mises, has also been free-market-oriented, taking a more principled stand in favour of the doctrine of laissez-faire. Three distinguishing features of Austrian economics are: (1) social science is the study of purposeful human action; (2) only individuals are the appropriate sources of study (methodological individualism); and (3) value is in the eye of the beholder (subjective theory of value). We will be focusing on the thoughts of Hayek who was the most influential Austrian with his wide-ranging contribution to political philosophy and scientific methodology. Relevant writings of Hayek, for our limited purpose, are *The Road to Serfdom* (1994), *The Fatal Illusion* (1989), *Law, Legislation and Liberty* (1973), and *The Constitution of Liberty* (1960).

The major themes that recur in his thought are: (1) society is a spontaneous order; as evolved, spontaneous order is to be preferred to a planned society; (2) liberty has instrumental value because it makes best use of widely dispersed knowledge and provides for the unpredictable growth of knowledge, allowing individuals to experiment with new ideas and techniques; (3) socialism is undemocratic and impossible. What will be produced is determined by a few and not by the mass of consumers. There is no agreed common purpose in society. The recognition of private property or the rules of contract exist to enable individuals to pursue their own goals and not to reach common goals. As regards planning, socialist planning has no way of predicting consumer demand without the role of prices—the planner does not know what to produce and at what cost; and (4) one of Hayek's controversial arguments was that the concept of social justice is meaningless. As a principle of state action, social or distributive justice, requires agreement on 'who deserves what' and existence of sufficient power in the hands of the state to determine it. It is implied that some concept of 'merit' should be the determinant of the distribution of goods and income. It is difficult to have 'unanimity' on this question because everyone has a different view on merit. In a free society, there is no consensus on what would be the correct distribution of goods.

Again, when the state assumes the role of a decider—to determine who gets what—whoever controls the state would determine what they thought people deserved. Income-distribution policy would be determined not by the ability to satisfy consumers but by political influence. In this situation, government becomes a scramble between the interest groups for influence over the political allocation of income. In Hayek's view, justice is procedural. Just rules of income is critical to societal stability. Since these rules are ingrained in a 'free society', the government has no 'pressing reasons' to intervene insofar as the distribution of income among citizens is concerned.

Hayek became interested in the establishment of a principle of a liberal constitution in which the role of government 'is to create a framework within which individuals and groups can pursue their respective ends, and sometimes to use its coercive power of raising revenue to provide services for which for one reason or another the market cannot supply'. Elected politicians, in his views, have increasingly come under the influence of interest groups who use political power for their own narrow purposes. Hayek was, therefore, in search of principles that would ensure that the state's activities did not go beyond certain limits.

We have now set the stage for direct entry into the 'public choice' debate. The thesis of limited government reaches its apogee in the public choice model, which is a theory of politics, also known as 'the economics of politics'. Political behaviour is sought to be explained and predicted on the assumption that political actors are 'utility maximizers', who seek to promote their self-interests. The public choice subset of rational choice theory has played a strategic role in supporting the privatization movement and the application of market rationality in government's decision making processes. This is a stark contrast to theories that view politics as 'the pursuit of public interests'. Most public choice writers converge on the main point that government has grown much larger than what the general public would wish it to be, because it has grown to meet the preferences of politicians, bureaucrats, and interest groups.

The Virginia school of public choice started an intellectual tirade against the nature of politics and bureaucracy. James Buchanan drew attention to the 'misfortunes of modern political life' in the welfare state. In his view, 'the basic structure of property rights is now threatened more seriously than at any period during the two-century history of the United States'. Again, as he argues, 'government failure against standard efficiency norms may be demonstrated analytically and empirically, but I see no basis for the faith that such demonstration will magically produce institutional reform. I come back to constitutional revolution as the only attractive alternative to the scenario that we have seen but to act out'. In an almost similar vein, Gordon Tullock underlines that 'we are saddled with a large and basically inefficient bureaucracy. Efficiency in this sector could, looking at the matter economically, raise our national income and improve our rate of growth. Politically, it could both increase the degree of control over citizens, *qua* voters and thus restrict his freedom'. The Virginia school has, thus, had its unique interpretation of advanced societies with liberal democratic constitutions, and their thrust is toward the rejection of the welfare state. In this view, the public sector has been suffering from inherent systemic failure in terms of policy making and implementation, and political failure is being more overtly felt than market failure.

The public choice, *prima facie*, emerges almost as a science of political failure—a right-wing perspective on the public sector. In his authoritative interpretation, Mueller has sought to present an apparently value-neutral definition: 'Public Choice can be defined as the economics of non-market decision making or simply the application of Economics to Political Science. The subject matter of public choice is the same as that of Political Science: the theory of state, voting rules, voter behaviour, party politics, the bureaucracy, and so on. The methodology of public choice is that of economics however'. The Mueller formulation seems ethically neutral and does not imply that public choice is the science of the public sector as social misfortune.

The Virginian version of the public choice approach has two underlying epistemological commitments: (1) public sector actors behave as if they maximize their own interests, and (2) all social entities are fundamentally sets of individual actors. As Buchanan writes, 'the basic units are choosing units, acting, behaving persons rather than organic units such as parties, provinces, or nations', and again, 'persons seek to maximize their own utilities, and...their own narrowly defined economic well-being is an important component of these utilities'.

Thus, the doctrine of methodological individualism and model of self-interest-maximizing behaviour together seek to explain the structure of the public sector and the motivation of public action. Premised on these two fundamental assumptions, the Virginian version of the public choice approach represents a positive theory about the public sector. Additionally, in this version, there is a normative theory of the state which is a straightforward right-wing ideology of a neo-liberal kind. The foundation of this normative approach was laid by the elements of a state theory proposed by Wicksell in 1896. Considerations of efficiency in taxation were at the heart of the Wicksellian state theory, which pleaded strongly for a *quid pro quo* rule on an individual basis. The only mechanism that will guarantee optimal taxation for public goods provision is the unanimity rule or the individual veto principle in a legislative context.

Following the Wicksellian principles governing decision making, Buchanan has derived two normative rules which are, in his views, constitutive of the public choice approach: (1) politics as exchange, and (2) economic constitutionalism or contractarianism as the basis of public policy making. The first normative rule—politics as exchange—means that every public policy must be based on the consent of all citizens. It is the application of the Wicksellian unanimity rule to politics. To quote Buchanan, 'in the absence of individual interest, there is no interest [and individuals are] motivated by self-interests'.[41] By definition, therefore, politics does not entertain any idea of the common good. Just policies are those that meet with unanimous consent from individual citizens. The second normative principle of constitutional economics is a mechanism for the expression of political criticism. As Buchanan writes, 'existing constitutions or structure of rules, are the subject of critical scrutiny. The conjectural question becomes: could these rules have emerged from agreement by participants in an authentic constitutional convention?' In the absence of any system of constitutional revisions on a permanent basis, it is a matter of conjecture as to what would be acceptable to the citizens, had they been in a constitutional setting. The public choice approach forbids all evaluative exercises (in respect of public policies) except those based on the unanimity principle. Again, in Buchanan's language, 'there is no criterion through which policy may be directly evaluated. An indirect evaluation may be based on some measure of the degree to which the political process facilitates the translation of expressed individual preferences into observed political outcomes. The focus of evaluative attention becomes the process itself, as contrasted with end-state or outcome patterns'.

AN ALTERNATIVE MODEL

Basically what the public choice proponents seek to do is to point out inconsistencies in the classical model of representative democracy and to suggest an alternative basis for decision making in government or public choice. Peter Self, while explaining the shift in public choice theory, points out that the Buchanan-Tullock combination mounted a frontal attack on any idealist theory of politics. On the assumption of political individualism or egoism of an instrumentally rational type, the conventional myths surrounding the public spiritedness of bureaucrats and politicians were explained, and 'we were back in Bentham's world of conflicting egoisms but without Bentham's assumption that democracy would solve the problem'. Tracing the evolution of public choice thought, Peter Self observes that the writings of the public choice school were also relatively mild and optimistic at first. Anthony Downs' path-breaking work— *An Economic Theory of Democracy*[42] (1957)—reached the fairly comfortable conclusion that there were sound reasons of rational egoism for voters to trust their representatives with considerable discretion, and for parties to satisfy the median preferences of voters. In *The Calculus of Consent*, Buchanan and Tullock provide a design of an ideal constitution which could establish a satisfactory trade-off between the rational individual requirements for public goods and the injury to his interests from state coercion. 'The collectivization of an activity', they argue, 'will be supported by the utility-maximizing individual when he expects the interdependence costs of this collectively organized activity...to lie below (to lie above) those involved in the private voluntary organization of the activity'.[43] According to this formulation, 'decision making costs' are what the self-seeking individuals willingly agree to incur in exchange of what he/she derives while participating in the decision-making process. However, 'the relative cost of collective organization of activity can be expected to be much greater in a community lacking some basic consensus among its members on fundamental values'.[44] Two important points emerge out of this calculus of consent: (1) decision-making costs are proportionate to individuals' satisfaction, and (2) the cost is less if there is a consensus among them on some basic values of democratic governance. Instead of interpreting 'the calculus of consent', in pure technical terms, Buchanan and Tullock seem to have underlined simultaneously the importance of 'consensus' which is linked with the prevalent social, economic milieu and political awareness of the participants in the decision-making process. Hence it is argued that the exporting of the Anglo-American governmental institutions may be not only inappropriate, but suicidal in an environment where they are hardly organically rooted.

The central issue in public choice model is how to limit government and to check the natural tendency for over-government. One favoured strategy has been to bring about constitutional reforms to place limits on government growth. Another strategy has been to reduce the influence of interest groups on government policy. Still another strategy is to decentralize political power. Individuals would then have the option to 'exit' by moving to another jurisdiction when dissatisfied with the mix of taxation and services provided in their area. To mitigate the evils of bureaucratic monopoly, Niskanen[45] suggests the following steps: (1) stricter control on bureaucrats through the executive or the legislature; (2) more competition in the delivery of public services; (3) privatization or contracting-out to reduce wastage; and (4) dissemination of more information for public benefit about the availability of alternatives to public services, offered on a competitive basis and at competitive costs.

The public choice school has been successful in pointing out that there are alternatives available for the delivery of services to the citizens. The role of 'market' as a competing paradigm has challenged the hegemonic position of the state. Also the power of bureaucracy has been similarly slashed, opening up possibilities of non-bureaucratic citizen-friendly organizational options. It is not, however, a state versus market debate, as it is often made out to be. The real issue is how to make the state more democratic and citizen-friendly and not to relegate it to the background altogether and install the 'new god' of market in its place. The assumptions of the public choice school are not above board, nor are the arguments in favour of the market always justified. Again, the situations may differ from country to country and their prescriptions to check governmental overgrowth may not be of universal relevance. The state-led development activities in the Third World, for instance, are not everywhere amenable to public choice prescription. It is probably true that the growth and complexity of government and perhaps a decline in the force of social opinion and sanctions have given increased opportunities for politicians and bureaucrats to pursue their own gain at the general expense. '[B]ut the extent to which they actually do', argues Peter Self, 'is another matter which is unlikely to be settled by formal models of behaviour based upon simple assumptions'.[46] The notion of a rational individual and the idea of a vote-catching politician and a budget-maximizing bureaucrat are not always real-life prototypes. Self-aggrandizing nature of man haunts public choice philosophy as did the selfish individual in the Hobbesian state of nature. Public interest and welfare state are rejected by the public choice writers; yet human institutional development in history has been toward these concepts. The ideals of communitarianism and people's welfare have not evaporated from our societies; rather, indications are that ideals of healthy collective life in the global village are more and more gaining in acceptance.

It will be in order to enter two important caveats at this stage: one drawn on Herbert Simon's cautionary observation 'to stop defaming the public service' and the other relating 'the state rollback theory' to the conditions of developing societies. According to

Simon[47], the argument that the activities of society aimed at satisfying its economic needs, as its needs for public order and for various kinds of public goods and services should be satisfied, to the maximum degree possible, through privately owned business firms operating in competitive markets, is badly flawed. First, as Simon observes, the major motivational premise of public choice theory—methodological individualism—is false because 'human beings make most of their decisions, not in terms of individual self-interest, but in terms of the perceived interests of the groups, families, organizations, ethnic groups, and national states with which they identify and to whom they are loyal'. It is unrealistic to accept that the profit motive is the only reliable motive for welding organizational actions to social needs. Second, it is wrong to suggest that privatization will always increase productivity and efficiency. Such empirical evidence as we have on the relative efficiency of private and public organizations shows no consistent superiority of one over the other. Again, as Simon argues, it is not enough that a society works efficiently and productively. There is also the expectation that the society must ensure fair distribution of goods and services, and fairness of distribution necessitates involvement of all members of society in the distribution process. A democratic society is one where power is dispersed, and not concentrated. 'A society dominated almost wholly by business interests does not provide a stable equilibrium of power', as Simon emphatically argues. There are also available concrete evidences of the contributions of creative and dedicated public servants, as against the self-aggrandizing ones who are especially picked up to run down the institution of bureaucracy. As Simon concludes, 'it is time to stop defaming the public service. Whatever the rhetoric about bureaucracy, organizations are not enemies. They are the most effective tools that we humans have found for meeting human needs'. Almost in a similar vein, it has been argued, rebutting the government-shrinkage viewpoint, that the market approach betrays a serious lack of understanding of the scope of public services. 'The market approach to the management of public services, which gives priority to the service–client relationship and satisfying individual preferences, or setting up a quasi market where a market is not possible, overshadows the other essential functions of public services, especially in developing countries: maintaining social cohesion and promoting citizenship'.[48]

Whatever be the arguments in favour of a rollback state in the developed West, the state in the developing world, as it emerged out of colonial experience, in most cases, has yet to grow as a stable institution governed by market-centric calculations. And hence, the state-weakening argument is palpably untenable given the critical importance of state in governance. The problem of the Third World state is its stability and institutional capacity to guard against its possible capture by pernicious, large, petty, interests, including business interests.

CRITIQUE

The Third World critique of governance seeks to provide an alternative, challenging the universality of the model. Rooted in the historical specificity of the Third World development, public administration was hardly an engine for development. Bureaucracy-obsessed administration and disillusionment with state-led development fuelled the search for people's need-based governance and people-led development. Conceptualizing development as 'freedom', the Third World critique articulates people's participation in the wider 'bottom-up' discourses, which redefine 'decentralization' in the era of globalization. Efforts are directed at 'reaching out' to the people and with their conscious involvement in the socio-political processes, they are also emerging as 'actors'. Issues of poverty and environment remain crucial for obvious reasons. These are the issues that bring to the forefront the localized intensive ground-based efforts, natural resource management, and environmental management (*Brundtland* Commission, Rio Earth Summit, and Agenda 21 endorsing the idea of 'thinking globally but acting locally').

A profitable way of understanding the emergence of the 'governance' paradigm would be to invoke Foucault's concept of 'governmentality'.[49] Drawn from the analysis of power, governmentality offers a view on power beyond a perspective that 'centres either on consensus or on violence [linking] the technologies of the self with that of domination [and] the constitution of the subject with the formation of the state'.[50] Governmentality is 'an array of technologies of government' [51] and a political rationality, both of them influencing each other. What it suggests is that the term governmentality or technique of government does not refer merely to the state but denotes 'a rationality of governance linked to systematized technologies engaged in the conduct of conducts'.[52] Foucault's concept of 'governmentality' provides a powerful argument against the universal claim of governance as a model. Based on the distinction between 'reason of the state' and 'art of the state', governmentality juxtaposes state as 'a macro authority' with micro-power in dispersed localities. What it suggests is that there are two important dimensions of governmentality. On the one hand, there is a set of 'political rationalities' embedded in governmental programmes, plans, and other guiding documents; there is, on the other hand, what Foucault underlines as 'technologies of government' dealing with the whole range of techniques—including computing, numbering, and accounting—that sustain the forms of administration, supported by specific kinds of schooling, training, and generating knowledge, appropriate for the system-sustenance and persistence.[53] The Third World public administration in the era of globalization is perhaps illustrative here: a bureaucratic state fulfilling its regulatory role with a high level of human subjectivity through both 'coercion' and 'persuasion'. Governmentality is thus a way of thinking

about how populations—that is societies—can be regulated, and it becomes the basis of modern forms of political thought and intervention [seeking] to capture the rationale of ruling and its techniques [a concept that] has served both as a macro-level conceptualization of states' regulation of their inhabitants and as meso- or micro-level conceptualization of governance in large and small-scale organizational forms.[54]

As evident, governmentality is a powerful and perhaps appropriate construct to meaningfully define the changing contours of contemporary governance. In contrast with the sovereign power of traditional top-down managerial control, governmentality articulates governance through 'individual self-regulation', through particular types of human subjectivity with high levels of human autonomy and self-management. Seeking to capture roots of 'rabid' individualism, the Foucaultian notion is perhaps an appropriate theoretical tool to grasp the nature of governance and identify its socio-economic and political roots in the contemporary global order reflective of the apparent 'end of history',[55] as some analysts tend to endorse.

GOVERNANCE-DECENTRALIZING INTERLOCKING (?)

It may not be an exaggeration to say that ours is an age of decentralization. Academics, administrators, and planners are virtually unanimous that decentralization takes the heavy load of governance off the shoulders of the central government, brings 'government' to the doorstep of the people, and empowers them and makes them active participants in their own local-area governance, and, in the process, deepens democracy. There is presently emerging a strong countermovement of 'inclusive management'[56], focusing on public managers building relationships with the public and making connections and building trust. Essentially, inclusive management aims at building 'social capital' by lending support to the process of enhancement of community capacity for democratic governance. Many diverse experiments and initiatives are now on to create spaces for citizens to directly participate and influence decisions affecting their lives. Admittedly, decentralization and local community governance would be most suitable sites for these kinds of people-led and citizen empowered approaches, allowing greater deliberation of policies and actual implementations through inclusion of a variety of social actors engaged in planning and decision making. Inclusive management may not supplant other 'big' management models. Its utility and salience lie in issuing a timely reminder that public management is embedded in the 'legitimacy' of the state and democratic governance.

The *World Development Report (WDR) 1999–2000* devoted one whole chapter–chapter V—to a detailed discussion on 'decentralization'. It opened with the significant remark that globalization and localization—the integration of the world economy and the increasing demand for local autonomy—are two of the most important forces shaping development as we enter the twenty-first century, and in this context, the role of institutions are of crucial significance. 'Sustainable development should be rooted in the processes that are socially inclusive and are responsive to changing circumstances'. Highlighting the role of 'decentralization', the WDR has this to say:

Localization is praised for raising levels of participation in decision-making and for giving people more of a chance to shape the context of their own lives. By decentralizing government so that more decisions are made at subnational levels, closer to the voters, localization nourishes responsive and efficient governance. But it can also jeopardize macroeconomic stability. Local governments that have borrowed heavily and spent unwisely, for example, may have to be bailed out by the national government.[57]

Thus the WDR takes a balanced view of decentralization: its merits in terms of accessibility, participation, responsiveness, and efficiency are acknowledged; but, at the same time, its potentiality to 'jeopardize macroeconomic stability' is also pointed out. By recognizing decentralization as integral to governance, this World Bank report endorses views which are critical of the Weberian notion of hierarchical and centralized public administration. While in the Weberian 'ideal form of organization', accountability is fixed internally, in the governance paradigm, besides internal sources, accountability draws its meaning also from external sources, denoting that the stakeholders have a significant say on how authority articulates itself in given circumstances. The following section, thus, focuses on the relationship between accountability and governance in a globalizing world in which public administration seems to be 'market-driven' as well.

ACCOUNTABILITY UNDER 'GOOD GOVERNANCE'

Accountability, though simple sounding, is an extremely complex concept. Traditional public administration considered it, basically, as an internal organizational issue seeking to bring about a congruence between top-down policy and bottom-line implementation. There have been many constitutional and institutional changes to enhance public accountability of government agencies. In the developed countries initially and later in the developing nations, the philosophy of 'new public management' has undergone a radical change, although, as discussed earlier, the focus has continued to remain on 'management'. For the developing 'third world' in the group of those countries in serious debt crisis, the World Bank came out with the new 'good governance' prescription, with its accompanying micro-accountability and macro-accountability formula. Institutional capacity building became the central point, and the World Bank's primary objective has been to promote sound development management by removing, as far as possible, the possibilities of 'capture' of benefits by the socially powerful. This is of crucial significance because the Third World has inherited a colonial administrative model, which is hard to destroy. Administrative hegemony has been further reinforced by a powerful socio-economic elite that is as keen as the administrative class to 'privatize' government. Accountability-enforcing institutions, such as the legislature and the judiciary, are too distant and cumbrous to bring about a climate of real pro-people accountability in governance. Decentralization has been formally (constitutionally) assured and philosophically celebrated. But, the grassroots institutions are yet to grow into autonomous institutions in a hostile surrounding of centralizing administration and inequitable resource distribution. So far accountability has remained, in any variant, a managerial concept for application by 'external' managers, be it internal organizational managers or outside donors like the World Bank. This runs contrary to what is critical to democratizing administration by empowering people. Nonetheless, it has raised new issues in the debate on accountability, which is not merely structural but also sociological involving those who matter in a specific administrative context.

Good governance is itself an accountability-oriented concept applicable to a specific target group of the Third World countries. To follow the line of thinking of its sponsor (the World Bank), good governance is synonymous with sound development management; it is an essential complement to sound economic policies. Governments are the main producers of public goods, and they frame rules for the market to work efficiently. The institutional frameworks conducive to growth and poverty alleviation do not evolve on their own; rather the emergence of such frameworks needs incentives and adequate institutional capacity to create and sustain them. It is in this context that the World Bank pinpoints accountability as an essential prerequisite of 'good governance'.[58]

The concern of the World Bank for accountability, in the context of the structural adjustment policy, has pervaded both public and private sectors. The phenomenon of 'capture' of public services and resources by relatively narrow special interests has been a common feature in most countries. Governments often keep their transactions secret and the public, in general, is not inclined to demand information about performance. Accountability assumes importance in respect of ensuring efficiency in investment as well as in production and distribution of public goods and services. The government has also to ensure accountability in the private sector through appropriate company and securities legislation, competitive policy, and regulatory oversight, especially when 'down-sizing' of government takes place through disinvestments, privatization, and contracting.

Public accountability,[59] the World Bank document points out, involves three interrelated groups:

1. the general public and particularly recipients of public services, who are interested in service providers being accountable to them;
2. politics leaders and supervisors of service providers who would like the service providers to be accountable to them; and
3. the service providers themselves, whose objectives and interests often differ from those of (1) and (2).

To follow the bank's argument, historically, accountability has revealed three features: (1) the salience of microlevel accountability, as, owing to expansion of state activity, it has become difficult to apply broad political accountability to numerous functions of government; (2) the focus in accountability tends to be on inputs, especially public expenditure, rather than outputs of effects; (3) accountability has mostly been by internal administrative controls exercised by political leaders, government agencies, and bureaucrats acting as proxies for the public.

Two broad types of accountability identified by the Bank are: Micro-accountability, and macro-accountability. Micro-accountability remains critical, especially in ensuring government responsiveness to the views and needs of the public for which services are intended. The concepts of 'exit' and 'voice' which originated in Albert O. Hirschman's classic work, *Exit, Voice, and Loyalty: Responses to Decline in Firms, Organizations, and States*[60] have been used to underscore the importance of micro-accountability. Competition or scope for the public to 'exit' when dissatisfied with a service, for instance, may have a salutary effect on the agency concerned by reducing its revenues and, thus, making the careers or pay of the staff less secure. Similarly, 'voice', in the sense of participation of the public, may influence the quality or volume of a service through some form of articulation of preferences or demand. Accountability is increased, if such 'voice' makes the public agency more responsive to public demands. Voice may take the form of protest, non-cooperation, or the rejection of political representatives through the ballot process. Collective action in any of these forms can 'act as an instrument of accountability, signalling the authorities that they must listen to the people's voice and take remedial action'.[61] It has been the Bank's policy to find out ways of increasing 'exit' and 'voice' at the design stage of service-delivery projects. Accountability at the microlevel can, however, be sustained only when the government and society at large are committed to ensuring it.

Decentralization in the form of strengthening local government has been widely viewed as essential to ensure greater responsiveness and accountability for many kinds of infrastructure and services that have hitherto been in the control of the central government. The other kind of accountability—macro-accountability—has two major dimensions: financial accountability and accountability for overall economic performance. Financial accountability involves, as the Bank document identifies: (1) properly functioning government-accounting system for effective expenditure control and cash management; (2) an external audit system which reinforces expenditure control by exposure and sanctions against misspending and corruption; and (3) mechanisms to review and act on the results of audits and to ensure that follow-up action is taken to remedy problems identified.

As it has been rightly emphasized, without a well-functioning system of financial accountability, government efficiency is poor, and the probability of corruption increases greatly. Accountability for economic performance involves review of resource-use in public investment programmes and general strengthening of the capacity of governments to monitor and evaluate their own economic performance including proper resource-use.

The question that is now being raised by quite a few social activists and civil libertarians is: can there be, as an alternative, a people's campaign for transparency and accountability: One such example of a search for grassroots accountability is the Mazdoor Kisan Shakti Sangathan (MKSS), which is just one of many such people's organizations developing in different parts of India to transform public administration into people's administration.[62] To quote the proceedings of the MKSS, the effort has been to transform the demand for a right to livelihood, wages, and employment into a

demand to know from the government agency/panchayat (local government), how much money was allocated and where and how it
was spent. The slogan was: '*Hamara paisa, hamara hisab*'. Through
people's awakening, the institution of *Jan sunwaii* or public hearing
turned out to be an effective forum where the people could speak
and be heard. 'The public hearings on development expenditure at
the panchayat level have led to a crystallization of issues and given
a tangible quality to the abstract notion of transparency and the
right to information'.[63]

The right to information campaign in India began with the MKSS
movement insisting on transparency in village accounts, especially
with regard to paying minimum wages in rural India. Ghost entries
in muster rolls were a sign of rampant corruption in the system,
which prompted MKSS to demand official information recorded in
government files. The movement soon spread across India. From a
very modest beginning in the villages in Rajasthan, the success of
MKSS has been a source of inspiration to activists in India and
throughout the world. It led to 'the genesis of a broader discourse
on the right to information in India'.[64] After dithering over this issue
for years, the central government finally introduced the Freedom of
Information Bill 2000, in parliament on 25 July 2000. The bill was
certainly a significant step in the process of democratization, though
Madhav Godbole apprehended that the 'the bill, as presented in
parliament, [was] hardly [adequate] to bring transparency to issues
of governance'.[65] This bill finally became the Freedom of Information
Act, 2002, that has now been replaced by the Right to Information
Act, 2005 (RTI Act) that seeks

to provide setting out the practical regime of right to information for citizens
to secure access to information under the control of public authorities, in
order to promote transparency and accountability in the working of every
public authority, the constitution of Central Information Commission and
State Information Commission and for matters connected therewith or
incidental thereto.[66]

The right to information is derived from Part III of the Constitution
of India guaranteeing the freedom of expression under Article 19.
Hailed as the *Magna Carta of Freedom*,[67] this act is the codification
of a right that empowers citizens to receive information within a
specific time frame of thirty days. As a 'path to swaraj',[68] this is an

important pillar of democracy in ensuring 'transparency' and 'accountability'. There are, however, doubts about the extent to which this act will help the people in getting the information they seek, despite the institution of the Central Information Commission and State Information Commission, presumably because 'of the typical colonial mindset of the bureaucracy', which, by denying access to information to the people, seems to sustain its hegemony in public administration. The validity of the 1923 Official Secrets Act even after the passing of the RTI Act seems to be puzzling though the act suggests punitive measures to check 'the errand officers', though that will hardly be effective unless the mindset is less 'bureaucratic' and more 'developmental'.

GOVERNANCE REFORM AND ACCOUNTABILITY

One of the core issues of governance reform is accountability of those involved in public affairs.[69] Lack of accountability defeats the primary goal for which governance is seen as an appropriate model in public administration. In most of the developing countries, this deficiency results in 'misguided resource allocation and arbitrariness and corruption in government [that] have deterred private sector investment and slowed growth and poverty-reduction efforts in numerous settings'.[70]

The accountability question needs to be cast in the background of the paradigm shift in public administration. Classical public administration, based on the functioning of bureaucracy within the framework of democracy, has so far been the staple of accountability theory. In the practical world of public administration of today, two closely competing but contemporary paradigms seem to hold sway: one is new public management and the other is known as 'good governance'. 'reinventing government', although an innovative expression falls in line with the main current of thought advocating 'quality' (as against size) of governance and entrepreneurial spirit.

Historically, the liberal-democratic set-up evolved basic mechanisms of accountability such as ministerial control, parliamentary debate, legislative committees, media security and ombudsmanic system. In recent times, there have been some major changes—a sort of paradigmatic shift—in the mode of public governance under the rubric of 'new public management', 'reinventing government' or 'reengineering government'. In essence, what is being advocated is a market-centred, neo-liberal approach to governance under which its objectives are shifted to economic growth and productivity, and its normative standards are redirected toward efficiency, competition, profit, and value for money. The standards that are being set for public governance are those of business management. This makes a radical departure from the traditional norms and objectives of governance; enhancing human progress, maintaining law and order, removing poverty and unemployment, providing public welfare, ensuring impartiality and equal treatment, safeguarding citizens' rights, and guaranteeing justice and fairness.

Therefore, in contemporary public administration, the new diction is, as Haque has rightly pointed out, 'the language of the market, of competition, of enterprise, customers and in a nutshell, of entrepreneurial management'.[71] There has thus emerged a unique set of challenges to the realization of accountability in the current phase of public administrative changes everywhere. The people-centred tradition of accountability had evolved with the emergence of broader civil society, an organised working class, and an increase in the entitlements or rights of common citizens. Under the new dispensation, citizens have been redefined as customers or clients—which is a commercial view of citizenship, reducing social rights associated with collective citizenship to narrow commercial prerogatives of individual customers governed by exchange relationship.

Under this reductionist interpretation, as Haque argues, 'public governance is accountable for the effective delivery of its services to customers who can pay, while it may remain indifferent towards low-income citizens who are not in a position to use such services due to their financial incapacity'. Accountability under this consumerist mode of governance is to private, affluent customers rather than to the collective public; and, in consequence, the economically underprivileged citizens, who often depend on the state for basic services, do not qualify as customers for not being able to afford user charges. Thus, the customer view tends to diminish citizens' rights vis-à-vis the state and excludes common citizens from the equation of public accountability. What therefore holds good is the argument that governance, today, has become more accountable and responsive not to the lay public but to the affluent business community. In this context, the currently fashionable citizen's charter, to enhance responsiveness and accountability of the public service to its clients as customers, needs to be viewed as 'a top-down device without public participation'. It is a managerial tool to enhance customer attractiveness in order to increase sales. The charter is, in reality, a manager's charter and not a citizen's. It empowers consumers rather than citizens. As Haque observes, 'in the prevailing context of governance, public accountability, in effect, has become more fragmented and class-biased accountability'.[72] The third dimension—means of accountability—has been under challenge in today's context of the neo-liberal mode of governance that has brought in its trail new sets of institutions, structures, and norms. Following Haque, the first change to note is the growing power of ministers or political executives to exert influence on the public service, which is leading to the politicization of civil servants by ministers in violation of the principle of political neutrality. Recent policy to do away with permanent tenure for civil servants and introduce contract-based appointments makes the public servants more vulnerable to political executives, who exercise control of job contracts and careers. Ministerial control as a means of accountability makes public servants extremely loyal to ministers, thus ignoring their accountability to the general public. Furthermore, under the new public management regime, many developed and developing countries have shifted from process-oriented to result-oriented performance of public agencies, with increasing focus on outcome than inputs. On the face of it, the result-oriented administration may look attractive, but such a mode of governance is likely to render the existing means of accountability ineffective. As Haque observes, it is difficult to put such an outcome-based administrative system under legislative scrutiny owing to the qualitative and controversial nature of public sector outcomes such as environmental security, poverty alleviation, and community development. The result-oriented public administration tends to focus more on 'what' is being achieved. In consequence, there is likely to be 'the diminishing relevance' of such means of public accountability as internal control and supervision over various inputs and processes in the public sector.[73]

As evident, a critical evaluation of accountability in the context of the World Bank strategy of governance reveals the extent to which this idea is linked with the contemporary neo-liberal agenda of the developed world. In the entire gamut of the World-Bank-inspired thinking on administrative reform, accountability is a most crucial dimension. The primary concern here is to do away with 'dysfunctional and ineffective public institutions—broadly defined to include all institutions that shape the way public functions are carried out—[that] are seen to be at the heart of the economic developmental challenge'.[74] While in traditional public administration, accountability is basically an internal organizational issue seeking to bring about a congruence between top-down policy and bottom-line implementation, under the new public management rubric, its focus is on the 'management' of the institutions in accordance with the set World Bank objective to promote sound development management by removing, as far as possible, the possibilities of 'capture' of benefits by the socially powerful. Accountability is a specific managerial device, exercised both internally and externally. While in a typical Weberian organization, accountability is ensured by strictly adhering to the hierarchic boss–subordinate network, in the context of globalization, conditional aid stipulates a well-defined mechanism to make the recipients of aid accountable to the donors. Accountability thus articulated as inimical to the processes of 'empowerment', which are critical in people-centric governance. This is crucial in the context of the Third World that has inherited a colonial administrative model endorsing the administrative hegemony of a powerful socio-economic elite that is as keen as the administrative class to 'privatize' government. Decentralization has been formally (constitutionally) assured and philosophically celebrated. But the grassroots institutions are yet to grow into autonomous institutions in a hostile surrounding of centralizing administration and inequitable resource distribution. Given the complexity in the evolution of institutions in a Third World context, administrative reform is more than a technical exercise; it is essentially a political intervention which takes into account the complex socio-economic relationships in which these polities are enmeshed. Whether the reform is externally imposed or internally induced there is neither a short-cut nor an escape route. What is needed is to critically assess the importance of these relationships in making public administration reform citizen-centric in the genuine sense of the term.

ETHICS AND GOVERNANCE

Governance and ethics are intertwined. A government functions within certain broad moral and ethical parameters, integrally linked with the sociological foundation of the polity in which it is articulated. In that sense, governance is both an 'art' and a 'science': it is an art because it connotes a specific style of functioning relative to those wielding power and authority; it is also a science because there are always well-defined principles and techniques in which it manifests in practice. The importance of ethics in political authority has acquired a significant place in contemporary theoretical discussion more so because of the growing decadence in governmental practices largely owing to a decline of ethical values in public administration, which is perhaps singularly responsible for the rise of 'corruption' in a virulent form. This is a matter of serious concern for not only the practitioners of administration but also for those seeking to locate its roots to provide a plausible explanation. A possible way out, as the theorists conceptualize, is probably to articulate public administration as 'governance'. Historically induced socio-economic circumstances, especially following the collapse of the Soviet Bloc, led to a search for alternative theoretical paradigms in governance, the alternative forms of administration drawing on planned economic development. Within the developed capitalist countries, almost simultaneously, there was a rise of strong anti-bureaucratic and anti-state criticism directed against what came to be called 'government overload' as a consequence of 'welfare backlash'. The state, it was alleged, has over the years taken upon itself a large array of activities that inflated its budgetary and financial commitment and led to the 'overgrowth' of bureaucracy that became rent-seeking, ignoring completely the Benthamite notion of 'benevolent guardian' of society. The battle cry now is to 'downsize' and allow free play to the market and civil society—giving rise to the new ideology of 'neo-liberalism'.

ETHICAL CONCERNS

That there are important ethical concerns underlying major 'development' decisions—be it a dam construction or a programme of eviction of slum-dwellers for city improvement—is, however, often glossed over by planners and administrators. Development is not something that happens automatically; development is purposive action, and behind such action there must be an ethic of some kind— implicit or explicit. Again, it is not usually admitted that the issue of 'power' is inherent in development decisions. The ruling class really rules. Particularly, in the postcolonial Third World situation, democracy has, in most cases, remained more a procedural matter than a real, substantive, and open exercise of people's power. Development decisions, under the circumstances, are, more often than not, 'top-down', non-participative, elite decisions that are intended to serve the interests of the 'powerful'. When 'power' decides, ethics becomes the handmaiden of power.

Still, there is no denying that some sort of ethical norms actually inform any policy decisions related to development made by any agency, public or private (generally, of course, public or government agency). In this context, the observations of Nigel Dower, President of the International Development Ethics Association (IDEA) are worth quoting. As he puts it, two related things are involved in ethics: (1) ethics is a 'set of norms or values together with some justifying story supporting those norms and values'; and (2) along with this there is 'systematic reflection on the nature and justification of such norms and values'. In this formulation, *norms* stand for 'certain rules or principles about what is morally right (and is thus required to be done) and what is right in the sense of what is morally permitted or what one has a right to do'. Values are 'certain elements of human well-being which are regarded as worth pursuing or promoting for members of one's society (and usually for human beings generally)'. In Dower's view, development is based on purposive or deliberate public policy initiative and as such it 'must presuppose an ethic of some kind', and 'the pursuit of development will be all the more effective if people acknowledge the importance of explicit ethical debate about the ethical foundations of development'.

NEED FOR ETHICS

In continuation of what has been stated above, it can now be asserted that in the context of development, ethics is concerned with what we choose to do (including not to do) intentionally or on purpose. Ethics is about choice, employing determinations and judgements about values. The choices of concern in ethics are those giving rise to significant 'good' or 'bad' in the world or in the larger society. Surely this is an extremely sketchy presentation of a very large subject. What is important for our purposes is the ontological status of 'development' involving questions such as: 'development' would mean what kind of existential transformation, for whom and how, and in terms of what scheme of distributional gains and losses, and even intended or unintended cultural mutations; and, very subtly, in terms of what consequences for the 'environment' as the womb of both human and non-human life. As Dennis Goulet puts it, 'Development is above all else a question of human values and attitudes, goals self-defined by societies, and criteria for determining what are tolerable costs to be borne, and by whom, in the course of change. These are far more important than modeling optimal resource allocations, upgrading skills, or rationalizing of administrative procedures'. Looking back, one can clearly discern, at the beginning of the development discourse, an overarching concern among development theorists and practitioners about how to achieve economic growth and how to apply effective means to reduce poverty within the growth model. It was not considered at that stage that a simplistic notion of 'development' as mere economic growth might evade issues like composition and distribution of 'products' of growth and that the processes or means of bringing about growth through democratic or non-democratic ways and at the cost of the 'environment' would thereby endanger 'sustainability' in future. In short, the essence of development ethics is critical ethical reflections on the means and ends of socio-economic change that is designed and implemented to bring about planned transformation of the lives of peoples in the 'developing' countries, with special emphasis on the lives of the poor and the marginalized. To quote Nigel Dower's most appropriate formulation in this context: 'Development ethics as sustained ethical enquiry into the nature and justification of the values underlying development and engagement both with the ethical dilemmas in development policy and practice and with the contested nature of development as a concept plays an important part in helping to make development discourse adequate to the enormous task before it—the challenge of world poverty and the general betterment of humankind.' At this stage, it needs to be asserted that development scholars today are firmly of the view that development decisions are a mix of 'ethical' and empirical-cum-policy issues.

GOVERNANCE: PREREQUISITES FOR 'DEVELOPMENT' (?)

Since the emergence of the 'Third World', 'development' (whatever it meant at that point of time), besides being the direct business of the 'developing' nations, had become a major international concern. How to bring about speedy socio-economic 'development' to improve the quality of life of peoples in the Third World assumed major significance for the leaders of the newly independent countries as well as for the international donor countries and institutions. There was hardly any debate at that time in history about what defined 'development' and how can vital choices be made about what would be the result of 'development' as a process. At best, there was a straightforward acknowledgement that 'economic growth' had to be attained using 'technology' and other work methods and techniques that the Western 'developed' nations (supposedly) had historically mobilized to grow as models of 'modernity'. That there are important 'ethical' considerations involved in adopting the 'processes' that would, it would be hoped, lead to the kind of societal transformation (called 'development') as an end. State was not of much concern to the 'development' practitioners.

The earliest phase may well be called 'developmentalism' connoting development as an essential means to 'modernize' and 'change' the traditional lifestyle of the peoples of the Third World. It was born with the Third World itself. This was the era of postcolonialism when the leaders of the new world—Nehru, Nkruma, or Sukarna—had been unanimous in the search for speedy amelioration of the living conditions of the masses. The international donor agencies, and the United States of America in particular (being concerned about the potential threat of the spread of communist influence) had also expressed concern about the 'development' of the new nations for which funds were mobilized, and 'planners', technicians, area and subject experts—a new breed of 'development pundits'—fanned out in different directions to advise and guide the 'underdeveloped' countries in their pursuit of planned change and 'development'. It was an era of unprecedented euphoria and optimism about the prospect of planned change in the 'Third World'. At least, initially, development was thought of in macro or holistic terms—to bring about qualitative change in the lives of the peoples, covering, apart from economic improvement, removal of poverty, malnutrition and ill health, and illiteracy. While strategizing development, the economic aspect—enhanced productivity in different sectors—did, however, loom large, and there was a firm belief that once wealth would be produced, the distributive aspect would be taken care of in due course. In the 1950s and 1960s, there were debates about development strategy centring around such themes as 'balanced or unbalanced growth', 'dualistic development processes', proper role of 'human capital', and so on and so forth. The earlier view of conceiving economic growth in instrumental terms had, however, come under severe criticism, as the critics pointed to the need to focus directly on urgent social objectives, particularly income distribution, poverty amelioration, employment generation, and meeting essential basic needs. Importantly, the development dialogue, during this phase, was going on within the framework of the nation state as a sovereign category.

Since the late 1960s the economic condition of much of the Third world started deteriorating fast leading to the rise of the 'dependency theory' that challenged frontally the reigning modernization paradigm. The conclusion of the dependency theorists was that the capitalist market relations, instead of stimulating economic development, had been actually retarding it in much of the Third World. The dependency theorists forcefully argued that the market power exercised by the industrialized 'core' was exploitative in nature and prevented the industrialization of the Third World 'periphery'. Economic power and political power had been hand in glove with each other. Reactionary leaders and classes in the developing countries made common cause with 'core' political and economic interests in order to retain their own power and enjoy monopoly rents. The dependency theory, thus, came to hold an extremely pessimistic view of economic development of the Third World as it stood in relationship to the First World.

The early 1980s witnessed a radical shift from the post-World-War-II era of state-led 'developmentalism' to a new phase of 'neo-liberal counterrevolution' in the context of the Third World's deepening debt crisis. The World Bank and the International

Monetary Fund, with their vastly increased power, clamped down on most of the Third World countries, with strict loan conditionalities, invoking a redefinition of the state in a changing world. It signalled a radical change in the framework of development thinking from the earlier 'national frame' to 'international' and 'globalized' frame. Development came to be unequivocally viewed as 'economic development' to be measured in terms of per capita economic growth. The central means for the purpose were declared as efficient markets, 'privatization' and 'deregulation', and a severely restricted role of the state in welfare provision and economic regulation. The state's distributive goals were de-emphasized with subsidies and welfare systems relegated to the background and the state itself was regarded as a predatory and rent-seeking agency. While the state's role is reduced or withdrawn, several regulatory institutions are created to deal with the anticipated abuse of market power by private producers. The Securities and Exchange Board in India (SEBI) and Telecommunications Regulatory Authority of India (TRAI) for instance, are illustrative of how regulatory institutions perform the twin functions of managing the market and also protecting citizens from abuse by the service providers in near monopolistic sectors.[75]

The 'rollback' concept of the state coincided with the emergence of another idea of 'bringing the civil society back in'. Development, it came to be realized, has often been top-down and bureaucracy driven without much care for what the 'people'—particularly the poor and the marginalized sections of society—genuinely need but cannot always demand as a result of voicelessness and lack of capabilities (owing to poverty, illiteracy, ill health, and 'gender' exclusion, for instance). Also, there was a growing realization that besides state and market, civil society (in multiple formations such as NGOs and CSOs) has a big role to play in societal problem solving, be it literacy campaigns or health provision or other facilities creation such as water conservation, forest maintenance, and the like. Since the 1980s, the shift from 'government' to 'governance' in development vocabulary was not a mere semantic change. On close scrutiny of the performance balance sheet of formal government, it transpired that the general trend had been toward cornering of development gains by the elite and the influential and consequent deprivation of the poor and the socially marginalized. Also, as far as the latter groups were concerned, 'access' to services and facilities was often a problem for them in most government-run programmes. Institutional response at this stage had been to correct the imbalance in social mobilization by introducing decentralization, people's participation, empowerment, 'engendering development', and an array of imaginative efforts to extend the ambit of government (hence 'governance') as well as to make development more participative, transparent, and accountable.

An extreme reaction in recent times has come from the post-developmentalists (Wolfgang Sachs, for instance) who would rather abandon the concept of 'development' lock, stock, and barrel. In their view, 'development' has from the beginning been aimed at not improving human condition but extending Western hegemonic control over the Third World. Note in this context the caustic comments of Sachs, 'The idea of development stands today like a ruin in the intellectual landscape. Its shadow obscures our vision'. Development, in this kind of perception, has been unethical.

NATURE OF DEVELOPMENT ETHICS

Policy makers, administrators and planners at any level who are actively engaged in 'development' activities of any kind face moral questions such as: What is going to be the end objective of a project or programme? What means should be adopted to actually bring about the desired results? What are the consequences of the programme or project when implemented? And, who will benefit from changes that will come about? To give an illustration, when the big dam project was being planned in the Narmada valley in the state of Madhya Pradesh, India, the anti-dam protesters were pointing out that it would involve large-scale deforestation and consequent loss of rare flora and fauna; and, more importantly, there will be the displacement of thousands of local tribal population from their age-old habitat along with their rich cultural tradition. The famous 'Chipko Movement' in the Uttarakhand State (earlier a part of Uttar Pradesh), which was spearheaded by local women activists, raised a similar question: the denudation of the hill forest for the benefit of some business people in the plains would deprive the local people of the benefit of firewood and, from a longer time point of view, soil erosion would endanger local cultivation and habitations. These are familiar stories known to most development practitioners everywhere.

Theories of 'development' or 'underdevelopment' in the social sciences are always a mix of practical policy issues and ethical or moral concerns. Moral assessment of the theory and practice of development is at the heart of what may be called 'development ethics'. Again, to quote Goulet, 'Ethical judgments as to the good life, the just society, and the quality of relations of people among themselves and with nature always serve, explicitly or implicitly, as operational criteria for development planners and researchers. Development ethics is the interdisciplinary *ex-professo* study of such value-laden issues.'

Acknowledging the signal importance of ethical issues in development, the International Development Ethics Association (IDEA) was formed in 1980, and Nigel Dower as its president has been justifiably ambitious to suggest that development ethics should be accorded the status of a separate discipline altogether. His proposal deserves serious consideration in view of the immense complexities involved in 'development' conceived as 'visioning' and 'implementation' of deeply value-laden programmes of massive societal change. As he has argued forcefully, 'value assumptions behind development and poverty alleviation are far more complex and indeed controversial, and so ethics as critical engagement with these normative issues is actually important'. Dower is right in pointing out that there is more 'justice sensitivity' today in development thinking. As he puts it, 'mainstream thinking about development has become more normatively complex—interest in the rights agenda, in transparency, in good governance, in greater regulatory regimes vis-à-vis labour relations and the environment, all show a greater recognition that development is not just about economic growth, but "just economic growth"which is politically appropriate and sociologically meaningful'.

SOURCES OF ETHICAL ASSESSMENT

The theory and practice of development are amenable to assessment from a variety of standpoints with regard to their ethical status. Referring to the work of Anglo-American development ethicists,

David Crocker has identified four important 'sources' for moral or ethical assessment.

1. Activists and social critics—Mahatma Gandhi in India, Raul Prebisch in Latin America, and Franz Fanon in Africa—who were critical of colonial and/or orthodox economic development.

2. The seminal contribution of Denis Goulet, who was influenced by the French economist Louis-Joseph Lebret and by social scientists like Gunner Myrdal, and who forcefully argued that 'development needs to be redefined, demystified, and thrust into the arena of moral debate'.

3. The effort of Anglo-American moral philosophers who have deepened and broadened the philosophical debate about conventional famine relief and food aid and transformed it into a more comprehensive 'ethics of Third World development'.

4. The pioneering work of economists like Paul Streeten and Amartya Sen, who addressed the problems of global economic inequality, hunger, and underdevelopment in terms of a novel and much broader conception of development based on deeper ethical principles.

Each of these sources has its own strength and salience in the development debate, and as such each needs to be examined much more elaborately. Admittedly, there are many other well-known activists and social critics in every country whose names can be added to the list provided by Crocker. Gandhi's contemporary, Rabindranath Tagore, a Nobel laureate widely known as a great poet, had been actively engaged in the development of the rural masses of the then Bengal, within his own conceptual frame of participative and human development-centric development ethics. To cite a few other eminent personalities, Julius Nayarare of Africa, Medha Patekar of India, Mohammad Yunus of Bangladesh had their distinctive thoughts and approaches to 'development'. Robert Chambers of the Institute of Development Studies, Sussex, who has spent a whole lifetime in active rural development and who brought about innovative techniques drawing on people's intrinsic planning knowledge, deserves special mention in this connection. In recent times, development ethics has been greatly enriched by the seminal contribution of the Nobel laureate Joseph Stiglitz, whose ideas, especially expressed in the context of 'globalization', need to be presented in some detail. Also, a fifth source may be added to Crocker's list—the grassroots people's movements—that have, at many locations, brought forth people's raw, home-grown, life wisdom about authentic 'development' and its inbuilt concept of development ethics. This was very eloquently expressed by Jose Saramago, the Nobel laureate, in the course of his concluding speech at the World Social Forum in Porte Alegre, Brazil in February 2002, when he referred to the 'multiple movements for resistance and social action that are fighting to establish a new, distributive and commutative justice that all people can come to recognize as intrinsically theirs, a justice that protects freedom and rights, and not any denial of them'.

E-/DIGITAL GOVERNANCE

In the context of globalization, the recent conceptualization of 'E-governance or digital governance'[76] is of significance in administrative reforms. Drawing on the latest Information and Communication Technology (ICT), the aim of e-governance is to open up government processes and enable greater public access to information. Both digital and e-governance are of recent origin, and there is hardly a universally acceptable definition. Digital/ e-government refers to the use of emerging ICT like internet, web page, and mobile phones to deliver information and services to citizens. It can include publication of information about government services on websites, and citizens can download application forms for these services. It can also deliver services, such as filling of a tax form, renewal of licenses, and processing on-line payments as well. The purpose of digital government is to create 'super counters in [the government departments] and eliminate the endless maze citizens have to negotiate in going from door to door, floor to floor, to obtain service'.[77] Appropriate use of various means of ICT will usher in a new era in public administration by seeking to make governmental functioning and processes more transparent and accessible.

Thus, e-governance through a technological innovation 'has changed the basic character of governance—its operational methodology, functional style, ideological orientation, even the spirit, heart and soul'.[78] In the developed countries, e-governance is a well-established mode in which governmental services are made available to the citizens through internet portals. In India, digital governance has been legalized by the Information Technology Act of 2000. The act provides 'legal recognition for transaction carried out by means of electronic data interchange and other means of electronic communication, commonly referred to as "electronic commerce" which involve use of alternatives to paper-based methods of communication and storage of information, to facilitate electronic filling of documents with the government agencies'.[79] Defining 'electronic form' as 'any information generated, sent, received or stored in media, magnetic, optical, computer memory, microfilm, computer-generated micro fiche or similar device', the act accords legal sanction to the following devices which are:

(a) the filling of any form, application or any other document with any office, authority, body or agency owned or controlled by appropriate government in a particular manner; (b) the issue or grant of any license, permit, sanction or approval by whatever name called in a particular manner; and (c) the receipt or payment of money in a particular manner.[80]

Legally endorsed, this act is a watershed in conceptualizing administrative reform in India. More importantly, e-governance is certainly an attack on bureaucratic red tapism, which causes unnecessary delay and corruption. It is a tool for achieving 'good governance especially with regard to improving efficiency, transparency and making interface with government user friendly'. The ultimate goal is 'to bring about better governance which has been termed as simple, moral, accountable, responsive and transparent (SMART)',[81] the aim of which is also to create a space for regular involvement of citizens who, as customers of public services, have now direct access to governmental activities through the ICT. Thus, the citizens can not only view on-line the governmental acts, they can also provide significant inputs through emails and electronic devices. Technology is, thus, an important tool for integrating citizens' input and transparency into one model. The ICT-based e-governance has ushered in a new era in government innovations with capacities to, (1) reduce the cost of government, (2) increase citizens' input into government, (3) improve public decision making, and (4) increase the transparency of government transactions. The object of e-governance is 'to arm the citizens to act as watch dogs to government'.[82] In view of these well-defined functional characteristics, e-governance is also a very meaningful step towards combating corruption. By reducing discretionary powers it curbs opportunities for arbitrary action, e-government also empowers the citizens by making their intervention in the transactions of governmental business regular through the ICT.[83] The project e-Sewa (service) that began in West Godavari district in Andhra Pradesh, India, is illustrative here. The project is a tool 'to bridge the digital divide in the rural areas' through extensive use of information technology 'for providing access to various citizen to citizen (C2C) and citizen to government (C2G) services to the people in rural areas'. Managed by a women's self-help group, the project is a class by itself as it enables 'the local women-participants' to emerge as 'information leaders', who remain critical in realizing the goal of e-Sewa.[84]

Drawing from the ICT, the e-governance articulates public administration in a refreshingly new way. Its application, however, is considerably limited in the public sector, simply because e-governance threatens mass retrenchment of workers involved in government. Therefore, the public sector cannot opt for e-governance to replace people for two reasons: first, access to internet is still limited even in the developed countries. Thus, while transactions through ICT cost less than they do by conventional devices, the government has to maintain both the old and new systems to sustain its 'public' character; otherwise, a large portion of the 'people' will remain outside governmental transactions. Second, downsizing and reducing public sector employment in many countries result in economic hardship for those losing jobs, which, for obvious reasons, has severe political repercussions. Thus, for the leadership, this is not a desirable option unless there is no option available.[85] In other words, given the obvious adverse consequences of e-governance in both the developed and developing countries, its applicability is uncertain and limited.

PUBLIC–PRIVATE PARTNERSHIPS

Governance is governing without government. Involving stakeholders in public administration, the governance paradigm is surely a break with the Weberian conceptualization of bureaucracy-centric public governance. In its redefined form, public administration is not allergic to civil society institutions which are critical of public service. Citizen's charter and also citizen report card are devices to articulate this new concern. The other crucial change is the involvement of private institutions in fulfilling a public obligation. And, hence, public–private partnerships have become significant in public governance. The issue is no longer about public sector control or privatization, not on who does what, but rather on how effectively the services get delivered to citizens. The focus of attention is on 'outcomes and not inputs'. This is a fundamental shift in approach and 'it calls for effective partnerships between public and private sectors [because] the problem cannot be solved unilaterally'.[86] In the developed countries, private corporations, especially the leading multinational corporations, contribute to public well-being by supporting public (or governmental) initiatives in those fields of their choice. More and more companies are being drawn to appreciate their 'social responsibility' owing to 'an element of self-interest as well [because] doing good for the community can be good for business, and doing bad can subject companies to expensive lawsuits'.[87] This is undoubtedly a paradigm shift in public governance because in the Weberian formulation, private initiatives are never considered appropriate for public well-being. In view of the growing importance of 'governance without government', the public–private partnership (PPP) is also suggestive of public–private cooperation in pursuing public good. It must be recognized that PPPs are not 'simply small interventions that are being used to put some systems right. PPPs are 'about changing the way the government does business and the manner in which it interacts with the private sector to ensure that the ultimate consumer—citizens get the quality of services they deserve'.[88]

There are various examples of public–private partnership in India. The most successful examples can be found in the health sector. With financial support from the donor agencies, especially the United States Agency for International Development (USAID) in its Innovations in Family Planning Services (IFPS) project, the PPP has led to remarkable improvement in health care, particularly, in this instance, among the poor in urban and rural areas of Uttar Pradesh, Uttaranchal, and Jharkhand. As the USAID reports spells out, the PPP was most effective in fulfilling the reproductive and child health needs in these areas. As a result, dependence on the private sector health care is considerably reduced. What is striking is that the IFPS project was most successful in those areas where communities are involved in executing the programmes. In other words, besides the government and the private health care providers, the PPP is also a mechanism specifically geared to involve the stakeholders in goals that traditionally belonged to the government. This is an alternative form of governance which is clearly not Weberian, but an expansion of public governance by including those who matter in the decision-making process, besides the traditional locus of administration, namely, the bureaucracy.

CONCLUDING OBSERVATIONS

Governance gained currency at a moment in the evolution of public administration when the complexity of societal problem solving demanded a multi-pronged search for the refashioning of mode of governing. As it eventually emerged, it came to represent transparency, accountability, integrity, and legitimacy of the institutions, rules, practices, and values on which a society functions. These characteristics are relative to the society in question because they cannot be articulated in absolute terms. But, what is critical is the process whereby citizens favourably link with governance, presumably because it generates trust and confidence among them. Governance is thus a mechanism involved in (1) 'the formation and propagation of values', (2) 'the creation and distribution of wealth', and (3) 'the emergence and consolidation of institutions'.[89] In the governance paradigm, the traditional governance process, with the state as supreme actor, is now heavily influenced by international organizations with a growing number of regulations formulated at the supranational level. These supranational policies travel across 'languages and cultures, framing and positioning local discourses and being translated by the local configurations of resources and ideas'.[90] As shown, the growing but critical importance of governance as both a technique and an agenda can easily be attributed to two important developments in global order in recent times: first, the disintegration of the Soviet Union, suggesting not only the weaknesses of Marxism-Leninism as a cementing ideology in diverse societies, but also the failure of the state-directed development model in mitigating basic human social, economic, and political needs. This apparent vacuum is being filled in by the consolidation of the neo-liberal discourse in which 'states should become commodified and marketized in their outlook and give way to the "market discipline" [paving the way for] governance without government'. The governance without government that is market discipline can be seen as 'governmentality of neo-liberal globalization'. Drawing on Foucault, governmentality includes 'mental and practical levels of governance'. Governmentality is 'a result of mentality and the organization of conduct that composes the art of governance'.[91] Drawn from 'the internalization of practices of governing', governmentality is a mechanism of policing the self 'according to existing conception of truth grounded in knowledge about the self'.[92] The second, and perhaps a more significant factor, is the remarkable technological advances that shrink distance and interdependencies that arise from much wider and deeper global economic integration. In the changed circumstances, without reorienting themselves substantially, the decision makers can hardly remain meaningful in governance. As a result, public administration is bound to undergo radical changes because of historical circumstances in which the idea of 'contextual' public administration seems to have lost its viability. The ecological view is replaced by the 'neo-Taylorist' philosophy of 'one best way' to organize public affairs. Neo-liberal values surged ahead predicting 'the end of history' and the natural emergence of capitalism as 'the sole' arbiter of the fate of the world. In the contemporary socio-economic milieu, 'management' and 'market' seem to be inbuilt in public administration redefining 'public' in a radical way.

As a paradigm reflective of the new challenges, governance has repositioned public administration as a field of enquiry. By responding to the modern challenges 'of high fragmentation and the disarticulation of the state', the new formulation of governance enables us to redefine public administration within 'the structural and contextual dynamics of the emerging global order'.[93] Two major trends—globalization and devolution—define the agenda of governance. They pose challenges as well as opportunities to redefine some of the major concerns of the traditional system of governance. Government must, as Donald F. Kettl emphasizes, 'not only devise new strategies for managing public programmes effectively in a globalized and devolved policy world [but also] build the capacity for doing so'.[94] Instead of altogether rejecting the Weberian hierarchical model of bureaucracy, Kettl argues for adaptation of the 'traditional vertical system' to the new challenges of globalization and devolution and also for integrating new horizontal systems to the traditional vertical ones. Being aware of the 'rigidity' in which the traditional hierarchical authority works and also that globalization and devolution 'scramble its foundation', Kettl thus insists on 'enhancing the capacity of the government to govern and manage effectively in this transformed environment'. There is another significant dimension that the governance agenda underlines: the problem of scale of various levels of government—from the local to the national. In a very perceptive comment, Daniel Bell drew our attention to this dimension of governance, as early as 1988, by saying that

[t]he common problem, I believe, is this: the nation state is becoming too small for the big problems of life, and too big for the small problems of life. It is too small for the big problems because there are no effective international mechanisms to deal with such things as capital flows, commodity imbalances, the loss of jobs, and the several demographic tidal waves that will be developing in the next twenty years. It is too big for small problems because the flow of power to a national political centre means that the centre becomes increasingly unresponsive to the variety and diversity of local needs. In short, there is a mismatch of scale.[95]

Within the governance discourse, several new concepts have gained salience underlining the shift from administration to management, from politics to market. In a 1987 OECD pamphlet entitled '*Administration as Service, the User as Client*, two market-governed ideas were introduced: *client orientation* and *service orientation*. In this conceptualization, citizens are clients and the public sector exists for those clients who use its services. And, public administration is reduced to being merely service providers to the clients or customers ignoring its purpose of which public administration is distinctly different from private administration. These two concepts constitute 'responsiveness' in public administration. Public administration becomes responsive, the OECD formula suggests, only if it is responsive to its users and satisfies them according to their expectations.[96] Governance is, thus, a mechanical act, governed not by any political ideal, but by the market where the satisfaction of the client is always primary to any other considerations. Public administration, in the new dispensation, is just a mechanism for the delivery of public services efficiently and with a smile to the individual customers, rejecting the role of 'political ideals' in its distribution. Politics lies in choosing 'what services to deliver, but implies nothing about how to deliver it'.[97]

If governance means interactional plurality in respect of collective societal problem solving, where do we place the phenomenon of gender as a constituent of governance? How does one explain women's empowerment in development by focusing on the concept of governance? In other words, does good governance or governance as such signify any specific standard of women's involvement in societal decision making? This is certainly a grey area that has not received adequate attention in the available conceptualization of governance. By insisting, however, on collective endeavours in development, the governance model seems to be theoretically receptive to 'gender' as a significant input. Several World Bank reports on this subject are illustrative here. As in the lack of adequate emphasis on gender, the governance model seems to suffer, largely since it has been identified as an ideological ploy of the 'developed' West to champion 'neo-liberalism' as a universal goal. There is sense in this argument. Since good governance is associated with loan conditionalities of the donors, with specific reference to accountability of the recipient countries, there has been an obvious criticism of governance being a Western-imposed concept of hegemonic nature. Despite the fact that it is a meaningful observation, what is intriguing is the explanation of governance exclusively in terms of the specified conditions on which economic aid is given, when the model seeks to articulate a general theory of public administration. One can trace the roots of such an obvious connection to the historical context in which governance was conceptualized. As shown, governance as model was devised by the World Bank in 1989 in the context of Sub-Saharan Africa where government was almost absent, if not missing entirely. What was true in Sub-Saharan Africa may not, for obvious reasons, be appropriate for the rest of world. Thus it would be conceptually limiting and theoretically redundant to apply the model of governance equally to the rest of world. Hence the hype for 'the universality' of this model does not seem to be logically tenable. What is striking about the concept, despite its various obvious limitations, is that governance or good governance has brought back some major issues in the development debate, especially the role of the state. One is not very clear, for instance, whether governance leads to loss of state control, since governance is merely suggestive of changes in governing. Similarly, linking 'goodness' with 'governance' is another theoretically significant issue given the apparent incompatibility between the two. While the former is 'ethics' or 'morality' related, the latter is primarily a technical act, informed by rules and regulations that have evolved over a historical period of time. These are some of the major governance-linked issues providing significant inputs to attempts at reconceptualising public administration in the 'globalized' international order.

There is no denying that governance has refashioned the contemporary debate on public administration by raising certain major critical questions. The primary goal, however, that remains at the core of this new dispensation in the World-Bank-sponsored model is to seek to champion universal goals within particular constraint where the role of politics is significantly minimal, if not entirely outlawed. Despite the formally apolitical stance of the World Bank on this question, 'there is little doubt that underlying even this limited vision of governance is a Western model, ringing with Weberian ethos, with its emphasis on free markets, individualism and a neutral but efficient public administration, subject to a legitimate government'.[98] Without politics, democracy has a restrictive meaning. Politics is the only social process of negotiation and contestation—politics as consisting of all the processes of conflict, cooperation, and negotiation involved in the use, production, and situation of resources. Hence John J. Kirlin argues that 'as long as democracy is valued the big questions of Public administration must go beyond the big questions of Public Management'.[99] Public administration diminishes its role in society if understood primarily in terms of managing public agencies. Both the Minnowbrook I Conference (1968) and the Blacksburg Manifesto have raised this issue of democratic governance in public interest. What is relevant in the context of the 'Third World' is that public administration is being crippled in the name of structural adjustment, which invokes more and more 'the market model' of governance in utter disregard of the crucial social developmental role of the state in the developing countries. The interests of public administration are no longer people related but capital related. And, here lies the perils of externally induced administrative reform through which most of the Third World countries are passing today. Hence Leftwich rightly argues that

the primacy of politics in development should not...be disguised any longer behind a technicist language about governance and management. For while no one would deny the importance of institutions and rules, it is political processes which bring them into being and crucially, which sustain them.[100]

In terms of administrative theory building, the current emphasis on 'public management' via the market model of governance needs to be viewed in proper historical perspective. Historically, two contrasting visions have guided the pursuits of administrative analysis: the managerial vision and the democratic vision. Both public/impersonal bureaucracy and democratic polity are critical to liberal democracy. But, administrative theorists, since the days of Woodrow Wilson and the authors of POSDCORB, have often been tempted to overemphasize 'managerialism' with its predilection for efficiency, economy, and effectiveness. The other more central pursuits in theories of public administration—such as achieving a democratic polity, improving the instruments of collective action, creating conditions for good citizenship, and increasing societal learning—are of no concern for those advocating public management. A major flaw in the managerial perspective is its inordinate interest in organizational concerns and measures of organizational performance. The interests of a democratic polity and maintenance of a legal order are substituted by the concern for organizational survival. There is in this effort a misplaced emphasis on 'the instrument' at the cost of 'the purpose' of public administration. As a result, the public choice perspective gains precedence over others. On the surface, the public choice theory seems to be the prime perspective in policy making, though it tends to push 'politics' out of the government by injecting the so-called market discipline. Hence, it is argued that rational models, including the public choice theory

are not merely seen as some bundle of techniques to do policy analysis. The mission of public/rational choice practitioners has become...far more ambitious; the objective for many devotees of rational models is to supplant the pushing, bargaining and noise of democratic politics with the putative elegance and parsimony of a rational calculus, the application of which will maximize cost-effectiveness and personal freedom.[101]

Public administration as management thus misses, altogether, the overarching perspective of a democratic polity. Sustained capacity of the political system for collective action, effective citizenship, and developing and nurturing the civic infrastructure to protect citizens' rights, and promoting collective life are of vital significance for any public administration in democracy. The new management cult is particularly ominous for Third World public administration, as it tends to strengthen bureaucracy, further impeding the development of alternative people's institutions so necessary for both generating social capacity to govern and creating more democratic spaces independent of bureaucratic administration. Characterized as 'neo-Taylorism', good governance seems thus a rehash of 'the one-best-way-principle' of the classical administrative theory which is a complete mismatch, for obvious reasons, with the contemporary global context that demands more 'open-endedness' in governance than rigidity of any kind.

WHAT THE VOLUME IS (NOT) ABOUT

The aim of this exercise is twofold: (1) to understand the concept of governance in its most complex manifestation. Is governance a mere practice or a conceptualizing mode striving to mould the practice of administration in a particular fashion? And, also (2) to identify its theoretical roots in the 'neo-liberal' mode of thinking, cutting across different sub-disciplines in the social sciences. Seeking to grasp governance as a complex manifestation of contemporary 'neo-liberal' search, the proposed work will fill up the gaps in the available literature that tends to reduce governance to just another mode of public administration undermining the ideological challenge that the mode articulates in the era of globalization.

The volume has two interconnected parts. Part I deals with the conceptual articulation of the phenomenon of governance, while Part II is devoted to a selective number of articles seeking to grasp the phenomenon empirically. Since the reader is also meant for graduate students, some of the chosen pieces deal with basic characteristics of the concept that is rooted in the neo-liberal form of global capitalism. Hence, Part I—with five articles—concentrates on the roots of governance as a conceptual tool of the international donor agencies, especially the World Bank. In his contribution, Mohit

Bhattacharya, one of the editors, argues that governance is essentially a neo-liberal articulation of public administration. Gerald E. Caiden locates the concept in the global context that saw a sea change, especially in the aftermath of the disintegration of the Soviet Union. In the same vein, H. George Frederickson is critical of the phenomenon which is articulated as 'contracting-out' of public administration. This strikes, as Frederickson feels, at the core of public administration which is guided by a purpose that governance can never approximate. Samuel Paul, in his contribution, expresses concern on the declining importance of citizens, given the reconceptualizing of citizens as 'clients' in market-driven societies. On the basis of his study of public service in Bangalore, the author has drawn our attention to 'the role of civil society or the stakeholders' in interactive governance. Drawn from their study of Tijuana municipal administration in Mexico and Newham Borough in the UK, Dorte Salskov-Iversen and others have pursued an in-depth analysis of 'the hegemonic governance discourse', in which human life is increasingly being conceived of 'in entrepreneurial terms'. What is most striking in their work is the attempt to theoretically address the issues of 'governmentality', 'globalization', and 'local practice' by reference to a critical study of two different localities.

In the empirical part, based largely on Indian experience, there are five articles. The section begins with an article by Kuldeep Mathur focusing on 'the shift from government to governance'. For the author, the adoption of the 1991 economic reforms is probably a watershed in public administration which no longer remains 'a hostage of bureaucracy'. The article on governance and civil service reform in India by Bidyut Chakrabarty is empirically grounded on a critical analysis of administrative reforms in India, including the 1997 Fifth Pay Commission. Drawing on the World Bank concern for 'downsizing' the rent-seeking public bureaucracies, the Fifth Pay Commission, as the editor argues, seems to have adopted a panoptical view of the Indian civil service that is not entirely 'postcolonial' in its ideological thrust. As a process of reform in the way government works, e-governance is perhaps an appropriate mechanism in building a SMART government, argues Subhash C. Bhatnagar on the basis of his study of the strategies that the Andhra Pradesh government had adopted to reform governance. In the globalizing world, Bhatnagar also underlines, governance is a 'function' that needs to be 'e-enabled' and 'e-driven' to capture its reinvented meaning. As an extensive study of a selective regulatory institutions by Saugata Bhattacharya and Urjit R. Patel has shown, the primary failure of these agencies 'has been the lack of attention to the reform of the market structure and an inadequate understanding of the nature of interaction between the market structure and the effectiveness of the regulatory process'. Furthermore, the fact that these regulatory institutions operate in 'a hostile environment' owing to the hostility of a well-entrenched bureaucracy also accounts for their 'inefficiency' in India, which is not exactly 'a free economy'. The volume concludes with an article on public–private partnerships (PPPs) in India. Based on a study of PPPs in Uttar Pradesh, Andhra Pradesh, Karnataka, and Bihar, the article demonstrates how effective the partnership is in family planning in these states. This article has also shown the role of stakeholders in implementing some of the health-related schemes involving both the public and private sectors.

Taken together, the introduction and selected articles seek to provide a critical analysis of the governance paradigm, which is not merely concerned with reform in public administration but also identifies new areas of research of a multidisciplinary nature. The governance paradigm has led to the recognition of the role of multiple agencies in organizing and undertaking the public's business. In addition to formal government, the role of non-governmental organizations and community-based organizations has been acknowledged as supplementary public agencies. Another significant development is decentralization and empowerment of localities for local resources and knowledge-based authentic grassroots governance. The Seventy-Third and Seventy-Fourth Constitutional Amendments (1992) signal momentous changes in terms of grassroots people's empowerment whose full potentialities are yet to be realized. The new instrumentalities like the Lokpal/Lokyukta for dealing with people's grievances against top functionaries in government still remain a distant dream. Corruption in many forms continue to plague the Indian public system, but its ability to successfully deal with corruption at different levels has fallen short of requirement. The other instrumentality is the 'Human Rights' institution at the national and state levels, which is quite recent in Indian public administration. There are both international and domestic pressures to uphold human rights and ensure effective 'rights regimes' at all levels in the interest of steady democratization of the public sphere.

Thus public administration has undergone a sea change in response to new inputs from the contemporary socio-economic and political scene. It is therefore difficult, if not impossible, to grasp the nature of public administration in terms of the Weberian conceptualization underlining its rigid, rule-bound, and hierarchic characteristics. Instead, the preferred form of administration is one which is accessible, transparent, and accountable, and the citizens are consumers. Furthermore, the notion 'public' in public administration has acquired new dimensions where the public–private distinction is more analytical than real since there is a growing support for both cooperation and healthy competition between these two sectors in the larger interests of societal development. Thus, public administration, if conceptualized in its orthodox mould, is both an inadequate tool of analysis and inappropriate to meaningfully articulate governance in which government is merely an actor in the complex web of public administration. By drawing attention to the changes in the theoretical domain of public administration— reflective of the metamorphosis of the realities where public administration is located—this reader is both a comprehensive review of the available literature and also a quest for 'new' directions in the unfolding and consolidation of the discipline.

We are aware that the volume is not exhaustive. The core theme—governance—has still been evolving and the accompanying literature is proliferating almost daily. Nonetheless, this reader is useful for at least two reasons: first, by including those articles which we think are seminal and instructive, we have placed before the readers a basic text which will contribute to further research in this growing field. Second, given the introduction of courses on governance in most of the major universities in the world, this compilation will be of use to the students, researchers, and practitioners of public administration. The long introduction by the editors will acquaint the readers with the theoretical roots and empirical manifestation of governance in 'the global village'. Not only is the introduction a thorough review of the literature, it also raises critical questions for further research on the subject. In this sense, the introduction is organically linked with those articles that are included in the volume.

Notes

[1] As mentioned, governance in contemporary academic discourses is exclusively the practitioners' contribution. Its definition by leading institutions and studies, however, converge on the term as referring to 'a process' by which power is exercised. Various definitions of governance is given in Appendix I.

[2] H. George Frederickson, 'The Repositioning of American Public Administration', the 1999 John Gaus Lecture, mimeo, p. 5.

[3] R.A.W. Rhodes, 'Governance and Public Administration', in *Debating Governance*, J. Pierre (ed.), Oxford: Oxford University Press, 1999; N. Rose, and P. Miller, 'Political Power beyond the State: Problematics of Government', *British Journal of Sociology*, 43 (2), 1992.

[4] Robert D. Putnam, *Making Democracy Work: Civic Traditions in Modern Italy*, Princeton: Princeton University Press, 1993.

[5] For an analytical study of civil society see Carolyn M. Elliot (ed.), *Civil Society and Democracy: A Reader*, Delhi: Oxford University Press, 2003.

[6] Jamil Jreisat, 'Governance in a Globalized World', *International Journal of Public Administration*, 27 (13 &14), 2004, pp. 1004–6.

[7] Manuel Castells, *The Rise of the Network Society*, vol. I, Oxford: Blackwell Publishing, 2000, pp. 1–2.

[8] Dorte Salskov-Iversen, Hans Krause Hansen, and Sven Bislev, 'Governmentality, Globalization and Local Practice: Transformation of a Hegemonic Discourse', *Alternatives: Social Transformation and Human Governance*, 25 (2), April–June 2000, p. 186.

[9] Hans Krause Hansen, and Jens Hoff (eds), *Digital Governance: Networked Societies: Creating Authority, Community and Identity in a Globalized World*, Nordicom: Samfundslitterathur Press, 2006, p. 21.

[10] Webster's *New Universal Unabridged Dictionary*, London: Dorset & Baber, 1979.

[11] *Random House College Dictionary*, revised ed., New York: Random House, 1984, p. 571.

[12] World Bank, *Sub-Saharan Africa: From Crisis to Sustainable Growth: A Long-Term Perspective Study*, Washington, DC: World Bank, 1989, p. 18.

[13] World Bank, *World Development Report*, New York: Oxford University Press, 1992, p. 29.

[14] World Bank, *The World Bank in Governance: The World Bank Experience*, Washington, DC: World Bank, 1992, p. 27.

[15] World Bank, *Governance and Development*, Washington, DC: World Bank, 1992, p. 9.

[16] World Bank, *Sub-Saharan Africa: From Crisis to Sustainable Growth: A Long-Term Perspective Study*, p. 192.

[17] Deborah Brautigam, 'Governance and Economy: A Review', Working Papers, Policy and Review Departments, Washington, DC: World Bank, December 1991, p. 8.

[18] Ibid., p. 9.

[19] World Bank, *Governance and Development*, p. 3.

[20] Ibid., p. 58 (See note 1).

[21] UNDP, *1997: Reconceptualizing Governance*, discussion paper 2, New York: UNDP, January 1997, p. 9.

[22] Deborah Brautigam, 'Governance and Economy: A Review', p. 6.

[23] UNDP, *1997: Reconceptualizing Governance*, p. 19.

[24] This section is drawn from *Human Settlements*, report prepared by United Nations Economic and Social Commission for Asia and Pacific, unless otherwise stated. *Source*: www.unescap.org/huset/gg/governance.html.

[25] The summary is drawn from the UNDP report, *Governance for Sustainable Human Development*, 1997.

[26] Lewis T. Preston's foreword to *Governance and Development*, Washington, DC: World Bank, 1992, p. v.

[27] World Bank, *Governance and Development*, pp. 11–12.

[28] These points are drawn from Philippe Keraudran and Hans Van Vicrlo, 'Theories of Public Management Reform and Their Practical Implications', in *Innovations in Public Management: Perspectives from East and West Europe*, Tony Verheijen and David Coombes (eds), Cheltenham: Edward Elgar, 1998.

[29] Drawn from 'Governance Barometer: Policy Guidelines for Good Governance', prepared by the National Party of South Africa, www.gdrc.org/u-gov/governance-understand.html.

[30] This is how governance is defined by The Institute on Governance, Canada. *Source*: www.log.ca/about.html.

[31] Lawrence E. Lyer, Jr., Carolyn J. Heinrich, and Carolyn J. Hill, *Improving Governance: A New Logic for Empirical Research*, Washington, DC: Georgetown University Press, 2001, p. 10.

[32] The discussion on 'engaged governance' is drawn from Dr Diane M. Gurthrie's 'Engaged Governance: An Institutional Approach to Government-Civil Society Engagement', Background Paper for United Nations Department of Economic and Social Affairs, Interregional workshop on 'Engaged Governance', Colombo, Sri Lanka, 9–11 December, 2003.

[33] Dorte Salskov-Iversen, Hans Krause Hansen, and Sven Bislev, 'Governmentality, Globalization and Local Practice: Transformation of a Hegemonic Discourse', p. 194.

[34] OECD, *Participatory Development and Good Governance*, Paris: OECD, 1995, p. 14.

[35] Lawrence E. Lyer, jr., Carolyn J. Heinrich, and Carolyn J. Hill, *Improving Governance: A New Logic for Empirical Research*, p. 1.

[36] UNDP, '*Decentralized Governance for Development*, UNDP Working Paper, New York: UNDP, 1997.

[37] Wolfgang Michalski, Riel Miller, and Barrie Stevens, 'Governance in the 21st Century: Power in the Global Knowledge Economy and Society', in *Governance in the 21st Century: Future Studies*, London: OECD, 2001, p. 9.

[38] World Bank, *The Bank and the Heavily Indebted Middle-Income Countries*, Washington, DC: World Bank, 1989, p. 49.

[39] Adrian Leftwich, 'Governance, Democracy and Development in the Third World', *Third World Quarterly*, 14 (3), 1993, p. 607.

[40] Ibid., p. 607.

[41] James M. Buchanan, and Gordon Tullock, *The Calculus of Consent: Logical Foundation of Constitutional Democracy*, Ann Arbor: The University of Michigan Press, 1965, p. 312.

[42] Anthony Downs, *An Economic Theory of Democracy*, New York: Harper Bros, 1957.

[43] James M. Buchanan and Gordon Tullock, *The Calculus of Consent: Logical Foundation of Constitutional Democracy*, p. 62.

[44] Ibid., p. 116.

[45] William A. Niskanen, *Bureaucracy and Representative Government*, Chicago: Aldine-Atherton, 1971.

[46] Peter Self, *Modern Theories of Government*, London: George Allen and Unwin, 1985, p. 31.

[47] Herbert Simon, 'Why Public Administration?' *Public Administration Review*, 58 (1), January/February 1998.

[48] Gerald Marcou, 'The Role of the State and the Future of Public Services Faced with the Problems of Transition and Development', in *Public Administration and Development: Improving Accountability, Responsiveness and Legal Framework*, Amsterdam: IOS Press, 1997 (a UN document).

[49] According to Foucault, governmentality has evolved 'from pastoral power, taking the functions and individualizing practices of the Church and taking them to a form that totalizes governance. The pastoral power of the Church was based on the idea of a good shepherd who had complete knowledge of the flock, who took care of the flock and watched over each of them individually and collectively. The pastoral power was a form of ultimate kindness in which the good shepherd through perfect knowledge, could attend to the flock's needs. In the neo-liberal dispensation, not only are states less able to protect their citizens, but they are also eager to remove obstacles to globalization, resulting in a situation in which relations among governments are replaced by reliance on market force governance. In such

a situation, individual identities and loyalties shift away from the state as the state's ability to provide welfare and other functions is reduced. Instead these functions are increasingly assumed by the private sector'. Elina Penttinen, 'Capitalism as a System of Global Order', in *Power in Contemporary Politics: Theories, Practices, Globalisation*, Henri Goverde, Philip G Cerny, Mark Haugaard, and Howard Lentner (eds), London and New York: Sage, 2000, p. 211. For a detailed exposition of Foucault's governmentality, see Andre Munro, 'Following the Market: Rational Choice Theory and Neo-Liberal Governmentality', paper presented to the 20 Years After Foucault Conference, New School University, 16th April, 2004.

[50] Thomas Lemke, 'The Birth of Bio-Politics–Michael Foucault's Lecture at the College de France on Neo-Liberal Governmentality', *Economy and Society*, 30 (2), 2001, p. 201.

[51] Graham Burchell, 'Liberal Government and Technique of the Self' in *Foucault and Political Reason*, Andre Barry, Thomas Osborne, and Nikolas Rose (eds), Chicago: The University of Chicago Press, 1991, p. 42.

[52] Andre Munro, 'Following the Market: Rational Choice Theory and Neo-Liberal Governmentality', p. 4.

[53] For an elaboration of this argument, see Dorte Salskov-Iversen, Hans Krause Hansen, and Sven Bislev, 'Governmentality, Globalization and Local Practice: Transformation of a Hegemonic Discourse', p. 191.

[54] Ibid.

[55] Francis Fukuyama, *The End of History and the Last Man*, New York: Avon Books, 1992.

[56] Martha Feldman, and Anne Khadimain, *Inclusive Management: Building Relationships with the Public*, Centre for Study of Democracy, Repository of the University of California Irvine, 2004.

[57] World Bank, *The World Development Report, 1999-2000*, vol. 1, Washington, DC: World Bank, 2000, p. 19.

[58] World Bank, *Governance and Development*.

[59] For definitions of public accountability, see Richard Mulganm 'The Process of Public Accountability', *Australian Journal of Public Administration*, 56 (1), 25–36, March 1997; M. Hayller, 'Accountability, Ends, Means and Resources', *Asian Review of Public Administration*, 3 (2), 1991.

[60] Albert O. Hirschman, *Exit, Voice, and Loyalty: Responses to Decline in Firms, Organisations, and States*, New Haven: Yale University Press, 1970.

[61] Samuel Paul, 'Auditing for Social Change: Learning from Civil Society Initiatives', paper presented in 6th Global Forum on Reinventing Government: Towards Participatory and Transparent Governance, 24–27 May 2007, Seoul, Republic of Korea, p. 3.

[62] The outcome of this movement is momentous in terms of both theoretical and practical significance, as Rob Jenkins and Anne Marie Goetz have shown in 'Accounts and Accountability: Theoretical Implications of the Right-to-Information Movement in India', *Third World Quarterly*, 20 (3), pp. 603–22.

[63] Aruna Roy, Nikhil Dey, and Shanker Singh, 'Demanding Accountability', *Seminar*, April 2001.

[64] Working paper entitled 'National level R[ight] T[o] I[nformation]', Commonwealth Human Rights Group, 2005, p. 2.

[65] Madhav Godbole, 'Unending Struggle for Right to Information', *Economic and Political Weekly*, 12 August 2000, p. 2899. Godbole further observed that 'though five years of dithering over the bill on the right to information, the position of the Central Governments which have been run by two United Fronts, the BJP and its allies, has remained the same. [It] is disconcerting that in this important area of governance, the interests of bureaucracy and the ruling elite seem to converge against the empowerment of common man'.

[66] Government of India, *The Gazette of India*, Part II (section 1), Ministry of Law and Justice, New Delhi, 2005.

[67] Working paper titled 'National level R[ight] T[o] I[nformation], p. 2.

[68] *The Hindu* characterized the Right to Information as 'a path to Swaraj', The *Hindu*, 7 October 2005.

[69] In the World Bank's 1994 report *Governance: the World Bank's Experience*, 'good governance is epitomized by predictable, open and enlightened policy-making (that is transparent processes); a bureaucracy imbued with a professional ethos; an executive arm of government accountable to its actions, and a strong civil society participating in public affairs, and all behaving under the rule of law'.

[70] *Reforming Public Institutions and Strengthening Governance: Main Strategy*, A World Bank Strategy, November, 2000, Public Sector Group, poverty Reduction and Economic Management (PREM) Network, p. 1.

[71] M. Shamsul Haque, 'Significance of Accountability under the New Approach to Public Governance', *International Review of Administrative Services*, 66, 2000, p. 57.

[72] Ibid., p. 61.

[73] Ibid., pp. 63–5.

[74] *Reforming Public Institutions and Strengthening Governance: Main Strategy*, p. 1.

[75] These institutions cannot afford to be 'pure' since they operate and are also rooted in a specific socio-economic and political milieu, as Leena Srivastava argues while articulating the World Bank views on the regulatory institutions, especially in the 'third world' context. Leena Srivastava, 'Issues in Institutional Design of Regulatory Agencies' paper presented in, On

Infrastructure Regulation and Reform, World Bank, New Delhi, 4–15 December 2000.

[76] Both of these terms are broad enough to include the use of ICT by government and civil society to promote greater participation of citizens in the governance of political institutions. Thus,for instance, they cover the use of internet by politicians and political parties to elicit views from their constituencies in an efficient manner or by propagating the views by civil society organizations which are in conflict with the ruling authorities. E/digital government is, by contrast, a narrowly conceptualized idea focusing only governmental steps to improve government functions.

[77] Jagdish C. Kapoor, 'IT and Good Governance', *Indian Journal of Public Administration*, XLVI (3), July–September, 2000, p. 394.

[78] Bata K. Dey, 'E-Governance in India: Problems, Challenges and Opportunities—A Future Vision', *Indian Journal of Public Administration*, XLVI (3), July–September, 2000, p. 306.

[79] Government of India, *The Information Technology Act, 2000*, New Delhi: Government of India, 2000 chapter 1, p. 2. The act is reproduced in the *Indian Journal of Public Administration*, XLVI (3), July–September, 2000, pp. 417–55.

[80] Ibid., chapter III, (1), p. 10.

[81] Government of India, *The Tenth Five Year Plan,* approach paper, 2002, ch. 6, p. 187.

[82] Sameer Sachdeva, 'White Paper on E-Governance Strategy in India', World Bank, Washington, December, 2003 (unpublished), p. 5.

[83] For details of this argument, see Subhash Bhatnagar, 'Administrative Corruption: How does E-Government Help?', Global Corruption Report, 2003, Transparency International, New York, 2003, pp. 8–9.

[84] I owe this information to Mr. Sanjay Jaju, an IAS officer working as Vice Chairman and Managing Director, Infrastructure Corporation of Andhra Pradesh.

[85] For details of the argument, see Elaine Kamarck, 'Government Innovations around the World', Faculty Research Working Paper, John F. Kennedy School of Government, Harvard University, February, 2004, p. 36.

[86] Nasser Munjee, 'India: A Partnership Agenda for the Next Decade', in *India: the Next Decades*, Manmohan Malhotra, New Delhi: Academic Foundation, 2006, p. 268.

[87] Joseph Stiglitz, *Making Globalization Work: The Next Steps to Global Justice*, London: Allen Lane, 2006, p. 198.

[88] Nasser Munjee, 'India: A Partnership Agenda for the Next Decade', p. 271.

[89] Daniel Tarschys, 'Wealth, Values, Institutions: Trends in Government and Governance', in *Governance in the 21st Century: Future Studies*, OECD, 2001, p. 28.

[90] Dorte Salskov-Iversen, Hans Krause Hansen, and Sven Bislev, 'Governmentality, Globalization and Local Practice: Transformation of a Hegemonic Discourse', p. 188.

[91] Elina Penttinen, 'Capitalism as a System of Global Order', p. 211.

[92] Paul R. Brass, 'Foucault Steals Political Science', *American Reviews of Political Science*, 3, 2000, p. 318.

[93] H. George Frederickson, 'The Repositioning of American Public Administration', p. 710.

[94] Donald F. Kettl, 'The Transformation of Governance: Globalization, Devolution and the Role of Government', unpublished discussion paper prepared for the Spring Meeting of the National Academy of Public Administration, 1–3 June 2000, p. 11.

[95] Daniel Bell, 'Previewing Planet Earth in 2013', *Washington Post*, 3 January 1988.

[96] OECD, *Administration as Science. The Public as Client*, Paris: OECD, 1987, p. 97.

[97] Dorte Salskov-Iversen, Hans Krause Hansen, and Sven Bislev, 'Governmentality, Globalization and Local Practice: Transformation of a Hegemonic Discourse', p. 196.

[98] Adrian Leftwich, 'On the Primacy of Politics in Development', in *Democracy and Development: Theory and Practice*, Adrian Leftwich (ed.), Cambridge: Polity Press, 1996, p. 16.

[99] Jonh J. Kirlin, 'The Big Question in a Democracy', *Public Administration Review*, September–October, 1996, p. 217.

[100] Adrian Leftwich, 'On the Primacy of Politics in Development', p. 20.

[101] Max Neiman and Stephen J. Stambough, 'Rational Choice and the Evaluation of Public Policy', *Policy Studies Journal*, Autumn, 26, p. 450.

APPENDIX I

Governance is basically a definitive process in which power is exercised, as the following definitions demonstrate:

UNDP: Governance is viewed as the exercise of economic, political and administrative authority to manage a country's affairs at all levels. It comprises mechanisms, processes and institutions through which citizens and groups articulate their interests, exercise their legal rights, meet their obligations and mediate their differences (UNDP 1997).

World Bank: Governance is defined as the manner in which power is exercised in the management of a country's economic and social resources. The World Bank has identified three distinct aspects of governance: (1) the form of political regime, (2) the process by which authority is exercised in the management of a country's economic and social resources for development, and (3) the capacity of governments to design, formulate and implement policies and discharge functions (World Bank 1997).

OECD: The concept of governance denotes the use of political authority and exercise of control in relations to the management of its resources for social and economic development. This broad definition encompasses the role of public authorities in establishing the environment in which economic operators function and in determining the distribution of benefits as well as the nature of the relationship between the ruler and ruled (OECD DAC 1995).

DFID: The Department for International Development adopts the same approach as that provided by the OECD's Development Assistance Committee (DAC) which identifies four key elements in governance: (1) legitimacy of government (political systems), (2) accountability of political and official elements of government (public administration and financial systems), and (3) competence of governments to formulate policies and deliver services (public administration) and (4) economic systems and organizational strengthening.

Asian Development Bank (ADB): The definition of governance, adopted by the ADB echoes that of the World Bank. Accordingly, the ADB regards good governance as synonymous with sound development management. It involves both the public and private sectors. It is related to the effectiveness with which development assistance is used, the impact of development programmes and projects (including those financed by the Bank). Thus irrespective of the precise set of economic policies that find favour with a government, good governance is required to ensure that these policies have their desired effect. In essence, it concerns norms of behaviour that help ensure that governments actually deliver to their citizens what they say they will deliver.

USAID: Governance encompasses the capacity of the state, the commitment to the public good, the rule of law, the degree of transparency and accountability, the level of popular participation and the stock of social capital. Without good governance, it is impossible to foster development. No amount of resource transferred or infrastructure built can compensate 'bad governance'.

Institute of Governance, Ottawa, Canada: Governance comprise the institutions, processes and conventions in a society, which determine how power is exercised, how important decisions affecting society are made and how various interests are accorded a place in such decisions.

Commissions on Global Governance: Governance is the sum of the many ways individuals and institutions, public and private, manage their common affairs. It is a continuing process through which conflicting or diverse interests may be accommodated or cooperative action may be taken. It includes formal institutions and regimes empowered to enforce compliance, as well as informal arrangements that people and institutions either have agreed to or perceive to be in their interest.

Source: Drawn from Adel M. Abdellatif, 'Good Governance and its Relationship to Democracy and Economic Development', *Workshop IV, Democracy, Economic Development and Culture*, held on the occasion of the congregation of the Global Forum III on fighting and safeguarding integrity, Seoul, 20–31 May 2003.

APPENDIX II

The Sequence of Good Governance

What comes first? Good governance or human rights? In this instance, the answer is neither. Good governance and human rights develop together. Outlined below are some key principles of good governance and an explanation of how each is linked with a particular type of human right.

Good Governance Principle	Human Rights Link
Democratic government and processes	A truly democratic government cannot occur unless individuals have guaranteed civil and political rights. This means they can freely express their views without fear of being arrested, tortured or discriminated against.
Effective public sector institutions	These institutions are developed through good government policy but they cannot be administered effectively unless the staff has access to economic human rights, such as adequate pay. Adequate pay enables people to support themselves properly and so reduces corruption. This improves governance.
The primacy of the rule of law and an impartial and effective legal system	The primacy of the rule of law and an impartial legal system protects the civil rights of all people in relation to their property, personal security and liberty. The legal and judicial system should be independent of the government so that it can serve the interests of its citizens rather that a particular political party. In this way it protects the civil rights of its citizens against a predatory state.
A strong civil society	Civil society is about people contributing to the governing of their country through their participation in the community. It is difficult to participate if you are poor, unemployed, hungry, homeless and uneducated. People who live under

Contd...

... Contd

Good Governance Principle	Human Rights Link
	these conditions are being denied their economic, social and cultural rights. Good governance cannot truly occur until these rights are guaranteed by a government willing to take responsibility for the social security of its people.
A high priority on investing in people	Investing in people means creating a skilled workforce. This cannot occur unless basic economic and social human rights are met including the right to adequate education, health services, food, and shelter.
Careful management of the national economy	A government, which does not manage its economy well will not have enough resources to guarantee basic human rights. However, if these rights are not met it is difficult to create the accountable and transparent institutions so vital to good governance and to sustainable development.

Source: Global Education: Australia Aid Programme, http://globaled.ausaid. gov.au/secondary/casestud/governance/1/governance.html.

PART I

CONCEPTUAL UNDERPINNING
OF GOVERNANCE

2

Contextualizing Governance and Development*

Mohit Bhattacharya

ETIOLOGY OF GOOD GOVERNANCE

Development assistance to Third World countries in the post-cold-war era has been subjected to the new politics of 'good governance' with its roots in neo-liberalism. In 1989, the concept of 'governance' was for the first time highlighted in a World Bank document on Sub-Saharan Africa. By good governance it was meant, at that time, sound development management. Four key dimensions identified in this context were: (1) public sector management; (2) accountability; (3) legal framework for development; and (4) information and transparency. The bank document on Sub-Saharan Africa had this to say: 'Improving governance would begin with an assessment of the institutional environment (with emphasis on the key governance elements of accountability, rule of law, openness and transparency) which determines the patrimonial profile of the country: high when all other factors are absent and low when they are present.'

WORLD BANK'S CONCEPTUALIZATION

As the World Bank document, entitled *Governance and Development* (1992), puts it, 'governance is defined as the manner in which power is exercised in the management of a country's economic and social resources for development'. From its lending experience in many

* Originally published as 'Contextualizing Good Governance', in *Indian Journal of Public Administration*, XLIV (3), July–September 1998.

developing countries, the bank came to realize that 'good governance is central to creating and sustaining an environment which fosters strong and equitable development, and it is an essential complement to sound economic policies'. Three distinct aspects are identified in the conceptualization of 'governance': (1) the form of political regime (parliamentary or presidential, military or civilian, and authoritarian or democratic); (2) the process by which authority is exercised in the management of a country's economic and social resources; and (3) the capacity of governments to design, formulate, and implement policies, and, in general, to discharge government functions. The first aspect, admittedly, falls outside the bank's mandate. The focus of 'governance' is, therefore, basically, on the second and third aspects.

Recounting its wide experience, the bank document narrates vividly the problems of 'governance'. Despite technical soundness, for instance, programmes and projects have often failed to produce desired results. Laws are not enforced properly and there are often delays in implementation. Privatized production and market-led growth do not succeed unless investors face clear rules and institutions. In the absence of proper accounting systems, budgetary policies cannot be implemented or monitored. Many a time, procurement systems encourage corruption and distort public investment priorities. Again, failure to involve beneficiaries and others affected in the design and implementation of projects has often led to substantial erosion of their sustainability.

Against this background of malgovernance, the bank has attempted to focus on some of the key dimensions of 'governance', such as a public sector management accountability, the legal framework for development, and information and transparency, as already stated.

Economic, human, and institutional development are considered important in bringing about sound development management. The conditionalities of 'good governance' have been carefully spelt out, as the bank document sums up:

Governance' is a continuum, and not necessarily unidirectional; it does not automatically improve over time. It is a plant that needs constant tending. Citizens need to demand good governance. Their ability to do so is enhanced by literacy, education, and employment opportunities. Governments need to prove responsive to those demands. Neither of these can be taken for granted. Change occurs sometimes in response to external or internal threats.

It also occurs through pressures from different interest groups, some of which may be in the form of populist demands. Although lenders and aid agencies and other outsiders can contribute resources and ideas to improve governance, for change to be effective it must be rooted firmly in the societies concerned and cannot be imposed from outside.

What is surprising is that the World-Bank-touted 'good governance' thesis looks so unWorld-Bank-like, as conventionally the bank has been concerned with technical and economistic solutions. Hence, at first glance, the governance agenda seem rather 'naive and simplistic', to quote Leftwich (1994). Fundamentally, however, it is in continuation of the bank's 'technicist illusion', a kind of neo-managerialism, encompassing the more difficult spheres of political management of 'development' in Third World countries. 'Governance' is now being defined in terms of an autonomous administrative capacity, reminding one of the first-generation administrative theory centred around the administration-politics dichotomy. Governance is sought to be 'detached from the turbulent world of politics and the structure and purpose of the State'.

OECD'S DEFINITION

A definite political meaning of 'governance' appeared in the policy directives of the OECD countries, laying down conditionalities for receiving economic assistance. The OECD policy (1997) sought to link development assistance with (1) participatory development, (2) human rights, and (3) democratization. The key components of 'governance' were identified as:

1. legitimacy of government;
2. accountability of political and official elements of government;
3. competence of governments to make policy and deliver services; and
4. respect for human rights and the rule of law (including individual and group rights and security, a legal framework for economic and social activity, and participation).

What emerges out of the combined efforts of aid-giving countries and international funding agencies is that entitlement to aid would depend on the degree to which a client country would be having a liberal democratic state with a pluralist polity in which legislatures are constituted through free and fair elections.

STATE-SOCIETY RELATIONS

The governance agenda, as set by the World Bank, subsume a set of state-society regulating disciplinary procedures. There is an underlying belief that accountability or government through checks and balances available under a liberal democratic system would ensure that state activity meets the needs and expectations of society. So, the right kind of state and the right kind of society are both posited as end objectives in terms of the overarching neo-liberal agenda.

Prima facie, this kind of policy stance of Western donor agencies (particularly of the World Bank) looks innocuous. Promotion of the cause of liberal democracy seems to be the objective. However, critical comments on the bank's policy range from encroaching upon sovereignty to spreading the gospel of capitalism. Therefore, the question has been raised: What are the real intentions of the World Bank? Is it 'democracy' concern or 'domination' concern? Also, selling a single model of governance is like resurrecting the old 'one best way' of management of the classical theory vintage. The assumption that all is good in the First World, and all is bad in the Third seems to underline the bank's governance prescription. That there are alternatives in collective societal problem solving does not seem a tenable proposition to the dictating donor agencies.

OPERATIONAL DIFFICULTIES

There are genuine operational difficulties as well in translating the new concept of governance into actual practice. As Bob Currie comments:

Like democracy, governance remains a particularly difficult variable to operationalise. At present 'good governance' is seemingly defined in terms of a checklist of criteria (transparency, accountability, public sector management, etc.) that governance must broadly satisfy in order to justify receiving loans. However, it is not made explicit which, if any, of these are prioritised and how they should be measured and compared. Governance is not a binary variable and cannot be defined in terms of 'on/of' or 'present/ absent' criteria. There is little clear guidance as to how well or badly a government must perform in the above categories before it is granted or disqualified from funding. If quality of governance is to represent a standard for making vital decisions about international lending, there is a need for greater clarity about what this actually means in practical terms (1996).

WHITHER PEOPLE-DRIVEN DEVELOPMENT!

As earlier explained, the World Bank's (and the donor agencies') concern for 'good governance' has been linked to the problem of sound development management in Third World countries. And, very explicitly, the bank dictates terms and conditionalities for being eligible for assistance, oblivious of the fact that 'development discourse' has since moved away from the earlier 'top-down' approach to a distinct 'bottom-up' one. Imposed development has, since the 1980s, been substituted by an autonomous people-driven development concept. It seems the World Bank wants to reverse this trend.

A MORE CREATIVE APPROACH

Whatever might have been the institutional compulsions compelling the adoption of 'governance' paradigm by the First World countries, good governance need not be narrowly conceived in terms of a set of structural and processual dimensions as the World Bank and other funding agencies have sought to present them. Keeping in view the distinctive context of most Third World countries a more creative approach would be to treat the issues as new opportunities to have a fresh look at state-society relationships in today's complex world of governance in context-specific situations. To quote Kooiman in this connection:

In many countries, the main tendency in recent years has been to shift the balance between government and society away from the public sector and more towards the private sector. Partly, this added up to privatisation and sometimes to deregulation. But there are also efforts to shift the balance towards a sharing of tasks and responsibilities; towards doing thing together instead of doing them alone (either by the 'State' or by the 'market'). New patterns of interaction between governments and society can be observed in areas such as social welfare, environmental protection, education and physical planning. These new patterns are apparently aimed at discovering other ways of coping with new problems or of creating new possibilities for governing (1993).

It is this search for 'new possibilities' that brings out the true meaning of good governance. The issues involved rake up some of the old discourses on state-society relationships since the beginning of political theory. As mankind moves towards the new century, these relationships are being reopened for a fresh dialogue to fashion a new paradigm of governance amidst turbulent existential conditions. Obviously, it is going to be a multilevel and cross-national intellectual enterprise aimed at rehabilitating and enriching humanism within the parameters of a newly fabricated state-society relational architecture in search of a just society.

GOVERNANCE DISCOURSE AND DEVELOPMENT DISCOURSE

As can be inferred from the discussions so far, the governance discourse has generally been oriented towards institutional issues—issues of responsive, accountable, transparent, and open governing with the involvement of multiple actors, of which formal government (possibly a lean and thin one) would be one among many actors. Beyond institutional shaping there are other vital issues involved here—governing is not simply a structural problem; more importantly the question is—governing for what purpose and for whose benefit. Mahbub ul-Haq, one of the chief protagonists of 'human development' philosophy in development, posed the question: 'increased productivity is necessary; but let us ask the questions, increased productivity of whom and for whom?' (1988) The reorientation of 'development' that took place under his leadership and vision led to the publication of successive volumes of Human Development Report (HDR) carrying the imprint of his development philosophy. Note, for instance, the essence of the HDR (1990):

Human development is a process of enlarging people's choices. The most critical of these wide-ranging choices are to live a long and healthy life, to be educated and to have access to resources needed for a decent standard of living....Development enables people to have their choices. No one can guarantee human happiness, and the choices people make are their own concern. But the process of development should at least create a conducive environment for people, individually and collectively, to develop their full potential and to have a reasonable choice of leading productive and creative lives in accord with their needs and interests.

The contemporary 'governance discourse', contrastingly, has been engaged in the niceties of structural arrangements, without taking into account the vital questions of 'development ethics'.

DEVELOPMENT ETHICS

Decisions about 'development' are decisions about 'good or beneficial change', not just mere change. These decisions are bound to affect the society as a total life system of a collectivity or a segment of it. For centuries, ethical inquiry has revolved round the nature of human well-being and concerns about freedom, social equity, and justice. Therefore, a discussion of development ethics boils down essentially to an effort of having a fresh look at the concept of 'development' itself. At a very general level, it can be said that ideas about development involve at least three elements: (1) a macro-conception of the kind of society that is sought to be built, (2) a set of policies that would bring about both enhanced economic productivity and distributive justice aimed at the promotion of social equity, and (3) a set of clear measures that would protect, prevent, and enhance environmental quality (guarding against environmental degradation). Whether development decisions in a particular country situation have brought about 'good change' would always be debatable, depending on the definition of 'good' and who defines it.

ETHICAL CONCERNS

That there are important ethical concerns underlying major 'development' decisions—be it a dam construction or a programme of eviction of slum-dwellers for city improvement—is, however, often glossed over by planners and administrators. Development is not something that happens automatically; it is purposive action, and behind such action there must be an ethic of some kind—implicit or explicit (Bhattacharya 2006). Again, it is not usually admitted that the issue of 'power' is inherent in development decisions. The ruling class really rules. Particularly, in the postcolonial Third World situation, democracy has, in most cases, remained more a procedural matter than a real, substantive, and open exercise of people's power. Development decisions, under the circumstances, are, more often than not, 'top-down', non-participative, elite decisions that are intended to serve the interests of the 'powerful'. When 'power' decides, ethics becomes the handmaiden of power.

Still, there is no denying the fact that some sort of ethical norms actually inform any policy decisions related to development made by any agency, public or private (generally, of course, public or government agency). In this context, the observations of Nigel Dower (1998), President of the International Development Ethics Association (IDEA) are worth our quoting. As he puts it, two related things are involved in ethics: one, ethics is a 'set of norms or values together with some justifying story supporting those norms and values'; two, along with this there is 'systematic reflection on the nature and justification of such norms and values'. In this formulation, *norms* stand for 'certain rules or principles about what is morally right (required to be done) and what is right in the sense of what is morally permitted or what one has a right to do'. *Values* are 'certain elements of human well-being which are regarded as worth pursuing or promoting for members of one's society (and usually for human beings generally)'. In Dower's view, development is based on purposive or deliberate public-policy initiative and, as such, it 'must presuppose an ethic of some kind', and 'the pursuit of development will be all the more effective if people acknowledge the importance of explicit ethical debate about the ethical foundations of development'.

NEED FOR ETHICS

In continuation of what has been stated above, it can now be asserted that in the context of development, ethics is concerned with what we choose to do (including not to do) intentionally or on purpose. Ethics is about choice, employing determinations and judgements about values. The choices of concern in ethics are those giving rise to significant 'good' or 'bad' in the world or in the larger society. Surely this is an extremely sketchy presentation of a very large subject. What is important for our purposes is the ontological status of 'development' involving questions as, 'development' would mean what kind of existential transformation, for whom and how, and in terms of what scheme of distributional gains and losses, and even intended or unintended cultural mutations, and, very subtly, in terms of what consequences for the 'environment' as the womb of both human and non-human life. As Dennis Goulet puts it, 'Development is above all else a question of human values and attitudes, goals self-defined by societies, and criteria for determining what are tolerable costs to be borne, and by whom, in the course of change. These are far more important than modeling optimal resource allocations, upgrading skills, or rationalizing of administrative procedures' (1995). Looking back, one can clearly discern, at the beginning of the development discourse, an overarching concern among development theorists and practitioners about how to achieve economic growth and how to apply effective means to reduce poverty within the growth model. It was not considered at that stage that a simplistic notion of 'development' as mere economic growth might evade issues such as composition and distribution of 'products' of growth and the processes or means of bringing about growth through democratic or non-democratic ways and at the cost of the 'environment', endangering, thereby, 'sustainability' in the future. In short, the essence of development ethics is critical ethical reflections on the means and ends of socio-economic change that is designed and implemented to bring about planned transformation of the lives of peoples in the 'developing' countries with special emphasis on the lives of the poor and the marginalized. To quote Nigel Dower's most appropriate formulation in the context: 'Development ethics as sustained ethical enquiry into the nature and justification of the values underlying development and engagement both with the ethical dilemmas in development policy and practice and with the contested nature of development as a concept plays an important part in helping to make development discourse adequate to the enormous task before it—the challenge of world poverty and the general betterment of humankind' (1988). At this stage, it needs to be asserted that development scholars today are firmly of the view that development decisions are a mix of 'ethical' and empirical-cum-policy issues.

THE BEGINNING

The theme of 'development' or 'progress' is as old as human history. 'Development' assumed special salience, however, with the emergence of the 'Third World' on the international scene after World War II. There have been several 'paradigms' of development in the sense that the meaning of a construction of 'development', search for causalities of 'underdevelopment', and the adoption of means to bring about speedy change have, from the very beginning of development efforts, been highly polemical. Practices in different country situations including their impact on the ground, changing social scientific conceptualizations, shifting stances of international donor agencies, and above all, the developing nations' evolving interactions with the changing global techno-economic scene have all steadily served to render the practical job of 'development' as well as its conceptualization more and more complex and controversial.

THE ERA OF DEVELOPMENTALISM

Since the emergence of the 'Third World', 'development' (whatever it meant at that point of time), besides being the direct business of the 'developing' nations, had become a major international concern. How to bring about speedy socio-economic 'development' to improve the quality of life of the peoples in the Third World assumed major significance for the leaders of the newly independent countries as well as for the international donor countries and institutions. There was hardly any debate at that time in history about what is 'development' and how can vital choices be made about what would be the result of 'development' as a process. At best, there was a straightforward acknowledgment that 'economic growth' had to be attained using 'technology' and other work methods and techniques that the Western 'developed' nations (supposedly) had historically mobilized to grow as models of 'modernity'. That there are important 'ethical' considerations involved in adopting the 'processes' that would, it would be hoped, lead to the kind of societal transformation (called 'development') as an end state was not of much concern to the 'development' practitioners.

The earliest phase may well be called 'developmentalism', connoting development as an essential means to 'modernize' and 'change' the traditional lifestyle of the peoples of the Third World. It was born with the Third World itself. This was the era of postcolonialism, when the leaders of the new world—Nehru, Nkruma, or Sukarna—had been unanimous in the search for the speedy amelioration of the living conditions of the masses. The international donor agencies, and the United States of America in particular (being concerned about the potential threat of the spread of communist influence) had also expressed concern about the 'development' of the new nations for which funds were mobilized, and 'planners', technicians, and area and subject experts—a new breed of 'development pundits'—fanned out in different directions to advise and guide the 'underdeveloped' countries in their pursuit of planned change and 'development'. It was an era of unprecedented euphoria and optimism about the prospect of planned change in the 'Third World'. At least initially, development was thought of in macro or holistic terms—to bring about qualitative change in the lives of people, covering, apart from economic improvement, removal of poverty, malnutrition and ill health, and illiteracy. While strategizing development, the economic aspect—enhanced productivity in different sectors—did, however, loom large, and there was a firm belief that once wealth would be produced, the distributive aspect would be taken care of in due course. In the 1950s and 1960s, there were debates about development strategy centring round such themes as 'balanced or unbalanced growth', 'dualistic development processes', proper role of 'human capital', and so on and so forth. The earlier view of conceiving economic growth in instrumental terms had, however, come under severe criticism, as the critics pointed to the need to focus directly on urgent social objectives, particularly income distribution, poverty amelioration, employment generation, and meeting essential basic needs. Importantly, the development dialogue, during this phase, was going on within the framework of the nation-state as a sovereign category.

Since the late 1960s, the economic condition of much of the Third World started deteriorating fast leading to the rise of the 'dependency theory' that challenged frontally the reigning modernization paradigm. The conclusion of the dependency theorists was that the capitalist market relations, instead of stimulating economic development, had been actually retarding it in much of the Third World. The Dependencists forcefully argued that the market power exercised by the industrialized 'core' was exploitative in nature and prevented the industrialization of the Third World 'periphery'. Economic power and political power had been hand in glove with each other. Reactionary leaders and classes in the developing countries made common cause with 'core' political and economic interests in order to retain their own power and enjoy monopoly rents. Dependency theory, thus, came to hold an extremely pessimistic view of economic development of the Third World as it stood in relationship to the First World.

The early 1980s witnessed a radical shift from the post-World-War-II era of state-led 'developmentalism' to a new phase of 'neo-liberal counterrevolution' in the context of the Third World's deepening debt crisis. The World Bank and the International Monetary Fund, with their vastly increased power, clamped down on most of the Third World countries' strict loan conditionalities, invoking a redefinition of the state in a changing world. It signalled a radical change in the framework of development thinking from the earlier 'national frame' to 'international' and 'globalized' frame. Development came to be unequivocally viewed as 'economic development' to be measured in terms of per capita economic growth. The central means for the purpose were declared as efficient markets, 'privatization' and 'deregulation', and a severely restricted role for the state in welfare provision and economic regulation. The state's distributive goals were de-emphasized, with subsidies and welfare systems relegated to the background, and the state itself was regarded as a predatory and rent-seeking agency.

The 'rollback' concept of the state coincided with the emergence of another idea of 'bringing the civil society back in'. Development, it came to be realized, has often been top-down and bureaucracy-driven without much care for what the 'people'—particularly the poor and the marginalized sections of society—genuinely need but cannot always demand owing to voicelessness and lack of capabilities (because of poverty, illiteracy, ill health, and 'gender' exclusion, for instance). Also, there was a growing realization that besides state and market, civil society (in multiple formations such as NGOs and CSOs) has a big role to play in societal problem solving, be it literacy campaigns, or health provision, or any other facilities creation such as water conservation, forest maintenance, and the like. Since the 1980s, the shift from 'government' to 'governance' in development vocabulary was not a mere semantic change. On a close scrutiny of the performance balance sheet of formal government, it transpired that the general trend had been towards a cornering of development gains by the elite and influential and consequent deprivation of the poor and the socially marginalized. Also, as far as the latter groups were concerned, 'access' to services and facilities was often a problem for them in most government-run programmes. Institutional response at this stage had been to correct the imbalance in social mobilization by introducing decentralization, people's participation, empowerment, 'engendering development', and an array of imaginative efforts to extend the ambit of government (hence 'governance') as well as to make development more participative, transparent, and accountable.

An extreme reaction in recent times has come from the post-developmentalists (Wolfgang Sachs, for instance) who would rather abandon the concept of 'development' lock, stock, and barrel. In their view, 'development' has from the beginning been aimed at not improving human conditions but extending the Western hegemonic control over the Third World. Note in this context the caustic comments of Sachs, 'The idea of development stands today like a ruin in the intellectual landscape. Its shadow obscures our vision' (1992). Development, in this kind of perception, has *ab intio* been unethical.

From the initial first step in development conceptualization, that is, modernization theory to the contemporary mix of ideas— neo-liberal plus decentralist-participative 'governance'—the long conceptual journey of 'development' has at each stage had embedded ethical notions regarding both the means and the end of 'development'. As stated above, the post-developmentalists have been rather candid in revealing their ethical posture.

In this respect, we owe to Robert Chambers a more balanced view, which, to quote him, would be 'to recognize renewals and continuities in the landscape (of development) as well as ruins and rubble, and older trees as well as new sprouts'. Whichever posture is adopted in conceptualizing 'development', the normative undertone is, however, unavoidable.

ECONOMIC REDUCTIONISM

As mentioned earlier, initially at least, the question: what is 'development' and how can vital choices be made about what would be the result of 'development' as a process did not receive much attention. At best, there was a straightforward acknowledgement that 'economic growth' had to be attained using 'technology' and other work methods and techniques that the Western 'developed' nations (supposedly) had historically mobilized to grow as models of 'modernity'. That there are important 'ethical' considerations involved in adopting the 'processes' that would, it would be hoped, lead to the kind of societal transformation (called 'development') as an end state was not of much concern to the 'development' practitioners.

In the beginning, development studies had been basically concerned with 'economic development', which was accepted as good for the 'developing' nations. Study of development thus became the monopoly of the discipline of economics, particularly, as Amartya Sen points out, the discipline's 'engineering' stream of methodology and analysis. To quote Sen in this context,

...economics has had two different origins, both related to politics, but related in rather different ways, concerned respectively with 'ethics' (*in the Aristotelian sense*) on the one hand, and with what may be called 'engineering' on the other....The 'engineering' approach is characterized by being concerned with primarily logistic issues rather than with ultimate ends and such questions as what may foster 'the good of man' or 'how should one live'. The ends are taken as fairly straightforwardly given, and the object of the exercise is to find the appropriate means to serve them.

Sen questions the very methodology of so-called 'positive economics', which, in his view, 'has not only shunned normative analysis in economics, it has also had the effect of ignoring a variety of complex ethical considerations which affect actual human behaviour...' (1991).

Economic reductionism in development thinking has since been virtually abandoned. Note the significant comment of the Human Development Report, 1990: 'People cannot be reduced to a single dimension as economic creatures'. Thus the central message of the report was that growth in national production (GDP) is no doubt necessary to meet all essential human objectives. But the main issue is: how that growth translates or fails to translate into human development in various societies.

COMPLEXITIES OF DEVELOPMENT AND THE HUMAN CONCERN

Development practice over these long years has convincingly brought out the fact that a country's 'successful development' is contingent on several factors such as history, economy, politics, culture, geography, social psychology, resources endowment, level of skill and technology, and, of course, international interactions. There is almost universal awareness now that 'development' needs to be reconceived, essentially, in human terms and not mere material terms. To quote the World Development Report 2000:

The principal goal of development policy is to create sustainable improvements in the quality of life for all people. While raising per capita incomes and consumption is part of that goal, other objectives—eradicating poverty, expanding access to health services, and increasing educational levels—are also important. Meeting these goals requires a comprehensive approach to development.

This point has been very cogently and forcefully made in a seminal paper by Keith Griffin and A.R. Khan entitled, 'Globalization and the Developing World: An Essay on the International Dimensions of Development in the Post-Cold War Era', originally prepared for the UNDP as a background document for the Human Development Report, 1992. To quote Griffin and Khan:

The ultimate purpose of development is to expand the capabilities of people, to increase their ability to lead long and healthy lives, to enable them to cultivate their talents and interests, and to afford them an opportunity to live in dignity and with self-respect. The means by which this is achieved may be diverse—by increasing the stock of physical capital, introducing new techniques, changing institutions, altering incentives. Equally important, and sometimes more important, are investments in human capital—the provision of education and training, the creation of employment and opportunities to acquire skills while on the job, the provision of primary health care and adequate nutrition, expenditure in research and seeking out new sources of information. Both these ideas—development as capability expansion and as human capital formation—are captured in the phrase human development...

Thus, according to Griffin and Khan, development stands for human development.

NATURE OF DEVELOPMENT ETHICS

Policy makers, administrators, and planners, at any level, who are actively engaged in 'development' activities of any kind, face moral questions such as: What is going to be the end objective of a project or programme? What means should be adopted to actually bring about the desired results? What are going to be the consequences of the programme or project when implemented, and the changes that will come about are going to benefit whom? To give an illustration, when the big dam project was being planned in the Narmada valley in Madhya Pradesh, India, the anti-dam protesters pointed out that it would involve large-scale deforestation and consequent loss of rare flora and fauna; and, more importantly, there would be the displacement of thousands of local tribal people from their age-old habitat along with their rich cultural tradition. The famous 'Chipko Movement' in Uttarakhand (earlier part of Uttar Pradesh), which was spearheaded by local women activists, raised a similar question: the denudation of the hill forest for the benefit of some business people in the plains would deprive the local people of the benefits of firewood and, from a longer time point of view, soil erosion would endanger local cultivation and habitations. These are familiar stories known to most development practitioners everywhere.

Theories of 'development' or 'underdevelopment' in the social sciences are always a mix of practical policy issues and ethical or moral concerns. Moral assessment of the theory and practice of development is at the heart of what may be called 'development ethics'. Again, to quote Goulet, 'Ethical judgements as to the good life, the just society, and the quality of relations of people among themselves and with nature always serve, explicitly or implicitly, as operational criteria for development planners and researchers. Development ethics is the interdisciplinary *ex-professo* study of such value-laden issues.' Acknowledging the signal importance of ethical issues in development, the IDEA was formed in 1980, and Nigel Dower as its president has been justifiably ambitious to suggest that development ethics should be accorded the status of a separate discipline altogether. His proposal deserves serious consideration in view of the immense complexities involved in 'development' conceived as 'visioning' and 'implementation' of deeply value-laden programmes of massive societal change. As he has argued forcefully, 'value assumptions behind development and poverty alleviation are far more complex and indeed controversial, and so ethics as critical engagement with these normative issues is actually important.' Dower is right in pointing out that there is more 'justice sensitivity' today in development thinking. As he puts it, 'mainstream thinking about development has become more normatively complex—interest in the rights agenda, in transparency, in good governance, in greater regulatory regimes vis-à-vis labour relations and the environment, all show a greater recognition that development is not just about economic growth. But the issues now are not so much "is ethics relevant to development?" as "what ethic is relevant?" and "how important is ethics as critical sustained reflections on these questions?"'

THREE VALUE QUESTIONS

As a 'process', development is a continuous search for 'good life' in society. Hence, to follow Goulet's ideas, development is basically concerned with constructing the meaning of 'good life'. Three major 'value' questions identified by Goulet, in this context, relate to: (1) choice of model of community life, (2) foundations of justice in society, and (3) societal view of nature.

With regard to the first, two contrasting models of community life have crucial significance for the development debate. The first model can be called communitarian and the second liberal—individualistic. The former is oriented towards social solidarity, valuing collectivist social life and a high degree of equality based on 'a disciplined collaborative regime of resource-use'. The latter, by contrast, values 'individual comfort and enrichment and relies on competition and abundant material resources as its social motors'. Which of these two macro-models would be accepted as a sort of conceptual guide to the 'end state' of development involves a very basic 'value' question in any development exercise.

With regard to the second, the basic issue revolves round the foundations of justice in society. To quote Goulet, 'should civil and political rights ensuring individual freedoms enjoy primacy over collective socio-economic rights to have needs met and the common good of society pursued? Should human rights be treated as instrumental goods or end-values worthy for their own sake?'

The third value question is reminiscent of the recent 'sustainable development' debate. In other words, what criteria would be adopted toward nature in the course of development decision making? To borrow Goulet's imaginative expressions in this regard: 'Should humans view nature simply as raw material for Promethean exploitation by them or as the larger womb of life in which humans live, move, and have their being and whose rhythms and laws they must respect? Should the dominant human stance toward nature (to) be extractive and manipulative or harmony-seeking?' The World Development Report, 2003, echoed the same sentiment as it observed: 'Ensuring sustainable development requires attention not just to economic growth but also to environmental and social issues. Unless the transformation of society and the management of the environment are addressed integrally along with economic growth, growth itself will be jeopardized over the longer time.'

AREAS OF COMMON CONCERN AND COMMON BELIEFS

Despite considerable differences among development ethicists in approaches and philosophical stances, there are important *areas of common concern* among them that can be tied together to carve out an ethical core area in development discourse. In this context, one must refer to a set of closely interrelated questions (as areas of common concern) meticulously posed by David Crocker (1998):

1. What should count as (good) development?
2. Should we continue using the concept of development instead of, for example, 'progress,' 'economic growth,' 'transformation,' 'liberation,' or 'post-development alternatives to development'?
3. If development is defined rather neutrally as good socio-economic change, what basic economic, political, and cultural goals, and strategies should a society or political community pursue, and what values or principles should inform their selection? And a related issue is: how should the benefits and harms of development be conceived and distributed? Is the most fundamental category GDP, that is, income, or utility, social primary goods (Rawls), access to resources, human capabilities and functioning (Sen 2002), human flourishing, or human rights? Is it some basic composite measure of development success, such as economic growth or economic efficiency, or does social justice require maximizing the least well-off, getting all above a threshold, or reducing inequality?
4. Who (or what institutions) bear responsibility for bringing about development—a nation's government, civil society, or the market? What role—if any—do more affluent states,

international institutions, non-governmental associations, and poor countries themselves have or should have in development?

5. What are the most serious local, national, and international impediments to and opportunities for good development? How should the blame for development failures be distributed among global, national, and local agents?

This is a highly compressed version of Crocker's more elaborate presentation without missing (in the view of the present author) the most salient points.

Crocker's other admirable effort is the gathering together of *a set of common beliefs* or *commitments* among the development ethicists. These are:

1. Alongside the 'elevated affluence' of a few, there is the stark reality of grave deprivation for many; hence, one must be committed to understanding and reducing human misery and deprivation everywhere.

2. 'Development' has important ethical and value dimensions that need to be critically analysed; also, development has both descriptive (such as GDP growth, industrialization, etc.), and normative (hence adjectives like 'just', 'good', etc.), aspects.

3. Development is a multidisciplinary field; and one has not only to understand its nature, causes, and consequences but also to argue for specific conceptions of change.

4. Development practitioners should pay attention to concerns of both human well-being and a healthy environment.

5. Development ethics should assess, (i) basic ethical principles such as justice, liberty, autonomy, democracy, etc., (ii) development goals and models such as economic growth, basic needs, sustainable development, structural adjustment, human development, etc., and (iii) specific development institutions and projects, and strategies and policies.

6. Development strategies must be sensitive to specific 'contexts'; for instance, what constitutes best balance (between state, market, and civil society, etc.), would depend on a country's history, stage of development, and linkages with global forces.

7. Development benefits must accrue to everybody irrespective of caste, creed, gender, status, age, etc., and in this context, two models need to be repudiated: first, 'unaimed opulence' representing economic growth without concern for better living conditions for everybody, and second, 'authoritarian egalitarianism' that caters to physical needs at the expense of political liberties.

Like the preceding discussion on the areas of common concern, this enumeration is also a compressed, short-listed version of Crocker's imaginative ethicist vision.

SOURCES FOR ETHICAL ASSESSMENT

The theory and practice of development are amenable to assessment with regard to their ethical status, from a variety of standpoints. Referring to the work of Anglo-American development ethicists, David Crocker has identified four important 'sources' for moral or ethical assessment.

1. Activists and social critics—Mahatma Gandhi in India, Raul Prebisch in Latin America, and Franz Fanon in Africa—who were critical of colonial and/or orthodox economic development.
2. The seminal contribution of Denis Goulet, who was influenced by the French economist Louis-Joseph Lebret and by social scientists like Gunner Myrdal, and forcefully argued that 'development needs to be redefined, demystified, and thrust into the arena of moral debate.'
3. The effort of Anglo-American moral philosophers who have deepened and broadened the philosophical debate about conventional famine relief and food aid, and transformed it into a more comprehensive 'ethics of Third World development'.
4. The pioneering work of economists like Paul Streeten and Amartya Sen, who addressed the problems of global economic inequality, hunger, and underdevelopment in terms of a novel and much broader conception of development based on deeper ethical principles.

Each of these sources has its own strength and salience in the development debate, and as such each needs to be examined much more elaborately. Admittedly, there are many other well-known activists and social critics in every country whose names can be added to the list provided by Crocker. Gandhi's contemporary, Rabindranath Tagore, a Nobel laureate known as a great poet, had been actively engaged in the development of the rural masses in the then Bengal within his own conceptual frame of participative and human development-centric development ethics. To cite a few other eminent personalities, Julius Nayarare of Africa, Medha Patkar of India, and Mohammad Yunus of Bangladesh had their distinctive thoughts and approaches to 'development'. Robert Chambers of the Institute of Development Studies, Sussex, who has spent his whole life in the field of active rural development and who brought about innovative techniques, drawing on people's intrinsic planning knowledge, deserves special mention in this connection. In recent times, development ethics has been greatly enriched by the seminal contribution of Nobel laureate Joseph Stiglitz (2000). Also, a fifth source may be added to Crocker's list—the grassroots people's movements—that have, at many locations, brought forth people's raw, home-grown life wisdom about authentic 'development' and its inbuilt concept of development ethics. This was so eloquently expressed by Jose Saramago (2005), the Nobel laureate, in the course of his concluding speech at the World Social Forum in Porte Alegre, Brazil, in February 2002. He referred to the 'multiple movements for resistance and social action that are fighting to establish a new, distributive and commutative justice that all people can come to recognize as intrinsically theirs, a justice that protects freedom and rights, and not any denial of them'.

WHITHER DEVELOPMENT

L.J. Lebret, a famous French philosopher and social thinker, while commenting on the processes of 'contemporary development said that the world has fallen prey to "illusory anti-development" under which a small number of nations or privileged groups remain alienated in an abundance of luxury (facility goods) at the expense of the many who are deprived thereby of their essential (subsistence) goods'.

He made a novel distinction between *plus avoir* (to have more) and *plus etre* (to be more)—quite close to Fromm's To Have or To Be (1997)[1]. A society, according to Lebret, is more human and developed not when its citizens 'have more' but when they are enabled and endowed with capabilities 'to be more' (Goulet 1996)[2].

Against this blackcloth of basic concerns about human condition and 'development ethics', the contemporary 'governance discourse' looks rather inane and discordant.

Notes

[1] Among many of Fromm's writings on economic development, ethical concerns have been explicitly expressed in his address entitled 'Ethics, Economic Advice, and Economic Policy' at a conference at the Interamerican Development Bank in Washington, DC in December 2000.

[2] L.J. Lebret, one of the pioneers of 'human development approach' greatly influenced the writings of Goulet. See, in this connection, Goulet 1996.

Select References

Bandopadhyay, D., 'Administration, Decentralization and Good Governance', *Economic and Political Weekly*, 30 November 1996.

Bhattacharya, Mohit, 'Ethical Concerns in Development', in *Social Theory, Development Administration and Development Ethics*, New Delhi: Jawahar Publishers, 2006.

Braùtigam, Deborah, 'Governance and Economy: A Review', Working Papers, Policy and Review Departments, the World Bank, December, 1991.

Chambers, Robert, *Ideas for Development: Reflecting Forwards*, Brighton: Institute of Development Studies at the University of Sussex, 2004.

Currie, Bob, 'Governance, Democracy and Economic Adjustment in India: Concept and Empirical Problem', *Third World Quarterly*, 17 (4), 1996.

Curtis, Donald, *Beyond Government: Organization for Common Benefit*, Hong Kong: Macmillan, 1991.

Das, S.K., *Civil Services Reform and Structural Adjustment*, Oxford: Oxford University Press, 1998, ch. 5.

Dia, Mamadou, *A Governance Approach to Civil Service Reform in Sub-Saharan Africa*, Washington, DC: World Bank, 1993.

Dower, Nigel, *World Ethics: The New Agenda*, Edinburgh: Edinburgh University Press, 1998.

———, 'Towards Development Ethics', *World Development*, 19 (5), May 1991, pp. 457–83.

Fromm, Erich, *To Have or To Be?*, London and New York: Continuum International Publishing Group, 2005.

_____, 'Ethics, Economic Advice, and Economic Policy', Conference at the Interamerican Development Bank, Washington, DC, December 2000.

_____, *Development Ethics: A Guide to Theory and Practice*, New York: Apex Press and London: Zed Books, 1995.

_____, *The Cruel Choice: A New Concept in the Theory of Development*, New York: Anthenaeum, 1971.

Goulet, Denis, *Development Ethics at Work: Explorations 1960–2002*, Routledge, 2006.

_____, 'A New Discipline of Development Ethics', *Working Paper 231*, 1996.

Haq, Mahbub-ul-, 'Reinstating the Human Being as the End and Means of Development', Paul Hoffman Lecture, 14 April, UN Hdqrs., New York, 1988.

Jayal, Niraja Gopal, 'The Governance Agenda: Making Democratic Development Dispensable', *Economic and Political Weekly*, 22 February 1997.

Kooiman, Jan (ed.), *Modern Governance: New Government—Society Interactions*, New Delhi: Sage Publications, 1993.

Leftwich, Adrian, 'Governance, The State and the Politics of Development', *Development and Change*, 25, 1994, pp. 363–86.

Minocha, O.P., 'Good Governance: Concept and Operational Issues', *Management in Government*, October–December, 1997.

North, Douglass, *Institutions, Institutional Change, and Economic Performance*, New York: Cambridge University Press, 1990.

Organization for Economic Co-operation and Development (OECD), *Participatory Development and Good Governance*, Final Report, Paris, 1997.

Sachs, Wolfgang, *Development Dictionary: A Guide to Knowledge as Power*, London: Zed Books, 1992.

Saramago Jose quoted in Stephen Marks, 'The human rights framework for development: seven approaches', in Arjun Sengupta *et al.* (eds), *Reflections on the Right to Development and Human Rights*, Centre for Development and Human Rights, New Delhi: Sage Publications, 2005.

Sen, Amartya Kumar, *Capabilities Approach and Poverty Reduction*, Oxford: Oxford University Press, 2002.

Sen, Amartya Kumar, *Development as Freedom*, New York: Oxford University Press, 1999.

_____, *On Ethics and Economics*, Oxford: Basil Blackwell, 1991.

Sengupta, Arjun, Archna Negi, and Moushumi Basu, *Reflections on the Right to Development*, New Delhi: Sage Publications, 2005.

The *European Journal of Development Research*, 5 January 1993 (special issue on Political Conditionality).

United Nations Development Programme (UNDP), 'Overview', *Human Development Report*, New Delhi: Oxford University Press, 1990.

World Bank, *Governance and Development*, Washington, DC: World Bank, 1992.

Young, Oran R. (ed.), *Global Governance: Drawing Insights from the Environmental Experience*, Cambridge, Mass.: The MIT Press, 1977.

3

The Repositioning of Public Governance

Global Experience and Challenges

Gerald E. Caiden

In the face of an increasingly turbulent environment, governments the world over are reexamining their role in society and reassessing their ability to deliver and improve their public goods and services. This repositioning of the public sector reflects the shift in developed countries from the focus on government to an enlarged vision of integrated governance and in developing countries from government as *the* engine of development to alternative avenues for promoting development while strengthening government to deal with daily challenges and crises. Despite universalities, emphasis remains on the special needs and circumstances of each country. The difficulties of applying general rather than particular strategies are illustrated in the global campaign for democratization, which has had some success in the past two decades, and in the global anti-corruption campaign, which has been quite disappointing. Both campaigns confront deeply embedded institutional systems that will probably takes generations to reform and require radical changes in people's thinking and behaviour.

THE REPOSITIONING OF PUBLIC GOVERNANCE

...[G]overnance has become a central component in any explanation of economic and social development. It is both cause and effect, covering both independent and dependent variables in the evolutionary process. It is also linked to several different sides or aspects of our common history: to the formation and propagation of *values,* to the creation and distribution of *wealth,* and to the emergence and consolidation of *institutions.* (Daniel Tarschys 2001, 28)

All over the globe, countries are reconsidering how their present institutional arrangements meet current challenges and shape the future. The world moves at an ever-accelerating pace that bewilders, surprises, startles, and so often shocks. Nobody knows what to expect next. The past is no guide to the future. Technological prowess alone overwhelms the capacity to adopt and assimilate quickly and defies the ability to assess its impact. Everything is in a state of flux. New questions dumbfound traditional answers. Things seem to be spinning out of control and nobody knows what to do. People despair of their future and fear their fate. Where are we going? And what are they doing about it?

The 'they' used to mean government leaders, the legitimate societal authority that made the big decisions, imposed their will, and tackled current challenges. But, government seems to be getting out of its depth and has not been doing too well of late. Clearly, it has its limitations. It faces, as it has always done, competition and divided loyalties from other social institutions. Perhaps, it is trying to do too much with too few resources. Maybe, other institutions might do better if allowed, but are they any better qualified or equipped? Maybe, too many people are uncomfortable with what government is doing or trying to do, distrust its justifications, and feel discounted, abused, and even humiliated. It is time to rethink what government is and what it should do. This is what repositioning is all about.

Notice that repositioning has yet to become one of those buzz words that have been floating around the social sciences for some decades and that are valiantly making their way into popular parlance—words such as reorganization, reinvention, reengineering, and other words prefixed by 're'. Repositioning is a much more inclusive term that covers all of these, because, in repositioning, there may well have to be some reorganization, reinvention, reengineering, and a redistribution of power, a reallocation of responsibilities and obligations, a relocation of functions and activities, and a reform of institutional arrangements. Repositioning can cover all these other aspects involved in rethinking public governance.

Notice, too, that *public* governance implies the exclusion of *private* governance, which refers to voluntary arrangements enforced only by voluntary agreement without resort to public policing, public law, and public rewards and punishments. Thus, friendly societies that have their own formal and informal rules of conduct come under private governance, whereas business organizations subject to public regulation fall under public governance. But this distinction is often blurred. Probably, as public authority has extended its scope over most societal arrangements, including religious and family matters, private governance has been diminishing. Thus, any private body receiving public funds cannot expect, let alone claim, to be exempt from public authority of such funds with regard to how they were spent and whether they brought the anticipated return to the community and the public good.

So what's wrong with using the old-fashioned term 'government' instead of this newfangled 'governance'? Why the upgrade? What is this change in terminology? Why has it come about?

FROM GOVERNMENT TO GOVERNANCE

'Governance' is an old English word, referring to people who had authority over others, which in centuries past meant mostly religious and political leaders in the community, but it could, conceivably, also include leaders of other organizations. It fell out of common use after the eighteenth century, more particularly after the French Revolution when much of what was to become the modern administrative bureaucratic state evolved in Europe. Instead, the word 'government' replaced it to describe leadership of the nation-state, with its political arrangements heading a professional public service in an enlarging public sector.

The revival of the term 'governance' dates from the second half of the twentieth century, when opposition arose to Big Government, expressed: (1) ideologically, by fears of a forthcoming return to serfdom, as epitomized by totalitarian regimes; (2) politically, by mounting criticism of higher taxes and public expenditures; (3) pragmatically, by the increasing practice of hiving out government activities to a melange of non-governmental organizations; (4) socially, by complaints about the inadequacy of public sector performance that was failing to live up to political promises and public expectations; (5) globally, by increasing interdependence that poses challenges to existing governmental arrangements; and (6) academically, by a shift from the static approach of the positive paradigm focusing on objectivity to post-positivism that stresses complexity, interconnections, interactions, and processes.

Exactly when the term 'governance' was first used cannot be precisely established. But,

It was Cleveland who first used the words governing and governance as surrogates for the public administration he saw coming. In the mid-1970s I distinctly remember a speech given at an annual meeting of ASPA in which he said this: 'What the people want is less government and more governance.' (Frederickson 2003, 11)

Here, the reference is to Harlan Cleveland, who, in 1972, had just published *The Future Executive: A Guide for Tomorrow's Managers* in which he forecast that:

The organizations that get things done will no longer be hierarchical pyramids with most of the real control at the top. They will be systems-interlaced webs of tension in which control is loose, power diffused, and centers of decision plural. 'Decision-making' will become an increasingly intricate process of multilateral brokerage both inside and outside the organization which thinks it has the responsibility for making, or at least announcing, the decision. Because organizations will be horizontal, the way they are governed is likely to be more collegial, consensual, and consultative. The bigger the problems to be tackled, the more real power is diffused and the larger the number of persons who can exercise it—if they work at it. (Frederickson 2003)

Like many, Cleveland saw the blurring of the distinction between public and private organizations. He reasoned through what it meant as follows: 'these new style public-private horizontal systems will be led by a new breed of men and women. I call them public executives, people who manage public responsibilities whether in "public" or "private" organizations....'

Governance is an especially important word/concept because of the mismatch between jurisdictions on the one hand and social, technological, political and economic problems on the other hand. Cleveland understood this too.... Big problems, Cleveland believes, require big responses. These. responses will, however, be multi-organizational and will involve both public and private organizations. These responses will, post-Cleveland, be led by not one, but many leaders. (Frederickson 2003)

Cleveland's ideas struck a chord among political scientists already dealing with networks of organizations that were delivering public goods and services and among liberal economists, who preferred private enterprise, the market system, and capitalism to public enterprise, state bureaucratic planning and direction, and collectivism. To the latter, government was not *the* solution to societal problems but was itself a problem if not *the* problem. They objected to the overuse of government. The term 'governance' put government in its proper place as only one of several social institutions that alone or through mutual cooperation meets contemporary challenges. Cleveland's analysis fits nicely into a future that would de-emphasize government, the administrative state and public management, and strengthen institutional alternatives that would play a more important part in public policy and the delivery of public goods and services.

Since many multilingual liberal economists occupied top positions in both domestic and international economic policy, they readily adopted the new nomenclature to denote their switch from public enterprise and state direction to private enterprise, private initiatives, and private or non-governmental delivery systems. The whole matter came to a head within the World Bank when, at the start of the 1990s, a task force went beyond purely international economic development to deal with the issue of public management of development matters in recipient countries. Was this beyond the World Bank's jurisdiction and interfering with the internal affairs of member countries? The World Bank affirmed 'that efficient and accountable public sector management and a predictable and transparent framework for economic activity are critical to the efficiency of both markets and government interventions—and hence to economic development' (World Bank 1991, 1). Governance was definitely and definitively adopted.

...[G]overnance is defined as the manner in which power is exercised in the management of a country's economic and social resources for development. The Bank's concern with sound development management extends beyond the capacity of public sector management to the rules and institutions which create a predictable and transparent framework for the conduct of public and private business, and also to accountability for economic and financial performance....

The Bank's interest in governance arises from its concern for the effectiveness of the development efforts it supports. From this perspective, sound development management, in the broadest sense of the word, is

critical to ensuring adequate returns and the efficacy of programs and
projects that the bank finances, and so to the underlying Bank objectives of
helping countries reduce poverty and increase sustainable growth....

The Bank's experience has also shown that when programs and projects
appear technically sound but fail to deliver results, the reasons are sometimes
attributable to weak institutions, lack of an adequate legal framework,
damaging discretionary interventions, uncertain and variable policy
frameworks and a closed decision-making process which increases risks of
corruption and waste....

Recognizing the importance of sound development management, the
Bank's emphasis in recent years has shifted rapidly from its own
interventions to the overall country context within which those interventions
are taking place. In the area of public sector management, attention has
shifted from improving management of project-related agencies to more
general reform of the civil service and public enterprises, and to the central
economic agencies that are responsible for macro-economic policy. A similar
broadening of focus is now taking place in such 'areas' as accountability
and the legal framework. (World Bank 1991, i–ii)

The die was cast. Other international development agencies followed
suit, adjusting their definitions of governance and approaches
according to their special missions, different from those of the World
Bank. What they were acknowledging was that governance
was 'comprised of purposeful actions to guide, steer or control
society...[a] process [involving] both governmental and non-
governmental actors. Governance is the regularized, institutional
patterns that emerge from the interactions of these actors....Needs
are no longer confined to society, capacity to government. Needs
and capacities are both public and private and are embedded in
both state and society in their mutual interdependencies.' (Hyden
2001, 14–15).

Governance, then, transcends the conventional boundaries of public
administration....In the context of a 'disarticulated state', for instance, one
with reduced capacity to solve public problems, it is in governance theory
that public administration gets to wrestle with problems of representation,
political control of bureaucracy, and the democratic legitimacy of institutions
and networks. Governance links values and interests of citizens, legislative
choice, executive and organizational structures and roles, and judicial
oversight in a manner that suggests interrelationships among them that
might have significant consequences for performance....[T]here is still an
emerging consensus in the public administration field about the meaning

of governance as a process which, aimed at producing results for society, transcends conventional boundaries of public administration theory. (Hyden 2000, 15).

Thus, for instance, the Ford Foundation's 'program focus has evolved from a government-centered notion of public administration in the 1950s to the broader concept of "governance and civil society" that guides [its] efforts today'.

...For the Foundation, the concept of *governance* involves fostering effective, transparent, accountable and responsible governmental institutions guided by the rule of law and dedicated to reducing inequality. In *civil society* the Foundation seeks to strengthen the civic and political participation of people and groups in charting the future of their societies [and] help people make their government more accountable and responsive to their needs. (Ford Foundation 2002, 1–2)

Since the collapse of the Soviet Union, the way has been clear to push a liberal economic agenda and extend it beyond public policy and management to global liberalization, democratization, human rights, civic organization, citizenship, transparency, accountability (answerability for actions and use of public resources), and participation. Good government now becomes good governance, which covers all these together with legitimacy (consent of the governed), competence (appropriate public policies and efficient public services), rule of law, and protection of every single individual.

[G]ood governance aims to achieve much more than efficient management of economic and financial resources, or particular public services; it is also a broad reform strategy to strengthen the institutions of civil society, and make government more open, responsive, accountable and democratic.... [M]ajor aid donors...[attempt] to implement (some would say impose) these models of governance: there are considerable pressures on developing and transitional economies to adopt the whole range of governance reforms. Aid donors have always, to some degree, used economic conditionality to ensure the application of their preferred economic policies in recipient countries: now we see the use of political conditionality, which may involve limiting or withholding aid until political liberalization takes place in a recipient country, often in relation to the protection of human rights, or to processes of democratization....(Minogue, Polidano, and Hulme 1998, 6)

What is being incorporated into governance is establishing the preconditions for a strong civil society, maintaining the rule of law to strengthen modem markets, intergovernmental actions to solve common problems, and the growth of semi-autonomous agencies both within and without the machinery of government, a world away from the original use of the word 'governance.'

PUBLIC GOVERNANCE

Instead of government meaning just public organizations, governance refers to the way society governs itself, with the emphasis on society and not just on political or governmental authority. A simple explanation would be the switch from top-down to bottom-up, to look at government and every other social institution from the viewpoint of the ruled not just the rulers, the served not just the servers, the stakeholders and clients not just the professionals and careerists, the recipients not just the providers. This inverts the traditional bureaucratic pyramid and judges things not from the executive suite but from the street level, not from the convenience of the management but from the convenience of clients, not from the imperatives of authority but from the treatment of stakeholders, not from the perspective of protected insiders but from the perspective of the unprivileged and unsheltered outsiders.

Another interpretation is to recognize that the government is not the only institution that governs people's lives, plans for them, acts on their behalf, and possesses power that can reinforce or counteract governmental power, that is, that power is shared with or without government approval. Nowadays, society is so much more complex, complicated; people are assailed from many different directions from many different kinds of social institutions. Thus, governance can be seen as examining the interrelationships between public organizations and other social institutions, broadly in their external relations into traditional areas such as government and religion, government and business, government and non-governmental organizations, government and lobbyists/pressure groups, government and law, government and health, government and development, government and poverty, and it can also be confined just to the interrelationships within government itself, among overlapping agencies, between different agencies working within a common public policy arena, even between different classes of bureaucrats and careerists within a public organization, which does not depart so much from the traditional field of public administration.

A third interpretation is that governance embraces all the institutions and processes that inform and make collective decisions and solve (or attempt to solve) collective problems. Hence, it includes how public policy is formulated and how public services are delivered. It focuses on how government has been changing from the traditional styles of public administration to global reform as a result of:

fiscal pressures to lower the costs of public services, citizen frustration with ineffective services, and ideological interest in reducing the size of government...[prompting] governments to find more efficient ways to deliver public services. The resulting transformation has three key elements: a changing role for the state from direct provider to facilitator/coordinator, the devolution of decision making to empower citizens, and an increased role for the private sector in service delivery.

These governance changes raise concerns about our capacity to effectively design and manage the new systems. Public managers must now operate in both a vertical authority-based environment and a horizontal negotiation-based environment, which requires the ability to coordinate complex systems and to manage 'equal' partners. New organization forms—public-private partnerships and networks—have been created for collective decision making and service delivery. But how do we ensure accountability and citizen input while still improving efficiency? (Graddy 2005, 1).

Yet another more sophisticated explanation delves into the theoretical basis of the two dominant rival narrative schools—one being the rationality of neo-liberal economists and the other being the more pragmatic approach to institutional networks and networking by political scientists—but criticizes both of them for being incomplete and needing greater compatibility.

The neoliberal narrative, with its overlap with rational choice theory, defines governance in terms of a revitalized and efficient public sector based on markets, competition, and management techniques imported from the private sector. Behind this definition, there lurk neo-classical ideas of preference formation, utility, rationality, and profit maximization. Because social democracy, with its Keynesianism and bureaucratic hierarchies, did not allow for such ideas, it allegedly ran on problems of inflation and overload. Neoliberal reforms are thus needed to restructure the state in accord with these ideas. (Bevir 2005, 13)

Institutionalists often define governance as self-organizing, inter-organizational networks. Behind this definition, there lurks the idea that the emergence of governance embodies functional and institutional specialization and differentiation. Entrenched institutional patterns ensure that neoliberal reforms lead not to markets but to the further differentiation of policy networks in an increasingly hollow state. (Bevir 2005, 14)

And, the neo-liberals ignore 'the need for trust, diplomacy, and accountability in the public sector' (Bevir 2005, 22). The clash between these rival interpretations in the political arena 'will exhibit new failings, pose new dilemmas, and be the subject of competing proposals for reform...[and] a further contest over meanings' (16). Better governance should be understood 'in terms of a political contest resting on competing webs of belief, and to explain these benefits by reference to traditions and dilemmas' (17). Thus, 'governance is not new, then, in that it is an integral part of social and political life' (18) even if the concept might remain vague and its terminology somewhat abstract and metaphorical. What it does is to open an opportunity to redefine democracy.

It prompts us to search for patterns of devolution, participation, control, and accountability that better reflect our capacity for agency, the contingency of our identities, the importance of moral conduct as well as moral rules, and an aspiration toward an open community. (Bevir 2005, 28)

Lastly, there is the interpretation of governance that requires even greater sophistication. It also tries to be more inclusive of these other different interpretations and approaches. This uses a third term, namely 'governing,' defined as all interactions expressing societal diversity, dynamics, and complexity. It explores 'the utility of the governance concept as an instrument for conceptualizing issues on the boundary between the social and the political, or in current terminology, between state, market and civil society' (Kooiman 2003). Besides emphasizing interaction, it examines different elements of governance such as images, instruments, and action and analyses three types of governance, viz., self-governance, co-governance, and hierarchical governance. It reviews three different orders of governance, the first concerned with problems and opportunities, the second with institutions, and the third with metagovernance. All come together in a grand theory of governability, matching or joining previous explorations into the possibility that societies are becoming less governable (Dror 2001).

That said, some complications follow. First, the term remains fuzzy and ill-defined even by those who most use it. Unfortunately, different folks use the term differently. Here, besides the definitions already quoted, there are a few more. The Organization for Economic Development and Cooperation states that,

In the OECD context, it is defined in terms of relationships, and thus includes more than public administration and the institutions, methods and instruments of governing.

It also encompasses the set of relationships between governments and citizens, acting as both individuals and as part of or though institutions....

The Commission on Global Governance has defined the term as the sum of the many ways individuals and institutions, public and private, manage their common affairs. It is a continuing process through which conflicting or diverse interests may be accommodated and co-operative action may be taken. It includes formal institutions and regimes empowered to enforce compliance, as well as informal arrangements that people and institutions either have agreed to or perceive to be in their interest.

For the World Bank, governance consists of:

1. the form of political regime;
2. the process by which authority is exercised and the management of a country's economic and social resources for development; and
3. the capacity of government to design, formulate and implement policies and discharge functions. (OECD 1997)

THE UNITED NATIONS DEVELOPMENT PROGRAM

Governance can be seen as the exercise of economic, political and administrative authority to manage a country's affairs at all levels. It comprises the mechanisms, processes, and institutions through which citizens and groups articulate their interests, exercise their legal rights, meet their obligations and mediate their differences.

Good governance is among other things, participatory, transparent and accountable. It is also effective and equitable. And it promotes the rule of law. Good governance ensures that political, social and economic priorities are based on broad consensus in society and that the values of the poorest and the most vulnerable are heard in decision-making over the allocation of development resources.

Governance has three legs: economic, political and administrative. Economic governance includes decision-making processes that affect a country's economic activities and relationships with other economies. It clearly has major implications for equity, poverty and quality of life. Political

governance is the process of decision-making to formulate policy.
Administrative governance is the system of policy implementation.
Encompassing all three, good governance defines the processes and
structures that guide political and socio-economic relationships. (UNDP
1997, 2–3)

Second, the term is still unfamiliar to most people, more so if their
knowledge of English is limited. The term 'government' they know
but not 'governance', which dropped out of common usage two
centuries ago. Governance is now revived but in a totally different
context. It is likely that they will continue to use the more familiar
term. Even experts in business governance confine it in reality to the
government of business, and they narrow it in practice to improving
the accountability and transparency of business management. The
traditional term 'government' is simpler to use and more readily
understood by most people and that alone may delay the adoption
of the term governance.

Third, the word 'governance' is not easily translatable with
precision. Currently, it appears that most of the people who employ
it assume that others are as fluent in English as they are. As more
people become familiar with English through mass media and
computers, this may become less of a problem. Nonetheless, there
will be large numbers of people outside the English-speaking world
who will stick to 'government,' even those who most dislike public
intervention although some of these may well prefer the softer
sounding and more ambivalent 'governance.'

Fourth, although several international agencies press others to
employ the term 'governance', they exclude themselves and avoid
applying their own criteria for good governance to the international
level of government/governance. Few practise what they preach
outside of diplomatic niceties and self-justificatory public relations.
They are hardly models of openness, participation, accountability
(to whom?), rule of law (whose?), transparency, efficiency, and
integrity. If indeed there is now a global society for the first time in
history, then this superstructure of international institutions and
interrelationships cannot be exempt, certainly not if the global
community is moving in the direction of some form of world
government.

Fifth, even exempting the international level of government, the
governance approach tends still to be somewhat reductionist rather

than universal and place-based than global. To compare governance in more than a handful of countries that share many common features requires a thorough knowledge of applied social science just to formulate, let alone apply, universal criteria. Given that countries differ in context, history, and culture, the generalizations or lessons derived from a comparable few may not apply everywhere. In short, each country has to tailor its reforms according to its own needs. There may well be universal principles of good governance, but their application may differ from one country to another and in multicultural societies, from one part of a country to another. In large or populous countries, such as Russia, China, India, Canada, the United States, Brazil, and Nigeria, this is probably inevitable.

Thus, to repeat, what is behind the use of this revived term 'governance'? Simply, authority over individuals is exercised by many different social institutions—parental/familial, religious, educational, legal, military, market/business, voluntary, medical/health, fashion, entertainment, tourist, charitable—and none of them is (or should be) sovereign over any of the others. They overlap, compete, reinforce, undermine, contradict, and offset one another. Society would be better off if they recognized this fact, worked in the same direction, tried mutually to reconcile their differences, and acknowledged their interdependence. If this interpretation is correct, then the underlying ideology is liberal and democratic, cooperative if not consensual, tolerant and peacemaking. It is obviously anti-authoritarian, certainly anti-totalitarian. It opposes any authority that sets itself up as dominant and all encompassing. Its principal target is dictatorship or any similar regime that treats individuals as if they were mere puppets beholden to obey their leaders/rulers without question. But any government is to be feared because of its propensity to enlarge its jurisdiction, trample over opposition, overreach, and shut out others. The notion of governance does not deny the importance of government or political authority, only to limit it and remove it from activities where it has (or should have) no place. It is not libertarian and does not support the idea that the best government is least government.

The notion of governance acknowledges that individuals differ widely on how they view authority and government, what government should be employed to do, and how much government should interfere in everyday life. Its central concern is liberty.

How much freedom should individuals (and by implication associations) have against collective authority, in general, and against governmental authority, in particular? How much freedom should individuals have to pursue their own ends as long as they do not harm anyone else or themselves? Has governmental authority already gone too far? Has it gone far enough? If it has gone too far, then other social institutions have to be strengthened and repositioned to take some of the load off government. If it has not gone far enough, then government has to be repositioned and strengthened.

Whereas political scientists are prepared to accept that whatever countries decide for themselves is best, although Western-educated political scientists stump for liberal democracy, liberal economists believe that government has gone too far and should be reined in, particularly in economic arrangements broadly interpreted. Some (much?) of what it does could (should?) be transferred or delegated to other social institutions, if not completely then in delivery, simply because government is too inefficient, unproductive, and wasteful. Their agenda is not unbiased but slanted by those who have been disillusioned by the once internationally favoured notion that the state should be *the* engine of development. Now the pendulum for liberal economists has swung in the opposite direction, whereby private enterprise, the market system, and non-governmental organizations should be preferred instead, and their position in public policy puts them in the driver's seat.

HAS THE ADMINISTRATIVE STATE/GOVERNMENT GONE TOO FAR?

Any unbiased observer of totalitarianism, authoritarianism, and dictatorship has a clear answer. Tyranny, whatever its justification, support, and form, remains evil, a terrible curse on humanity, responsible for untold harm, with its so-called achievements at intolerable cost. The price it pays is:

1. foreign aggression, provoked wars, hate, conquest, occupation, plunder, exploitation, enslavement;
2. genocide, grand slaughter, death camps, mass starvation, horror;
3. terror, police state, spies and informers, concentration camps (gulags), torture, false imprisonment;

4. regimentation, enforced conformity, inhumanity, abject discrimination;
5. barbarity, evildoing, wickedness, gross misconduct, corruption; and
6. injustice, degradation, indignities.

Tyrannies engage in deliberately uncivilized behaviour without shame, or apology, or remorse. Their evil could not have been perpetrated on such a scale without their main instrument being the machinery of government. Revelations of what they do horrify people and remain sickening. Indeed, the abuse and misuse of government are scary even on its smallest scale. People, all peoples, must be vigilant at all times that government does not indulge in such gross behaviour. Thus, the answer to our question must be yes, and liberal democracy is an obvious answer. All government, indeed all governance, that is, all social institutions should operate on a truly democratic, humanitarian, compassionate basis. There is room in all for improvement, especially outside the public sector and political supervision, where many organizations tend to be run more on an authoritarian than democratic basis.

Even within liberal democratic regimes, there is reason to suppose government has overreached itself and needs some slimming as times change. Hence, every so often, governments do appoint special commissions to review their machinery of government to examine whether and how it could be more effective, what needs to be done to reorganize, and what functions and procedures have outlived their welcome. What is a carry over from the past that could be abandoned or released to other social institutions to perform? Why should the government still be doing this or that activity? Governments take on activities to meet the needs of the moment, but once they have been met, the activities linger on and become habitualized. In time, the original reason is forgotten, and the insiders are smart enough to perpetuate what they do or transform their activities into something else that does not draw outside attention. Admittedly, this does not seem to be the case. Usually, there has been such a political battle to get government or the public sector to add yet another activity that few are willing to reopen the fight, particularly if those within have proven themselves and built a dependent clientele who can be relied upon to prevent its discontinuance. Whenever the government announces cutbacks and elimination, it arouses opposition, and unless there is compelling reason, its proposals are dropped or compromised for the sake of political peace and quiet. Where they are not, the insiders are shrewd enough to recall the origins, history, and (engineered) successes of the activity, marshal stakeholders. and lobbyists, and bestir vested interests to rally behind them.

The issue gets transformed into not so much whether the government and the public sector should rid itself of some activity than how a better job might be done of it, by whom, and how the process could be minimally disruptive. This raises questions that need practical answers. Should the activity remains a monopoly of government or should it be opened to competition from other social institutions? If so, which and how? Should the activity be farmed out or delegated to some other government agency or contracted out? If so, which and how? Should the activity be shifted to some other social institution altogether, that is, privatized? If so, which and how and under what terms? And will there be any provision for renationalization if the private body reneges or fails to perform adequately?

Currently, there is much pressure from business and other organizations to take over completely or at least to have a share (or a bigger share) of governmental activities. They claim that government has grown too big and that they can do much better than government agencies. This has become their mantra because 'everyone knows private enterprise beats public enterprise every time', although there is not that much evidence to back such an assertion.

Private enterprise does indeed have its merits. But, business values and methods are not identical or preferable to public sector values and methods. Distrust of both Big Government and Big Business has given rise to an expanding third sector—non-governmental organizations (NGOs), which may or may not be for profit. In the United States, there are at least twenty-seven types of NGOs under federal law exempt from taxation, because the government wishes to promote their activities that in their absence would probably have to be assumed by the government and public sector. Many of these NGOs are willing to take on additional governmental activities, as, that way, they can assure themselves of a guaranteed (and subsidized) income. The American Red Cross is one such example. The drawback in expanding the role of the NGOs is that instead of getting the best of both Big Government and Big Business, the result maybe a combination of their worst, namely, unaccountable and poor performance at uncontrollable excessive cost and little consideration of public values such as justice, equity, honesty, decency, integrity, guardianship and all the other virtues of civilized conduct.

HAS THE ADMINISTRATIVE STATE/GOVERNMENT GONE FAR ENOUGH?

If by the administrative state, one now has to include the whole superstructure of international governance, taking into account that virtually every national government in the world is a member of the international community and every individual on the globe is affected by international authorities, then the answer is that it has not gone far enough yet. Many of a country's problems and challenges cannot be tackled without international cooperation and without being subject in some manner to international governance. That is why countries have chosen to become members of the United Nations encourage and other global bodies and have joined continent-wide associations and regional alliances. Even countries that have cut themselves off to isolate their inhabitants or have been excluded remain part of the global society subject to whatever may be decided elsewhere. And they well know this.

Given the shape of the world today, this international governance by its own criteria of good governance has not been doing well. Treaties and conventions that constitute solid components of international law and order are frequently and unabashedly treated with contempt by countries, which believe they can get away with their abrogation and defiance. The protection of universal human rights has become a farce as some of the worst offenders judge other countries and condemn them for the latter's alleged minor infractions. Hypocrisy is protected. Countries gang up together to pursue their own national interests even though these may be dysfunctional to international objectives, while spewing out unadulterated rhetoric. The world needs stronger international governance with real enforcement powers over recalcitrants but not in the way things are and not without fundamental reforms in the spirit of international operations.

It is not just the spirit that needs overhauling. The practices of many entrenched international agencies are a travesty not only of good governance but of good public administration and professional public service, too. Here is not the place to list all the justifiable criticisms of international operations—their non-performance, sinecures, waste, unwarranted privileges, corruption, venality, arrogance of power, even criminality. They claim that they do the best they can in the circumstances, because they are underfunded, can only go as far as member countries will allow them to (which is not far at all), poorly led, and overwhelmed. Though their critics have a field day, and they seemingly have an answer for everything, it remains that they appear to be too busy to put their own house in order even to employ the most elementary of good management practices. Perhaps, their better governance might improve their performance in tackling the crucial issues for humanity of war and peace, poverty, epidemic (and sometimes preventable) disease, illiteracy, unemployment, slavery, violent crime, environmental degradation, weapons of mass destruction, and protection of the vulnerable.

Returning to the more traditional area of governance at the country level, there remain the time-honoured functions of its civilizing mission, namely, security from external aggression and the issue of sheer survival, security from deviants of all descriptions, from violent criminals to interfering eccentrics, improvement in the quality and comfort of life for all individuals, and the socialization of the next generation in acceptable behaviour-edifying values. Each of these has undergone its own metamorphosis in the past twenty years or so, calling not for less governance or public intervention but more. Governments may take on additional activities, but these functions remain timeless and just as important as ever as they have been since the founding of the administrative state in Sumer some six thousand years ago.

The issue of sheer survival still dogs countries, peoples, and cultures. Not only are minorities jeopardized by the tyranny of the majority, but whole states can still be swallowed up by their neighbours without too much international concern or intervention. Likewise, minorities who want a country of their own to avoid extermination can also be abandoned without warning. They are forced to develop a state within a state to provide their own external security. How can any of these build up sufficient self-protection against overwhelming odds? How can they afford to counteract modern war machines? What deterrents can they muster against overwhelming force? They have to devote (sacrifice) enormous resources for self-defence and cultivating allies that will come to their defence in times of trouble. None of this comes cheap, for sophisticated weapons are expensive to obtain and deploy, military training and preparation absorb precious labour resources, and dependency exacts a heavy political price. The nature of modern warfare is continually changing and combat plans and methods have to be updated accordingly. Total warfare leaves none and involves everyone in some way as do surprise attacks, non-nuclear terrorism, germ warfare, and poison gases.

Internal security has gone beyond the simple policing of yesteryear to safeguarding the community against all manner of threats from natural disasters (and emergency preparedness) to technological accidents, from white-collar computer criminals to organized international gangs, from hazardous products to hazardous drivers. Urbanization compounds the challenge by herding people close together, offering more opportunities for evil intent, and providing ample hideouts. The paradox is that the more the security provided, the less the people feel secure, especially in the anonymous city where all are strangers to one another, turnover of neighbours can be fast, and where nobody can take proper care of themselves, not even the very wealthy who can afford private protection. Here is another area of governance where coverage is vast and costly to provide as it is too labour-intensive to be well done.

Every generation tries to ensure that the next generation will not have such a hard time of it as it had. Parents want a better future for their children than they had. It is not a matter of just a higher standard of living, that is, more material comforts. Today, it is improving the quality of life, which, again, has gone from being content with a simple way of rural living to adapting to the fast pace of the global tourist who tries to keep abreast of everything in invention, taste, and style. This one wants development and that one wants conservation. This one enjoys noise and that one craves for peace and quiet. All want to fly and yet be able to be caught in a rising safety net. All want the latest in medical advances to extend their lives but are not prepared to give up smoking, alcohol, and bad eating habits. Everyone wants to live better, those who supply employment, those who are employed, and those who cannot obtain employment or be employed. Business may meet economic demand, but governance has to meet community needs and, harder still, community aspirations. And to fulfil community expectations, governance has to invest heavily in research and development. All of this takes considerable public financing which in turn requires more economic, efficient, and effective money raising and allocation.

Every generation worries about its future and how the next generation is going to turn out. Every generation curses its legacy and worries about the legacy that it will pass on. How will the next generation behave? How will it fare? Will it have adequate coping abilities? Socialization becomes harder and harder. Parental guidance has many more competitors. Schools are not providing sufficient skills. Commercialism and mass media demote proper appreciation of the arts and the cultural inheritance of humanity. Despite all the professionalism, children or a significant portion of them still come out unprepared, even 'rotten,' meaning they still go too far astray from the acceptable. What should be done about this? 'They' aren't doing enough and probably never could, so pressures on governance just continue to mount.

In the global society, the wealthier countries, the bigger powers, the more advanced peoples, have more options than the poor, weak, underdeveloped peoples. And the gap between them grows, not diminishes, and it now seems that the gap between the privileged and the underprivileged within them follows suit. Their circumstances are so different. Whereas for the fortunate, the administrative state can he reduced and alternatives strengthened, the unfortunate may have to strengthen the administrative state until other social institutions reach the capability of assuming a wider role in contemporary society. In other words, they may still have to walk before they can run, let alone catch up if they ever will.

Some countries and peoples have done exceedingly well over the past two decades, moving up from right below until, now, they figure high up on human development indices, while others, no matter what attention is given them and no matter how much external aid they have received, still languish. The focus on governance rather than government gives us more clues why development has accelerated in some regions of the world and why it has actually receded in other regions. At least, we are now asking the right questions even if we still cannot provide the right answers. In any event, the administrative state still has its central role everywhere. It can be diminished in some fortunate countries, but it definitely needs strengthening elsewhere, and in all countries some areas of the administrative state can be diminished, but in other areas they still need to be expanded. Much depends on their own peculiar circumstances and how much government intervention their people demand and are prepared to tolerate. So the main question is, what are they repositioning public governance for? What kind of a future does each society at the different levels of government seek to shape for itself? How do they want their tomorrow to differ from today? What changes in direction do they want to make, for what purpose, for whom? From what do they wish to retreat? Where do they want to go? Why? How soon?

RESHAPING THE FUTURE

In reshaping the future, there are three different courses that can be taken. One is to let things just happen without interference. Changes are taking place in society all the time and people learn to adapt as they go along. Some changes they enjoy but others they resent and tend to resist as long as they can. This is the laissez-faire approach. It calls for minimum intervention and lets the chips fall where they may. Another takes the opposite course that preconceives the future, has a fixed agenda to achieve it, and tolerates no resistance. This is by *force-majeure*. It is radical, even revoluntionary, involving compulsion and violence and a break with the past. The third course takes the middle ground, the mean, the centre, that tries to be more selective than the laissez-faire approach and less traumatic than the radical approach. It is the path of reform, sometimes bold, other times cautionary, pushing society in a set direction using soft persuasive tactics rather than heavy-handedness although every so often straying into one of the other paths depending on public reaction on this or that issue.

Once again, the global society is split. There are very reactionary societies that look back rather than forward, cherish a lost past, and seek to return to what they believe once existed. These are prepared, or so they state, to give up much of what has transpired since and

sacrifice some (so-called) benefits of modernity, which they blame
for inculcating false values. At the other end of the scale are societies
that cannot rush quickly enough into a future quite different from
the present, prepared to try almost anything that promises to take
them away from their present misfortunes, and hoping that utopia
is just round the corner. Between these extremes are the great majority
of peoples who hope that the future will indeed be much better than
the present and support reforms that promise, with some degree of
reality, to bring that future so much nearer than would be the case
if nothing was done to speed it up. *In the context of public
governance. They do not want reforms to be imposed by distant,
anonymous, unresponsive, untrustworthy leaders but to be chosen
consensually with common understanding of reform goals,
appropriate values, and intended outcomes and carried out by
creative policy makers, sensitive regulators, conciliatory mediators,
and competent coordinators.*

In this respect, the global society does not start from scratch.
Reforms have been subject to scrutiny by many social scientists
according to their specialities. Here, I must be personal. I have
concentrated on administrative reform, that is, reforms confined to
the machinery of government and the inner workings of public
administration. Governance reform goes well beyond public sector
management and may soon bring quite different findings. In the
meantime, some generalities might be derived from the following
OECD Public Management Policy Brief No. 9 dated June 2001,
substituting governance for government.

Establish the Conditions for Reform

Determining the shape of reform depends on the government's ability to
anticipate the public's needs. Currently, most public reform is not developed
in anticipation of needs, but rather in response to crises that arise when
those needs are unmet. The challenge to government is to move away from
opportunistic reform towards more strategic reform: developing a clear
vision, building a constituency, devising tactics to achieve results, and
communicating this vision and anticipated results....

Communicate to Build Constituencies for Reform

Communicating the need for reform involves transmitting the values and
goals that underlie the reform vision and identifying and addressing the

public's fears. A compelling statement of values creates an emotional connection with the public by reflecting its own desires, and helps...overcome bureaucratic self-interest....Communicating the process helps government workers understand their role in reform and maintain the coherence of reform efforts...[and] provides a timeline for achieving results. Communicating reform successes builds public confidence and maintains the momentum of reform by bolstering political and public support.

CREATE A 'CHANGE CULTURE' BY CHANGING BEHAVIOUR

Reform should seek long-term change in government's behaviour by changing organizational culture...by building incentives into reform efforts....[S]tructural changes should foster leadership, innovation, flexibility and accountability for results.

WORK TO AVOID REFORM FATIGUE

...Governments can work to avoid reform fatigue by gaining stakeholder buy-in through feedback and consultation to create a sense of ownership in reform efforts....Instead of continuous reform, governments need to evolve organizations that can adapt to change.

STAY THE PATH BY FOSTERING CHAMPIONS OF REFORM

...Organisations should focus explicitly on leadership development by identifying and training leaders. Government can provide incentives for leadership by encouraging innovation and rewarding successes and by giving potential leaders the opportunity to develop leadership skills on the job. Leaders should be held accountable for outcomes, but also be allowed to make mistakes.

And a final word:

As society continues to change rapidly, the solutions of the past are no longer sufficient. Not only is there no 'one-size-fits-all' solution across countries, but countries should also use reform to create institutions that can constantly adapt to changes in their own societies and to changing outside forces. (OECD 2001, 1–6)

OECD's sage advice can also apply to the whole field of institutional reform. Potential reformers are better informed now than in any previous time in history about what does or does not work, under what circumstances the chances of success improve, according to what assumptions, and with what likely outcomes. It is not so much a question of *what* to do as to *how* to proceed and what needs to be done to reduce the odds against possible failure. Reformers have to compromise and stop short of what they plan and intend and return another day to try again in more auspicious circumstances. What follows is a sample of current on-going global attempts at institutional reform to illustrate how complicated the task of institutional reform is. A start is made with the democratization campaign followed by the anti-corruption campaign, both of which are receiving heavy international support.

DEMOCRATIZATION

Clearly, democratization favours the evolutionary Western liberal interpretation as opposed to the Marxist style people's democracy in which a single-party dictatorship transforms society by revolutionary means. How well has democratization been doing since the collapse of the Soviet Union? It has fared reasonably well. None of the former communist regimes has returned to the Marxist fold, and moves in that direction will rekindle the very fears that brought the Soviet Union crashing down, although democratization among the countries of the former Soviet Union may not have progressed as far as its advocates would have hoped. Outside the former Soviet Union, except for a few diehard states, the Marxist influence has been declining, and they have been moving away from communist style totalitarianism, the exception being in Latin America where populism has been reviving Marxist slogans without dismantling democratization.

Democratization faces a more serious challenge from its traditional non-Marxist absolutist opponents who steadfastly resist its overtures. Authoritarian regimes declare that democratization will worsen not improve their situation, and militant fundamentalists in the Middle East claim that Islam is being undermined by non-believers, who want to upset the whole social order. In Latin America, two decades ago or so, there were only a handful of genuine liberal democracies; today, the reverse is true, although several are quite fragile and could conceivably revert to authoritarianism. In Asia, the record is not so good with some notable successes and still too much fragility, where ghosts from the past along with their cronies have a habit of returning and reimposing their authority. Many claim to be on the path to democratization, but their reality remains somewhat hollow, and where threatened by terrorism they have been regressing. In Africa, the number of democracies in the same period has increased from four to sixteen out of a total of fifty-four countries, recording progress but failing to take into account regression through military coups and failure to implement real democratic reform.

The worst record is in the Middle East where democratization has had its ups and downs, mostly downs. Most peoples in this vast region have never really experienced genuine democracy, and their fundamentalists make no mistake about where they stand on views denying that democracy is incompatible with Islam by anointing man over Allah, allowing freedom of religion, belief, expression, and association no matter what, and on being secularist, separating religion from the state (Al-Zarqari 2005). Democracy 'does not take the unswerving legislation of Allah into account at all....' (Al-Burqari 1989). To dissociate themselves from such harsh opposition, moderate Muslim leaders are more likely to bow to democratization pressures in symbolic ways to please the international community but will give heart to their people to push for more. Thus, the momentum is probably shifting here as well as elsewhere in favour of democratization. The going will continue to be tough and some regression is also likely, especially if traditional democracies find themselves slipping into bad habits and discounting their own failings as they falter in dealing with popular feelings of powerlessness, alienation, indifference, and dissatisfaction with public leaders and social institutions.

COMBATING CORRUPTION

Whereas democratization can claim success for any advance in human rights, free elections, and the peaceful transition of power, reformers battling corruption have few benchmarks by which to measure their success. Corruption by its very nature is secretive unless institutionalized, whereby it is the regular way of conducting public business. Autocracy automatically is corrupt because those who exercise autocratic rule take advantage of the deprivation of inferiors' liberty, human rights, and representation. Naturally, autocratic regimes rate among the poorest as they do little to encourage societal investment over conspicuous consumption and reward immoral and unscrupulous conduct, especially exploitation and greed, while promoting the export of mobile capital and brains. Democratization runs up against the barrier of corruption because the corrupt benefit, as they are unlikely to have the political will to deprive themselves of their advantageous position and ill-gotten rewards. An integral part of democratization is dethroning the corrupt and building political will to end corrupt practices.

It has long been recognized that power and authority have a corrupting influence to which all office holders are prone. The insistence on institutional safeguards is an acknowledgement that democracy's moral imperative to rule impartially in the public interest is fragile in the best of governance systems, and temptations to deviate can be strong. Therefore, global campaigns to combat corruption look to exceptionally strong individuals of exemplary character and moral rectitude to lead and take a firm stand against the corrupt. Several international agencies give such leaders every protection, all manner of technical assistance, and global backing. But, too often, even these brave souls find they can go thus far and no farther because the corruption is just too embedded within society. As soon as one loophole is closed, another opens or the habitualized system continues only with different players. It is not as though the reformers attempt the impossible. They do not seek to put an end to all corruption, merely to reduce its prevalence, turning it from pervasive, harmful forms to minor inconsequential forms. They may have public opinion on their side but people are intimidated by the corrupt or feel hopelessly trapped to make a strong public stand. Yet, once the ball starts rolling, it gains a momentum of its own, and there are enough examples to show that with determination corruption can be thwarted.

One drawback to the global anti-corruption campaign is that it is pushed from the outside and associated with unpopular international agencies that fail to practise what they preach and whose (hidden) agenda is suspect. Another is that among the major backers are countries without a high reputation for clean hands as shown by too frequent scandals that embarrass them. And, it is not all that clear that it is all bad, for empirically some forms seem to promote progress or at least do not prevent development.

There is no doubt that corruption is a scourge. But there is also no doubt that many countries crippled by corruption are not sinking....Of course, it would be vastly superior for all these places to have an honest and independent judiciary, respect for the rule of law, and a sound educational system. But these are outcomes, not prescriptions. They represent hard-won progress from sustained efforts at all levels of society, typically over generations. Simply telling these countries to shake off the shackles of corruption...is worse than no advice at all. (Naim 2005)

The corrupt merely take advantage of what openings are available to them in any normally functioning society. To shut them off means interfering with the smooth running of society. Consequently, corruption remains a good business with rich countries probably deriving more from it than they spend on foreign aid (World Bank 2004, 25). Firm action against it may involve compromising democratic niceties. The conclusion to be drawn is that the anti-corruption campaign has not been faring at all well. There have been successes here and there but also an awful lot of back peddling, too much hype, and not that much impact in practice. Universal strategies do not seem to work well in local circumstance. The following questions have to be posed first:

1. Where is society being most victimized?
2. What forms of corruption most handicap development?
3. Which remedies are most likely to work without unforeseen effects?
4. Who is most reliable and trustworthy to follow through anti-corruption measures?
5. When has sufficient time passed to assess impact?
6. How can momentum be recharged?
7. How can miscalculations be corrected?
8. When is enough, enough?

Some reassessment of the global anti-corruption campaign is already justifiable. First, too much stress is placed on public sector corruption as if it were responsible for corruption in the private and third sectors and for corruption in the latter being much less important. One corrupts the others, although it is probably that much easier to tackle corruption in the public sector. Too often a one-sided picture is painted. Second, corruption in the public sector does not distinguish political from administrative corruption. While they are bound to-gether, they take different forms and can be tackled separately. Third, individual corruption has to be separated from institutionalized corruption. Whereas there are likely to be rotten apples in any barrel, they infect all within. It is institutionalized corruption that is the more serious as moral organizational norms are turned on their head. Fourth, to expect to eliminate corruption altogether is unrealistic as long as individuals and institutions are imperfect. In the absence of definitive proof either way, a good case can be made out for the corrupt simply because the circumstances in which they operate are so confusing and complicated and the corrupt are so convincing in their own defence that in a democratic society they must be given the benefit of the doubt.

The potential benefits of democratization and honest governance remain so worthwhile, that, like all reforms, they deserve any chance of success. The advice to institutional reforms is very simple: '*If at first you don't succeed, try, try, and try again.*' Persistence eventually pays off. Every advance becomes a launching pad for the next. A worthy goal would have been brought that much nearer, and newcomers will be forever grateful that they enjoy the fruits of victory. In these and other ways, the study of governance and the lessons to be derived therefrom will pay off handsomely.

Select References

Al-Burqari, Issam Muhhammad Taher, 'Democracy is a Religious Heresy', http://www.memri.org/bin/openerlatest.cgi?ID-SD85605, 1989, p. 3.

Al-Zarqari, Abu Mus'ab, 'Democracy is the Very Essence of Heresy, Polytheism, and Error', http://www.memri.org/bin/openerlatest.cgi?ID-SD85605, 2005, pp. 1–2.

Bevir, Mark, 'A Decentered Theory of Governance', Department of Political Science, University of California, Berkeley, CA, 2005.

Cleveland, Harlan, *The Future Executive; A Guide for Tomorrow's Managers*, New York: Harper & Row, 1972.

Dror, Yehezkel, *The Capacity to Govern*, London: Frank Cass, 2001.

Ford Foundation, *From Public Administration To Governance*, New Delhi, 2002.

Frederickson, George, 'The Prophet of Public Administration', *Public Administration Times*, American Society for Public Administration, Washington, DC, Aug. 2003, p. 11.

Graddy, Elizabeth, 'What is governance?', *Connections*, 1(1), School of Policy, Planning, Development, University of Southern California, 2005, p. 1.

Hood, Christopher, *The Art of the State: Culture, Rhetoric, and Public Management*, Oxford: Oxford University Press, 1990.

Hyden, Goran, 'Operationalizing Governance for Sustainable Development', in *Governance and Developing Countries*, Jamil Jeisrat, Boston: Brille, 2001.

Kooiman, Jan, *Governing as Governance*, Thousand Oaks, CA: Sage Publications, 2003.

Minogue, Martin, Charles Polidano, and David Hulme, 'Introduction: The Analysis of Public Management and Governance', in *Beyond the New Public Management: Changing Ideas and Practices in Governance*, Cheltenham: Edward Elgar, 1998, ch. 1, pp. 1–13.

Naim, Moises, 'Bad Medicine', *Foreign Policy*, March/April 2005, pp. 96–7.

OECD, *The State in a Changing World*, Paris: OECD, 1997.

_____, *Government of the Future*, Paris: OECD, 2001.

Rhodes, Richard, *Understanding Governance: Policy Networks, Governance, Reflexivity and Accountability*, Milton Keynes: Oxford University Press, 1997.

Tarschys, Daniel, 'Wealth, Values, Institutions: Trends in Government and Governance', in *Governance in the 21st Century*, Paris: OECD, 2001, ch. 2, pp. 27–41.

United Nations Development Program, *Governance for Sustainable Human Development*, New York: UNDP, 1997.

World Bank, *Managing Development; A Discussion Paper*, Washington, DC: World Bank, 1991.

_____, *Mainstreaming Anti-Corruption Activities in World Bank Assistance*, Report No. 29620, Washington, DC: World Bank, 2004.

4

Whatever Happened to Public Administration?

Governance, Governance Everywhere[1]

H. George Frederickson

For at least the last fifteen years, governance has been a prominent subject in public administration. Governance, defined by Lynn, Heinrich, and Hill as the 'regimes, laws, rules, judicial decisions, and administrative practices that constrain, prescribe, and enable the provision of publicly supported goals and services', holds strong interest for public administration scholars (2001, 7). This chapter reviews and evaluates the evolution and development of the concept of governance in public administration; then, using regime theory from the study of international relations, the concept of governance as applied in public administration is analysed, parsed, and framed.

The present scholarly and conceptual use of the concept of governance in the field tends to take one or more of the following forms: (1) it is substantively the same as already established perspectives in public administration, although in a different language, (2) it is essentially the study of the contextual influences that shape the practices of public administration, rather than the study of public administration, (3) it is the study of interjurisdictional relations and third-party policy implementation in public administration, (4) it is the study of the influence or power of non-state and non-jurisdictional public collectives. Of these approaches to public administration as governance, it is the third and fourth—governance as the public administration of interjurisdiction relations and third-party policy implementation, and the governance of non-state and non-jurisdictional public collectives—that form the basis of a usable theory of governance for public administration.

It was Harlan Cleveland who first used the word 'governance' as an alternative to the phrase public administration. In the mid-1970s, one of the themes in Cleveland's particularly thoughtful and provocative speeches, papers, and books went something like this: 'What the people want is less government and more governance' (1972). What he meant by governance was the following cluster of concepts.

'The organizations that get things done will no longer be hierarchical pyramids with most of the real control at the top. They will be systems—interlaced webs of tension in which control is loose, power diffused, and centers of decision plural. "Decision making" will become an increasingly intricate process of multilateral brokerage both inside and outside the organization which thinks it has the responsibility for making, or at least announcing, the decision. Because organizations will be horizontal, the way they are governed is likely to be more collegial, consensual, and consultative. The bigger the problems to be tackled, the more real power is diffused and the larger the number of persons who can exercise it—if they work at it' (13).

Like many, Cleveland saw the blurring of the distinctions between public and private organizations, and he associated this blurring with his conception of governance. He reasoned through what it meant as follows: 'These new style public-private horizontal systems will be led by a new breed of man and women. I call them Public Executives, people who manage public responsibilities whether in "public" or "private" organizations' (14).

Cleveland clearly understood the challenges of individual accountability associated with horizontal multi-organizational systems. Who, exactly, do these modern public executives work for and to whom are they accountable? Consider this remarkably bold argument: 'Public ethics are in the hearts and minds of individual Public Executives, and the ultimate court of appeals from their judgments is some surrogate for people-in-general' (117). Note, that he does not argue that accountability is ultimately to the people or to the elected officials of one's jurisdiction. Cleveland's idea of public responsibility is much bigger than that. The moral responsibility of public executives includes basic considerations of four fundamental principles: 'a sense of welfare; a sense of equity; a sense of achievement; and a sense of participating' (126–7).

What would be the results of such a grand conception of the moral responsibility of the public administrator? 'In a society characterized by bigness and complexity it is those individuals who learn to get things done in organizational systems who will have a rational basis for feeling free' (135). 'By the development of their administrative skills, and by coming squarely to terms with the moral requirements of executive leadership, individual men and women can preserve and extend their freedom. Freedom is the power to choose, and the future executive will be making the most choices— whom to bring together in which organizations, to make what happen, in whose interpretation of the public interest. Those who relish that role will have every reason to feel free, not in the interstices but right in the middle of things' (140).

Governance is an especially important word/concept because of the mismatch or disconnect between jurisdictions on one hand and social, technological, political, and economic problems on the other hand. Cleveland understood this, too: 'One of the striking ironies of our time is that, just when we have to build bigger, more complicated "bundles of relations" to deal comprehensively with the human consequences of science and technology, many people are seized with the idea that large-scale organization is itself a Bad Thing. My thesis is the reverse...' (139–40). Big problems, Cleveland believes, require big responses. Those responses will, however, be multi-organizational and will involve both public and private organizations. These responses will, post-Cleveland, be led by not one, but many, leaders.

In the thirty years since Cleveland's initial conception, it would be only a slight exaggeration to say governance has become the subject formerly known as public administration. A leading academic journal, now in its sixteenth year, carries the title *Governance: An International Journal of Policy and Administration*. A careful examination indicates that its contents have mostly to do with what was once called public administration. The most popular and widely read magazine for American state and local governments is *Governing: The Magazine of States and Localities*, now in its fifteenth year. The Brookings Institution recently changed the name of its highly regarded 'Governmental Studies' programme to

'Governance Studies' and launched a series of studies of governance (Benner, Reinicke, & Witte 2003; Birdsall 2003; Graham & Litan 2003; Woods 2003). Scholars at the Kennedy School of Government at Harvard are midway through a large project that has the title, ' Visions of Governance in the 21st Century.' Schools of governance, teaching graduate curricula not unlike public administration graduate curricula in both Europe and the United States, are now found at several important European universities. In the early 1990s, the National Academy of Public Administration essentially dropped the phrase 'public administration' in favour of the word 'governance,' although the work of the academy continues to be primarily public-administration consulting (Fosler 1998). 'In much of the modern literature in the field, governance has become a virtual synonym for public management and public administration' (Frederickson & Smith 2003, 225). The problem is that governance has dozens of meanings. Lynn, Heinrich, and Hill say it best:

The term 'governance' is widespread in both public and private sectors, in characterizing both global and local arrangements, and in reference to both formal and informal norms and understandings. Because the term has strong intuitive appeal, precise definitions are seldom thought to be necessary by those who use it. As a result, when authors identify 'governance' as important to achieving policy or organizational objectives, it may be unclear whether the reference is to organizational structure, administrative processes, managerial judgment, systems of incentives and rules, administrative philosophies, or a combination of these elements.

From Cleveland's tightly defined presentation of what governance was understood to be, and from his carefully set out descriptions of the implications of that understanding, governance is now everywhere and appears to mean anything and everything (Rhodes 2000). Because governance is a power word, a dominant descriptor, and the current preference of academic tastemakers, there has been a rush to affix to it all of the other fashions of the day. Governance is the structure of political institutions (National Research Council 1999). Governance is the shift from the bureaucratic state to the hollow state or to third-party government (Milward & Provan 2000; Salamon 2002; Frederickson 1997; Rhodes 1997). Governance is market-based approaches to government (Kettl 1993; Donahue & Nye 2002). Governance is the development of social capital, civil society, and high levels of citizen participation (Hirst 2000; Kooiman

2001; Sorensen 2003). Governance is the work of empowered, muscular, risk-taking public entrepreneurs (Osborne & Gaebler 1992). In the United Kingdom, governance is Tony Blair's 'third way,' a political packaging of the latest ideas in new public management, expanded forms of political participation, and attempts to renew civil society (Newman 2001).

Governance is the new public management or managerialism (Kernaghan, Marson, & Borins 2000; Considine & Painter 1997). Governance is public sector performance (Heinrich & Lynn 2000). Governance is interjurisdictional cooperation and network management (Frederickson 1999; O'Toole 2003; Peters & Pierre 1998). Governance is globalization and rationalization (Pierre 2000). Governance is corporate oversight, transparency, and accounting standards. Rhodes (2000, 55–60) found seven applications of governance in the field of public administration: the new public management or managerialism; good governance, as in efficiency, transparency, meritocracy, and equity; international and interjurisdictional interdependence; non-government driven forms of socio-cybernetic systems of governance; the new political economy, including shifting from state service provision to the state as regulator; and networks. There are many more applications of governance to the subject once known as public administration, but these few illustrate the capacious range of concepts, ideas, and theories associated with it.

There are as many definitions of the concept of governance as a synonym for public administration as there are applications. Kettl claims an emerging gap between government and governance. 'Government refers to the structure and function of public institutions. Governance is the way government gets its job done.'

'Traditionally, government itself managed most service delivery. Toward the end of the twentieth century, however, government relied increasingly on non-governmental partners to do its work, through processes that relied less on authority for control' (2002, xi). To Kettl, governance, as an approach to public administration, has primarily to do with contracting out and grants to sub-governments.

As was noted at the outset, Lynn, Heinrich, & Hill (2001, 15) use a much bigger approach to governance as an analytic framework. Their model, intended to be a starting point for research, is:

$$O = f[E, C, T, S, M]$$

Where:

O = Outputs/outcomes. The end product of a governance regime.

E = Environmental factors. These can include political structures, levels of authority, economic performance, the presence or absence of competition among suppliers, resource levels and dependencies, legal framework, and the characteristics of a target population.

C = Client characteristics. The attributes, characteristics, and behaviour of clients.

T = Treatments. These are the primary work or core processes of the organizations within the governance regime. They include organizational missions and objectives, recruitment and eligibility criteria, methods for determining eligibility, and programme treatments or technologies.

S = Structures. These include organizational type, level of coordination and integration among the organizations in the governance regime, relative degree of centralized control, functional differentiation, administrative rules or incentives, budgetary allocations, contractual arrangements or relationships, and institutional culture and values.

M = Managerial roles and actions. This includes leadership characteristics, staff-management relations, communications, methods of decision making, professional/career concerns, and mechanisms of monitoring, control, and accountability.

The problem is that it is difficult, following Lynn, Heinrich, and Hill, to conceive of anything involving government, politics, or administration that is not governance. That being the case, there appears to be little difference between studying the whole of government and politics and studying public administration. Put another way, public administration is ordinarily thought to have to do with 'treatments,' 'structures,' and 'management' in the Lynn *et al.* governance formula. They tuck the centrepieces of public administration into the broader context of governance. This chapter will later return to these distinctions and to a large-scale synthesis of governance research by Lynn, Heinrich, and Hill.

Peters uses an equally big definition of governance as 'institutions designed to exercise collective control and influence' (1995, 3). Peters, and Peters with Pierre (2000) settle on the 'steering' characteristics of governance as distinct from government. '...Public institutions continue to bear the primary responsibility for steering the economy and society. Government may, however, be able to discharge that fundamental responsibility through means other than direct imposition of authority, or use other instruments not requiring directly government involvement in the social processes being influenced. Governance, in the words of Walter Kikert (1997), is "steering at a distance." "This style of steering is more palatable politically in an era in which there is significant public resistance to the state and its more intrusive forms of intervention' (Peters 1995, 86).

Doubtless the most comprehensive synthesis of governance as public administration is found in B. Guy Peters' *The Future of Governing* (2001). Like many approaches to governance that use a narrow reading of public administration as a straw man, Peters 'sets up' public administration as the old-time religion, riddled with identity crises. Traditional public administration is 'five old chestnuts,' modeled on an institutionalized and apolitical civil service, organizational hierarchy and rules, a preoccupation with permanence and stability, and reams of internal regulations (Peters 2001, 4–13). These elements of the old-time public administration religion would be recognized by any of the members of that church, all of them having been part of the internal critique of the field long before governance ever appeared (Frederickson & Smith 2003). Traditional public administration, following Peters, floundered because of disappointments in governmental performance, changing demographics, overly large and cumbersome governments, and several other deficits. Governance reform, particularly as seen in Great Britain, New Zealand, Australia, and the United States is modeled on various contributions of four different approaches to public administration— markets and competition, participative administration, greater flexibility, and deregulation. In Table 4.1, Peters provides an excellent summation of the characteristics of these four governance models. Each of these models would be instantly recognized by any senior student of public administration as a part of the literature and theory of the field, entirely independent of applications of the models to governance. Public administration scholars have also long recognized the normative content of each of the models, as does Peters. The question is, does the application of governance as either a theory

	Market Government	*Participative Government*	*Flexible Government*	*Deregulated Government*
Principal Diagnosis	Monopoly	Hierarchy	Permanence	Internal regulation
Structure	Decentralization	Flatter organizations	'Virtual organizations'	No particular regulation
Management	Pay for performance; other private-sector techniques	TQM; Teams	Managing temporary personnel	Greater managerial freedom
Policy Making	Internal markets; market incentives	Consultation; negotiation	Experimentation	Entrepreneurial government
Public Interest	Low cost	Involvement; consultation	Low cost; coordination	Creativity; activism

Source: Guy Peters, *Governance: Four Emerging Models*, Lawrence: University Press of Kansas, 1996, p. 21.

or an analytic framework add value to broader long-standing approaches to public administration? (See particularly Wilson 1989; Frederickson & Smith 2003.)

Are these so-called governance concepts, with their attendant possible meanings, really useful to students of public administration and public management? Do they add anything of consequence to our understanding of the field? Do they merely repackage public administration in a newer and rather fuzzy language? Could the use of the governance concept have a negative influence on our theory building and research scholarship, obfuscating and confusing rather than clarifying and illuminating, and distorting by concealing bias rather than revealing and removing it? The validity and usefulness of the governance concept can be challenged on at least five rather fundamental grounds. These five points lead, in turn, to two implications or indirect criticisms that question whether further use of the concept of governance as an organizing concept for public administration and management has the potential to contribute substantially to our understanding of the field and ought to be encouraged by leading scholars in the field.

First, the concept of governance is fashionable, the favourite of academic tastemakers, the flavour not only of the month but also of the year and the decade. Does the governance concept bring anything particularly new to the public administration table? Much of the governance literature is 'a rehash of old academic debates under a new and jazzier name—a sort of intellectual mutton dressed up as lamb—so that pushy new professors...can have the same old arguments as their elders but can flatter themselves that they are breaking new ground by using new jargon' (Strange 1983, 341). Fashions change, and we may already have reached the half-life of the hegemony of governance as an organizing concept for the field. In the same way that miniskirts come and go, so too could governance.

Second, the concept is imprecise, woolly, and, when applied, so broad that virtually any meaning can be attached to it. As described earlier in this chapter, governance, at least at this point, does not have an agreed-upon meaning. Fortunately, some who use the term are serious about the matter of definition and precision; others however are not. Still, there is little doubt that the word governance is useful as a way to describe, as Cleveland does, patterns of interjusridictional and interorganizational relations. The matter of precision in definition is considered again at the close of this chapter.

Third, the concept of governance is freighted with values, values often stated in ways that imply that certain things are understood and agreed-upon when, in fact, they are not. Some approaches to governance as public administration tends to wrap together anti-bureaucratic and anti-governmental sentiments, preferences for markets over-governments, and preferences for limited government—all points of view masked as given, understood, and agreed-upon (Kernaghan, Marson, & Borins 2000; Osborne & Gaebler 1992). Not the least of the value problems generally associated with some uses of the concept of governance, are its democratic deficits. Standard models of democratic government involve a limited state that is controlled by representative government bound by the rule of law, and also a largely self-organizing civil society independent of the state but protected by the state's laws and administrative procedures. Some models of governance, however, either discount the significance of jurisdictionally based democratic traditions or fail to take them into account, most notably the Osborn and Gaebler reinventing government model (1992; see also Hirst 2000; Sorensen 2002). Other models are deeply contextual, based on constitutional, legal, organizational, and political influences and imperatives (Lynn, Heinrich, & Hill 2001). These models are state- and jurisdiction-centred understandings of governance in which public administration is contingent on artifacts of constitutions, rules, laws, and politics. This perspective on governance in public administration makes the subject both bigger and grander, a kind of un-public administration.

Fourth, scholars who use the word governance, particularly in Europe, claim that governance is primarily about change, about reform, about getting things right. In addition to the scholars, there are policy entrepreneurs using the word governance to lend importance to their policy projects. Such perspective almost always begins with the notion that things are broken and need to be fixed. Investments in our prevailing institutions, our cities, states, and nations and their established governments are devalued, as are the accomplishments of those institutions. Order, stability, and predictability are likewise undervalued. Governance, it is claimed, is about dynamic change, about reform. It is interesting to remember that the origins of American public administration were closely associated with reform and with the progressive project of the late-nineteenth and early-twentieth centuries.

In most of the more precise scholarly literature, despite the rhetoric of reform, governance is mostly about order and about how politicians and bureaucrats adapt in orderly ways to changing circumstances and values. There is a surface dynamic to governance as a form of orderly adaptation using the logic of the diffusion of innovation, and so-called best practices borrowed from other organizations or jurisdictions. But the underlying values of governance are not primarily about change, they are about order. Most descriptions of elements of governance—networks, interorganizational and interjurisdictional cooperation, power sharing federations, public-private partnerships, and contracting-out—are forms of institutional adaptation in the face of increasing interdependence.

Fifth, governance is often centred on non-state institutions—both non-profit and for-profit contractors, non-governmental organizations, intergovernmental organizations, parastatals, and third parties generally. State- and jurisdiction-centred theory and research is, from some governance perspectives, passé. In the name of the 'hollowed-out' thesis, many have criticized that part of the governance perspective that emphasizes privatization, contracting-out, and public–private partnerships (Rhodes 1997; Newman 2001; Milward & Provan 2000). In their convictions regarding the superiority of the market over the polity, advocates for this governance perspective appear to somehow imagine that there can be governance without government (Peters & Pierre 1998). At a minimum, when this perspective is implemented, it seriously diminishes the capacity of the core state executive to steer (Rhodes 2000). Indeed, it can be argued that under hollow-state conditions, steering is reversed, the state being steered by its governance partners (Kettl 1993; Frederickson 1999). It is the states and their sub-jurisdictions that deal with the vexing problems of race, poverty, and justice. In the words of Janet Newman, 'It is noticeable that theories of governance fail to deal adequately with the issues of diversity and patterns of inclusion on which it is based' (2001, 171).

From this sketchy critique of governance, two important implications arise. One is that the governance approach to the study of public management and administration emphasizes theory and research, explaining change and reform rather than the functioning of jurisdictions—cities, states, nations, and certain regional or global institutions—which are, after all, the dominant and preferred way to practise governance. Public administration, in practice, is about organization, bureaucracy, and management and the context in which they happen. What people often value about the jurisdictions in which they live and, by implication, the bureaucracies working for those jurisdictions, is the order, predictability, stability, and permanence they provide. National and local identity is important to the people. When will people sing an anthem to a contractor, wear the uniform of a network, or pledge allegiance to non-jurisdictional forms of governance? Probably not soon. Governance scholarship tends to ignore or at least de-emphasize the vast world of non-governance that lies deep in the folds of jurisdiction, organization, and bureaucracy. Are we better off as theorists who focus on governance and not on government organization, bureaucracy, and management?

Concepts of governance as public administration reflect a long-standing theoretical debate in the field, the matter of distinctions between politics and policy, on the one hand, and policy implementation or administration, on the other. Easy dismissal of the politics-administration dichotomy serves to focus the study of public administration, particularly by some governance theorist, on the constitutional and political context of the organization and management of the territorial state or jurisdiction. From this perspective, governance becomes steering and public administration becomes rowing, a lesser phenomenon in the scholarly pecking order, not to mention a lesser subject in governance. Public administration, thus understood, is the work that governments contract out, leaving governance as the subject of our study. Although the lines between politics, policy, and administration are often fuzzy and changing, and although we know, strictly speaking, there is no politics-administration dichotomy, it is nevertheless important to understand the empirical distinctions between political and administrative phenomena. Concepts of governance that advance our understanding of public sector administration and organization are helpful. Concepts of governance that simply change the subject of public administration to politics and policy making or not. In democratic government it is, after all, elected officials who govern. Bureaucrats have roles and responsibilities for governing or governance, but in democratic polities these roles and responsibilities are different than the roles and responsibilities of elected officials. Janet Newman says it well: 'Neither "good governance" nor "well-managed government" could resolve the contradictions around the popular role of government and the appropriate boundaries of governance' (2001, 170). In the name of stamping out bureaucracy and replacing it with what they describe as good governance, Osborne and Gaebler advocate a range of managerial prerogatives that would significantly intrude on the political and policy making prerogatives generally assumed to belong to elected officials, and particularly elected legislators, in a democratic polity (1992).

The second implication of the critique is that governance theorists persist in looking for an all-pervasive pattern of organizational and administrative behaviour, a 'general theory' that will provide an explanation for the past and a means to predict the future. Despite the accumulated evidence based on decades of work on theory and the empirical testing of theory in public administration, no such pattern has been found (Frederickson & Smith 2003). Does the governance concept beguile a generation of scholars to set off in the vain search for a metatheoretical EI Dorado (Olsen 2003)?

CONSTRUCTING A VIABLE CONCEPT OF GOVERNANCE FOR PUBLIC ADMINISTRATION

Although the critique of governance is a serious challenge, does it render the concept useless? The answer is no. There are powerful forces at work in the world, forces that the traditional study of politics, government, and public administration do not explain. The state and its sub-jurisdictions are losing important elements of their sovereignty; borders have less and less meaning. Social and economic problems and challenges are seldom contained within jurisdictional boundaries, and systems of communication pay little attention to them. Business is increasingly regional or global. Business elites have multiple residences and operate extended networks that are highly multi-jurisdictional. States and jurisdictions are hollowing out their organization and administrative capacities, exporting to contractors much of the work of public administration.

Governance, even with its weakness, is the most useful available concept for describing and explaining these forces. But, for governance to become anything more than passing fashion or a dismissive un-public administration, it must respond to the critique of governance. To do this, governance scholars must settle on an agreed-upon definition, a definition broad enough to comprehend the forces it presumes to explain but not so broad as to claim to explain everything. Governance theorists must be ready to explain not only what governance is, but also what it is not. Governance theorist must be upfront about the biases in the concept and the implications of those biases.

The lessons learned in the evolution of regime theory in international relations are relevant here because regime theory pre-dates governance theory and because the two are very nearly the same thing.[2]

To construct a practical and usable concept of governance for public administration, the field would profit by narrowing the subject to its most common usage and returning to Cleveland's original conception. In addition, the field would benefit by using regime theory from international relations to inform the development of governance theory. This would bring some precision to the concept and facilitate theoretical discourse around governance in public administration. In precise terms, then, governance in public administration should be defined as 'sets of principles, norms, roles, and decision making procedures around which actors (managers) converge in a given public policy arena' (Krasner 1983; March & Olsen 1997; Keohane 2002). It is important to note here that this definition includes many of the elements in the Lynn *et al.* definition of governance set out at the beginning of this chapter and does not include others (for example, outcomes as the dependent variable, environmental characteristics, client characteristics, regimes, judicial decisions, and the phrase 'administrative practices that constrain, prescribe, and enable the provision of public services'). Obviously, the definition of governance borrowed from the regime theory and applied to public administration significantly narrows the Lynn *et al.* definition.

The evolution of regime theory in international relations is guiding this insistence that to be useful, governance theory must be both narrowed and precise.

For a longer time than the concept of governance has claimed to be an organizing concept for public administration, the concept of regimes has informed research and theory in international relations

(Krasner 1983; Hasenclever, Mayer, & Rittberger 2000). The basic elements of the concept of governance in public administration are similar to the theory of international regimes, and international regime theorists are well ahead of governance theorists. The path that international relations scholars have taken in the development of regime theory serves as a useful guide for the development of governance theory in public administration.

Descriptions of international regimes are very close to the narrower description of governance being presented here. 'Regimes are deliberately constructed, partial international orders on either a regional or global scale, which are intended to remove specific issue-areas of international politics from the sphere of self-help behavior. By creating shared expectations about appropriate behavior and by upgrading the level of transparency in the issue area, regimes help states (and other actors) to cooperate with a view to reaping joint gains in the form of additional welfare or security. If we classify international issue-areas by the dominant value being at issue, we find that regimes exist in all domains of contemporary world politics: there are *security* regimes such as the nuclear non-proliferation regime; *economic* regimes such as the international trade regime; *environmental* regimes such as the international regime for the protection of the stratospheric ozone layer; and, finally, *human rights* regimes such as the one based on the European Convention on Human Rights' (Hasenclever, Mayer, & Rittberger 2000, 3–4). One might add to this list bureaucratic regimes, patterns of cooperation between jurisdictions conducted by appointed officials, almost always in specific policy domains (Haas 1990; 1992).

International relations theory went through a period not unlike the present period in public administration—anything and everything was claimed to be regime theory (Strange 1983; Rosenau 2003). In recent years the subject has returned to its original and narrower definition (Krasner 1983).

Adapting a theory of governance in public administration from international regime theory, suggests a governance theory in three parts: (1) vertical and horizontal injurisdictional and interorganizational cooperation; (2) extension of the state or jurisdiction by contracts or grants to third parties, including sub-governments; and (3) forms of public non-jurisdictional or non-governmental policy making and implementation.

The first of these, vertical and horizontal interjurisdictional and interorganizational cooperation, will be called *interjurisdictional governance*. Interjurisdictional governance in public administration is:

1. actors in systems of governance either based in jurisdictions representing jurisdictional interests or in non-governmental profit and non-profit organizations representing their interests;
2. participation in such systems of governance as a voluntary form of cooperation; and
3. almost always policy-area specific; for example environmental interjurisdictional governance, economic development interjurisdictional governance, public safety interjurisdictional governance, national defence interjurisdictional governance.

The second form will be known as *third-party governance*. Third-party governance has the following characteristics:

1. it extends the functioning of the state or the jurisdiction by exporting to third parties (the first party is the elected basis of democratic legislative authority, the second party is executive administration or public administration) jurisdictional tasks and responsibilities for policy implementation;
2. its precise governance roles and responsibilities are based upon formal contractual or grant documents upon which the contractor (the jurisdiction) and the contractee (the profit or non-profit organization or sub-government) agree;
3. its contracts and grants are time specific; and
4. its contract and grants are policy-area specific, as in health research grants or road construction contracts.

The third form will be known as *public non-governmental governance*.

Public non-governmental governance has the following characteristics:

1. policy making and implementation by non-governmental institutions or actors that bear on the interests or well-being of citizens in the same way and with the same consequences in state or jurisdictional outcomes; and

2. jurisdictional systems of jurisdictional regulation, oversight, or accountability have limited affect.

Governance in public administration may take these forms either singularly or in combination.

Interjurisdictional, third-party contract, and public non-governmental governance comprehend those aspects of governance most relevant to public administration and the largest and most common forms of governance. While other models of governance are interesting and may be relevant, it is interjurisdictional, third-party, and non-governmental governance that come closest to comprehending the traditional practices of public administration, theories of public administration, and the modern practices of governance. The critical point here is that instead of governance replacing public administration, governance is a kind of public administration. In simple terms, it could be said that in the day-to-day, internal management of a government agency, a person practises public administration. It could also be said that in the management of the extended state or jurisdiction, a person practises the public administration of governance. And it could be said that non-governmental institutions or organizations making and implementing policies that affect citizens in the same way as the policies or actions of the state are practising the public administration of governance (Frederickson 1997, 224). Therefore governance, as a distinct form of public administration, has to do with the extension of the state or jurisdiction either beyond its boundaries, through third parties, or by non-governmental institutions.

Three schools of thought have evolved in international regime theory, schools of thought that are particularly useful as a basis of comparison with the narrower description of governance theory in public administration—the *neo-liberal* school, the *realist* school, and the *cognitive* school.

Neo-liberals emphasize the role of international regimes in helping states and jurisdictions achieve common interests. In the neo-liberal schema, states and jurisdictions are rational egoists that care only for their own interests. Neo-liberals draw heavily on economic theories of institutions, focusing on the role of information and transaction costs. Regimes are likened to investments by the territorial state, investments determined by issue density. Game theoretic models such as the Prisoner's Dilemma are used by neo-liberal regime scholars to estimate the probability that, under conditions of mixed motives and in particular situations, a regime might emerge and institutionalize. Thus the 'structure of the situation' is central to the logic of the neo-liberal school of international regime theory (Hasenclever, Mayer, & Rittberger 2000, 5–9).

The neo-liberal school of international regime theory is very nearly the same as the public choice or rational choice school in public administration and policy studies. Consider, for example, studies of the commons (Ostrom 1998); the self-maximizing bureaucrat or bureaucracy (Tullock 1965; Downs 1967; Niskanen 1971); the self-maximizing citizen (Tiebout 1956; Lyons, Lowery, & DeHoog 1992); the conditions of both individual and jurisdictional cooperation (Axelrod 1984); and formal models or organizational or bureaucratic behaviour (Moe 1984; Knott 1993) as illustrative of the similarities between international regime theory and the governance perspective in that part of public administration having to do with public choice theory and the empirical work supporting it.

International regime theorists of the realism school emphasize political power and its exercise in the territorial state and argue that power is as important to interjurisdictional cooperation as it is to conflict. 'The overall result for realist students of international institutions is that international regimes are more difficult to create and harder to maintain than neo-liberals would have us believe. The likelihood for a regime to be put in place and to be stable is greatest when the expected gains are balanced (at least for the most powerful members) such that relative losses do not accrue' (Hasenclever, Mayer, & Rittberger 2000, 9–10).

The realist school of international regime theory is not unlike a similar school in public administration. In the public administration version the focus is on constitutions, laws, the separation of powers, formal structures and rules, and on the exercise of political and bureaucratic power in the context of such structures. The leaders in the study of the constitutional and legal foundation of public administration (Rohr 1986; Rosenbloom 2003; Cooper 2002; Gilmore & Jensen 1998) tend to focus on elements of third-party governance, (see especially, Cooper 2002) as well as interjurisdictional governance (see especially the federalism and intergovernmental relations scholars such as Wright 1997; Agranoff 1985; 2003).

Cognitivists (sometimes in regime theory called strong cognitivists) are critical of both neo-liberal and realist approaches to international regimes, 'for treating actors' preferences and (perceived) options as exogenous "givens", i.e., as facts which are assumed or observed, but not theorized about...(and) reject the conception of states as rational actors, who are atomistic in the sense that their identities, power and fundamental interests are prior to international society and its institutions. States are as much shaped by international institutions as they shape them' (Hasenclever, Mayer, & Rittberger 2000, 10–11).

Doubtless the most influential argument in the cognitive school of international regime theory is made by two political scientists primarily associated with public administration, James G. March and Johan P. Olsen (1998, 949). They apply institutional theory to international relations, insisting that 'on the one side are those who see action as driven by the logic of anticipated consequences and prior preferences. On the other side are those who see action as driven by the logic of appropriateness and senses of identity. Within the tradition of logic of appropriateness, actions are seen as rule based. Human actors are imagined to follow the rules that associate particular identities to particular situations, approaching individual opportunities for action by assessing similarities between current identities and choice dilemmas and more general concepts of self and situations. Action involves evoking an identity or role and matching the obligation of that identity or role to a specific situation. The pursuit of purpose is associated with identities more than with interests, and with the selection of rules more than with individual rational expectations' (951; see also March & Olsen 1984, 1995; Olsen 2003; Frederickson & Smith 2003).

The cognitive institutional perspective in both international regime theory and in public administration work from the premise that it is not possible to describe international political order, or organizational order, or interorganizational order in terms of the simple notion of rational intention and design. 'History is created by complicated ecology of local events and locally adaptive actions. As individuals, groups, organizations, and institutions seek to act intelligently and learn in a changing world involving others similarly trying to adapt, they create connections that subordinate individual intentions to their interactions....They coevolve with the actions they produce' (March & Olsen 1998, 968).

From this review of regime theory and its similarity to concepts of governance, it is evident that international relations scholars have about the same 'sharp disagreements with regard to both epistemology and ontology' (Hasenclever, Mayer, & Rittberger 2000, 33). The neo-liberalists and realists (sometimes together called the rationalists) can be synthesized with softer versions of cognitive regime theory in a form of 'contextualized theory' that rests positivist tests of truth in the folds of culture, history, demographics, and the general endogeneity of complex regime and governance forces. However, there does not appear to be enough common ground to hold both the strong cognitivists and their logic of appropriateness and the rationalists with their positivist truth tests.

The study of governance and public management is advanced considerably by a recent large-scale synthesis of the literature (70 journals, and 800 articles over a twelve-year period) by Lawrence E. Lynn and Carolyn J. Hill (forthcoming). They used a state-centric definition of governance adapted from their earlier work, a definition not unlike the standard Krasner definition of international regime theory (1983, 6). Like the regime theorists, they found that the governance research scholarship broke down about, (1) studies that are historical, descriptive, and institutional in the cognitive tradition; (2) studies of examples and 'best practices,' mostly in the institutional tradition; and (3) studies following the positivist social science canon. Their synthesis focused on studies of the third type. To operationalize the synthesis, they used an adaptation of their formula presented (134–5), a process hierarchical model from political power at the top to consequences, outputs, outcomes, results, and stakeholder assessments at the bottom.

In the order of their presentation, Lynn and Hill found that: (1) there is notably more research that explains frontline work than research on higher levels of governance; (2) the majority of studies adopt a top-down perspective on governance with little emphasis on outcomes, results, or stakeholders' assessments—studies of street-level bureaucracy and bureaucrat-client interactions are the exception; (3) structures of authority are used to explain, they are not explained; (4) governance matters or, put another way, there is a demonstrable hierarchy of influence from politics clear to the stakeholders, and at each step of the way structure, process, and management matter; (5) in governance studies results are most often described as institutional outputs and not social outcomes; (6) organizational structures and levels of management discretion influence organizational effectiveness; and (7) effectiveness and cost-savings associated with third-party governance are influenced by incentives and contract-review standards and processes.

Lynn and Hill's most important finding is that hierarchy and, as they put it, hierarchical governance, is alive and well and the primary means by which we govern. It appears that the networked, associational, horizontal, and conjuncted forms of governance are less important than governance scholars might think. '[T]he American political scheme remains hierarchical and jurisdictional,' and jurisdictional hierarchy is the predicate to networked governance (34). And, they identify the likely reasons: 'The seemingly "paradigmatic" shift away from hierarchical government toward horizontal governing (hence increasing the preference for "governance" as an organizing concept) is less fundamental than it is tactical: the addition of new tools or administrative technologies that facilitate public governance within hierarchical systems' (33). For this reason, it is argued here that the study of governance should focus on interjurisdicational, third-party, and non-governmental governance as a way to narrow the grandness of the governance project.

To return to the three categories of governance (145–6), in the cases of both interjurisdictional and third-party governance, it is important to get past the idea that there can somehow be a governance tree floating in space without governmental or bureaucratic roots. Peters and Pierre asked whether there can be, as Cleveland seemed to imply, governance without government (1998). The answer is no, at least following the narrower definition of governance argued here. This suggests a state or jurisdiction-centred approach to governance, an approach ready to accept the importance of hierarchy, order, predictability, stability, and permanence. Despite all the scholarly focus on governance, it appears, even from the synthesized research of governance scholars, that the old-time religion, traditional public administration, is the basis of policy implementation in government, and government is an essential precondition of governance.

It follows from this reasoning that one of the best hopes for an empirically robust theory of governance might be to turn somewhat in the direction of the cognitive and institutional research perspective. Lynn and Hill, in their justification for studying primarily the positivist-rationalist literature, acknowledge that their approach 'sacrifices verisimilitude and nuance but gains in transparency and replicability' (5). But they found 'the fact that relatively few studies examined more complex patterns of causality may reflect the paucity of data, but it may also reflect something more significant: conjunctions by hundreds of specialized investigators that the world of practice remains more hierarchical than many of us want to concede. When it comes to answering multilevel "why" questions, the evidence suggests that hierarchy "still" matters' (33–4).

It may be that causality is more likely to be found in the cognitive and institutional literature. The overarching descriptive synthesis by March and Olsen is an insightful understanding of democratic governance from the perspective of institutional theory, with an emphasis on the logic of appropriateness as an explanatory variable (1995; see also Wilson 1989). Keohane's application of the institutional perspective to international governance, particularly the formal intergovernmental organizations such as the United Nations, the World Trade Organization, and the European Union illustrates a conceptual approach that could be useful in the search for causality in public administration as governance (2002).

SUMMING-UP

From its prominence in the 1980s, regime theory would now be described as one of many important theories of international relations. International relations is, of course, the study of relations between nation-states whereas public administration is the study of the management of the state and its sub-governments. It could be said that regime theory accounts for the role of non-state actors and policy entrepreneurs in the context of the modern transformation of the nation-state. In public administration, it could be said that the modern transformation of states and their sub-governments explains the contemporary salience of theories of governance. Both regime theory and governance theory are scholarly responses to the transformation of states.

Government in the postmodern state involves multiple levels of interlocked and overlapping arenas of collective policy implementation. Governments now operate in the context of supranational, international, transgovernmental, and transnational relations in elaborate patterns of federated power sharing and interdependence. Therefore, it is now understood that public administration as governance is the best description of the management of the transformed or postmodern state (Sorensen 2004). Nationhood and community are transformed as collective loyalties are increasingly projected away from the state. Major portions of economic activity are now embedded in cross-border networks and national and local economies are less self-sustaining that they once were (Sorensen 2004, 162).

Harlan Cleveland understood very early how governments, economies, and communities were changing and how rapidly they were changing. His initial description of public administration as governance was designed to square the theory and practices of the field with the realities of a changing world. His governance model still serves as a compelling argument for plural interjurisdictional- and interorganizational-mediated decision making networks of public executives operating in the context of blurred distinctions between public and private organizations. Following Cleveland's treatise, the popularity of the word governance soared and while gaining altitude evidently also lost oxygen. In an oxygen-deprived state, many engaged in excesses and failures including fuzzy definitions and even no definitions of governance, the freighting of governance with anti-bureaucratic, anti-governmental, and pro-market values, often without acknowledging the weight, and the overuse of straw men with exaggerated claims that governance would tip them over. And, as is often the case with concept of entrepreneurs, governance was seen as the answer, *the* grand theory to replace public administration.

Lynn, Heinrich, and Hill brought governance back down to earth and oxygenated it with their analytic framework. And, more recently, they filled in much of their framework with a synthesis of empirical research literature. Many other leading scholars in public administration use the Lynn *et al.* framework, together building an impressive body of research.

Taking a page from the evolution of regime theory in international relations, it is here suggested that the longer-range prospects for the application of governance to public administration would be improved by narrowing the scope of the subject. It is suggested here that there be a fundamental distinction between public administration as the internal day-to-day management of an agency or organization, on the one hand, and public administration as governance, the management of the extended state, on the other. It is further suggested that the public administration of governance include the management of non-governmental institutions and organizations, insofar as their policies or actions affect citizens in the same way as state agencies. Once established, these distinctions lead to a three-part definition of governance in public administration. First, *interjurisdictional governance* is policy-area specific formalized or voluntary patterns of interorganizational or interjurisdictional cooperation. Second, *third-party governance* extends the functions of the state by exporting them by contract to policy-area specific non-profit, for-profit, or sub-governmental third parties. Third, *public non-governmental governance* accounts for those activities of non-governmental organizations that bear on the interests of citizens in the same way as governmental agencies. These three forms of governance are, after all, what is ordinarily meant when the word/concept governance is used in public administration.

The rapid transformation of the state and its sub-governments has profound implications for the practices of public administration. Governance theory, accounting as it does for most of the effects of state transformation, promises to contribute importantly to the development of public administration scholarship.

Notes

[1] The phrase 'public administration' is used here only as a convention. The phrase 'public management' could have been used, and would have had the same meaning.

[2] There is a second and less useful body of regime theory found in urban studies. Urban regime theorists tends to emphasize the role of business leaders in urban economic development and to de-emphasize the roles of elected and appointed government officials (Elkins 1987; Stone 1989). The work of Royce Hanson is a welcome exception to this generalization, and his work is rather similar to the use of regime theory in international relations and as it is used here (2003; see also Frederickson 1999).

Select References

Agranoff, Robert J., *Intergovernmental Management: Human Services, Problem-Solving in Six Metropolitan Areas*, Albany, NY: State University of New York Press, 1985.

Agranoff, Robert Y., 'Leveraging Networks: A Guide for Public Managers Working Across Organizations', in *New Ways to Manage Series*, James March Arlington, VA: IBM Endowment for The Business of Government, 2003.

Axelrod, Robert, *The Evolution of Cooperation*, New York: Basic Books, 1984.

Benner, Thorston, Wolfgang H. Reinicke, and Jan Martin Witte, 'Global Public Policy Networks', *Brookings Review*, 21(2), (Spring), 2005, pp. 18–21.

Birdsall, Nancy, 'Asymmetric Globalization', *Brookings Review*, 21(2) (Spring), 2003, 22–7.

Castells, Manuel, *The Rise of Networked Society*, 2nd ed. Oxford: Blackwell, 2000.

Cleveland, Harland, *The Future Executive: A Guide for Tomorrow's Managers*, New York: Harper & Row, 1972.

Cooper, Phillip J., *Governing by Contract: Challenges and Opportunities for Public Managers*, Washington, DC: CQ Press, 2002.

Dessler, David, 'What's at Stake in the Agent-Structure Debate?' *International Organization*, 43 (3), World Peace Foundation and the Massachusetts Institute of Technology, (Summer), 1989, pp. 441–73.

Downs, Anthony, *Inside Bureaucracy*, Boston: Little, Brown, 1967.

Elkin, Stephen L., *City and Regime in the American Republic*, Chicago: University of Chicago Press, 1987.

Fosler, R. Scott, 'The Global Challenge to Governance: Implications for National and Subnational Government Capacities and Relationships', *National Academy of Public Administration*, Presented to the NIRA-NAP A 1998 Tokyo Conference on The Challenge to Governance in the Twenty-First Century: Achieving Effective Central-Local Relations, 1998.

Frederickson, H. George, 'The Repositioning of American Public Administration', *PS: Political Science*, 1999, pp. 701–11.

———, *The Public Administration Theory Primer*, Boulder, CO: Westview Press, 2003.

Gilmour, Robert S., and Laura S. Jensen, 'Reinventing Government, Accountability, Public Functions, Privatization, and the Meaning of "State" Action', *Public Administration Review*, 58, 1998, pp. 247–58.

Graham, Carol, and Robert E. Litan, 'Governance in an Integrated Global Economy', *Brookings Review*, 21(2), (Spring) 2003, pp. 2–30.

Haas, Peter M., *Saving the Mediterranean: The Politics of International Environmental Cooperation*, New York: Columbia University Press, 1990.

———, 'Introduction: Epistemic Communities and International Policy Coordination', *International Organization*, 46, 1992, pp. 1–35.

Hanson, Royce, *Civic Culture and Urban Change: Governing Dallas*, Detroit: Wayne State University Press, 2003.

Hasenclever, Andreas, Peter Mayer, and Volker Rittberger, 'Interests, Power, Knowledge: The Study of International Regimes', *Mershon International Studies Review*, 40, 1996, pp. 177–228.

———, *Theories of International Regimes*, Cambridge: Cambridge University Press, 1997.

———, 'Integrating Theories of International Regimes', *Review of International Studies*, 26, 2000, pp. 3–33.

Heinrich, Carolyn J., and Laurence E. Lynn Jr. (eds), *Governance and Performance: New Perspectives*, Washington, DC: Georgetown University Press, 2000.

Hirst, Paul, 'Democracy and Governance', in *Debating Governance: Authority, Steering, and Democracy*, Jon Pierre (ed.), Oxford: Oxford University Press, 2000, pp. 13–35.

Keohane, Robert, 'International Organizations and Garbage Can Theory', *Journal of Public Administration Research and Theory*, 12, 2002, pp. 155–9.

Kernaghan, Kenneth, Brian Marson, and Sanford Borins, *The New Public Organization*, Toronto: Institute of Public Administration of Canada, 2000.

Kettl, Donald, *Sharing Power: Public Governance and Private Markets*, Washington, DC: Brookings Institution, 1993.

Kikert, Walter, 'Public Governance in the Netherlands: An Alternative to Anglo-American "Managerialism"', *Public Administration*, 75, 1997, pp. 731–52.

Knott, Jack, 'Comparing Public and Private Management: Cooperative Effort and Principal-Agent Relationships', *Journal of Public Administration Research and Theory*, 3, 1993, pp. 93–119.

Kooiman, J. (ed.), *Modern Governance*, London: Sage, 1995.

Krasner, Stephen D. (ed.), *International Regimes*, Ithaca, NY: Cornell University Press, 1983.

Lynn, Laurence E. Jr., Carolyn Heinrich, and Carolyn J. Hill, *Improving Governance: A New Logic For Empirical Research*, Washington, DC: Georgetown University Press, 2001.

Lyons, William, David Lowery, and Ruth Hoogland DeHoog, *The Politics of Dissatisfaction: Citizens, Services, and Urban Institutions*, Armonk, NY: Sharpe, 1992.

March, James G., and Johan P. Olsen, 'What Administrative Reorganization Tells Us About Governing', *American Political Science Review*, 77, 1983, pp. 281–96.

_____, *Rediscovering Institutions*, New York: The Free Press, 1989.

_____, *Democratic Governance*, New York: The Free Press, 1995.

_____, 'The Institutional Dynamics of International Political Order', *International Organization*, 52, 1998, pp. 943–69.

Milward, H. Brinton, and Keith Provan, 'Governing the Hollow State', *Journal of Public Administration Research and Theory*, 10, 2000, pp. 359–79.

Moe, Terry, 'The New Economics of Organization', *American Journal of Political Science*, 28, 1984, pp. 739–77.

Newman, Janet, *Modernizing Governance*, Thousand Oaks, CA: Sage, 2000.

Niskanen, William, *Bureaucracy and Representative Government*, Hawthorne, NY: Aldine de Gruyter, 1971.

Olsen, John P., 'Citizens, Public Administration and the Search for Theoretical Foundations', *American Political Science Association*, Annual Meeting, John Gaus Lecture. Philadelphia, August 29, 2003.

Osborn, David, and Ted Gaebler, *Reinventing Government*, Reading, MA: Addison-Wesley, 1992.

Ostrom, Elinor, 'A Behavioral Approach to the Rational Choice Theory of Collective Action: Presidential Address, American Political Science Association, 1997', *American Political Science Review*, 92, 1998, pp. 1–22.

O'Toole, Laurence J. Jr., 'Intergovernmental Relations in Implementation', in *Handbook of Public Administration*, B. Guy Peters and Jon Pierre (eds), Thousand Oaks, CA: Sage, 2005.

Peters, B. Guy, *Governance: Four Emerging Models*, Lawrence: University Press of Kansas, 1996.

Peters, B. Guy and Jon Pierre, 'Governance Without Government? Rethinking Public Administration', *Journal of Public Administration Research and Theory*, 8, 1998, pp. 227–43.

Pierre, Jon (ed.), *Debating Governance: Authority, Steering, and Democracy*, Oxford: Oxford University Press, 2000.

Rhodes, R.A.W., *Understanding Governance: Policy Networks, Governance, Reflexivity, and Accountability*, Buckingham: Open University Press, 1997.

_____, 'Governance and Public Administration', in *Debating Governance: Authority, Steering, and Democracy*, Jon Pierre, (ed.),Oxford: University of Oxford Press, 2000, pp. 54–90.

Rohr, John, *To Run a Constitution: The Legitimacy of the Administrative State*, Lawrence: University Press of Kansas, 1986.

Rosenbloom, David H., *Administrative Law for Public Managers*, Boulder, CO: Westview Press, 2003.

Sørensen, Eva, 'Democratic Theory and Network Governance', Paper presented at I workshop nr. 12 'Demokrati og administrative reform I norden' på NOPSA-konferencen 2002 I Ålborg.

Sorensen, Georg, *The Transformation of the State: Beyond the Myth of Retreat*, London: Palgrave Macmillan, 2004.

Stone, Clarence, *Regime Politics*, Lawrence: University Press of Kansas, 1989.

Strange, Susan, 'Cave! Hec Dragones: A Critique of Regime Theory', in *International Regimes*, Stephen D. Krasner (ed.), Ithaca, NY: Cornell University Press, 1983.

Tullock, Gordon, *The Politics of Bureaucracy*, Washington, DC: Public Affairs Press, 1965.

Wilson, James Q., *Bureaucracy: What Government Agencies Do and Why They Do It*, New York: Basic Books, 1989.

Woods, Ngaire, 'Unelected Government', *Brookings Review*, 21(2), (Spring) 2003, pp. 9–12.

Wright, Deil, *Understanding Intergovernmental Relations*, 3rd edition Washington, DC: International Thompson Publishing, 1997.

5

Auditing for Social Change
Learning from Civil Society Initiatives

Samuel Paul[1]

INTRODUCTION

Recent years have witnessed a growing concern in development circles about issues of governance and accountability in developing countries. There are several reasons behind this trend. First of all, there is mounting dissatisfaction with the manner in which the state has performed its functions in these countries. Both citizens and outside observers have questioned the efficiency and effectiveness of resource-use by governments. Public investments have resulted in meager returns and low productivity in many cases. Failures in terms of lack of transparency, rule of law, and corruption are often highlighted as the key contributory factors underlying this phenomenon. The plea for a restructuring of the state and its functions have been greatly influenced by these perceptions. Second, the failure of many developing countries to achieve significant poverty reduction and the consequent inequity and injustice suffered by millions of marginalized people is yet another reason for this global concern about governance. The weak bargaining power and organizational capabilities of the poor have no doubt contributed to this outcome. The global campaign under UN auspices in support of the Millennium Development Goals (MDGs) is a response to this reality. Third, there is a growing realization that existing mechanisms for ensuring public accountability have not been able to resolve these problems. Supreme audit institutions (SAIs) exist in almost all countries. But the efficacy of traditional accountability mechanisms and their impact on the functioning of governments have come in for serious questioning.

International development agencies and donors have given increasing attention to the issues of governance and accountability referred to above. Their responses can be divided into two categories. The first consists of international efforts to reform and restructure government systems and practices so as to strengthen their performance and accountability. It covers a mix of interventions that range from administrative reforms to the redesign of judicial and audit institutions. Many foreign aid projects include reform programmes of this nature. The second focuses on strengthening public accountability through pressure from outside of governments, especially through civil society institutions. The endeavour here has been to experiment with different types of pressure that civil society or citizens at large can bring to bear on their governments to be more accountable to the people. Some donors have begun to invest in the creation of civil society capabilities to play this role in specific-country contexts.

Since the purpose of this paper is to discuss ways and means for SAIs to enhance the relevance and impact of the audit function by drawing upon civil society perspectives and feedback, it aims to focus primarily on the current thinking on this approach to strengthen public accountability. This is not to deny the importance of restructuring governments. A lot of good work is going on in this regard, and it should continue to receive high priority. But, as noted above, in the context of this paper, linking the audit function to the potential of civil society pressure as an aid to accountability has greater relevance.

This chapter is divided into three sections. The first section presents some basic concepts and approaches that may help us to understand how civil society pressure can act as an influence on accountability. A narration of recent civil society initiatives to strengthen public accountability is provided in the second section. A case study of one of these initiatives, namely, citizen report cards on public services, in which this author was personally involved, is also presented here. The third section offers some ideas on how SAIs might draw upon these concepts and experiences to make their audit of social change more focused and effective.

ACCOUNTABILITY AND CITIZENS' VOICE

In a democracy, the state is the servant of the people. It performs many functions essential for the welfare and development of its citizens and provides an array of essential services many of which are 'public goods.' The state collects taxes from the people to discharge its functions and is accountable to society for the proper use of the resources entrusted to it. Periodic elections are seen as the ultimate lever that citizens can use to hold those wielding power in the name of the state accountable for their performance. But, the dilemma is that while much happens between elections in terms of transactions between the state and its citizens, there is little an individual citizen can do in the short run if things go wrong in the discharge of functions or services by the state's agencies. Waiting for the next election is of little help to a citizen who needs immediate corrective action. The problem arises because the citizens have no 'exit' unlike in the marketplace where they can exit from one supplier of a good or service to another. When citizens have no exit option, they can only vent their feelings through 'voice.' Voice may take the form of protest, non-cooperation, or the rejection of political representatives through the ballot process.[2] Collective action in any of these forms can act as an instrument of accountability, signalling the authorities that they must listen to the people's voice and take remedial action. Of these different forms of voice, the ballot process is the most difficult to access because of the long time gap between elections. Other forms of collective action (a form of voice) are more easily resorted to when people face problems continually with the functioning of governments, especially with the delivery of services.

There is a growing literature on the use of voice as an aid to accountability and on the evidence from numerous experiments based on this approach.[3] Illustrative of this trend is the framework for accountability presented in the *World Development Report* (*WDR*), 2004. WDR uses the term 'client power' to denote the voice of the users of public services. It is true that as customers of a service, citizens are clients. Nevertheless, it is important to note that their role as citizens is larger and has more power that what a mere client can command. Citizens, for example, have rights and avenues for action that may not always be available to mere clients. The preference of this author, therefore, is to use the term 'citizens' voice.'

Figure 5.1 presents a graphical representation of *WDR*'s framework for accountability.[4] Its focus is on accountability with respect to the services for the poor. But, its implications are by no means limited only to the services or functions that matter only to the poor. This framework brings together four sets of players, namely, citizens/clients, political leaders/policy makers, public-service providers, and frontline professionals. Citizens participate in the political process both individually and in groups. But they are also clients of the public agencies that provide different services. Their interests and goals need not always be the same and, hence, conflicts between groups cannot be ruled out. Elected leaders and policy makers have the power to formulate policies and laws and allocate and supervise resources and their use. Service providers are line departments and agencies charged with the responsibility for the design and delivery of public services. Providers may also be from the private sector but are required to function under the regulation of public authorities. Frontline delivery personnel such as teachers and doctors work under the supervision of service providers. But their goals and incentives need not always be in tune with those of their service providers or policymakers.

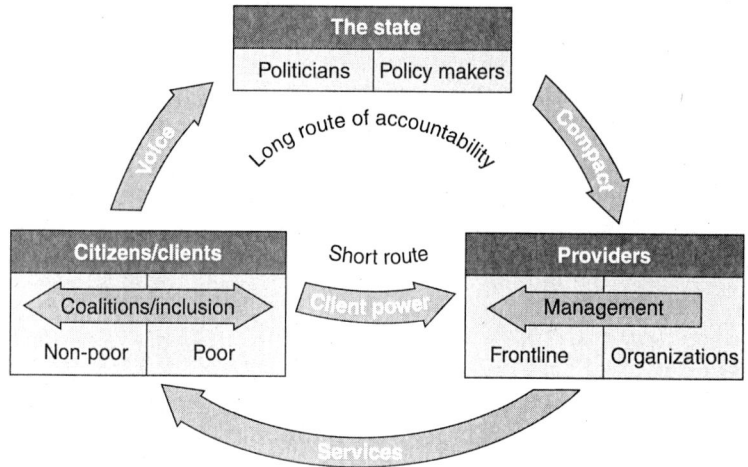

Figure 5.1   Key Linkages in Accountability

Source: Adapted from Chapter 5, *World Development Report*, 2004.

The WDR framework refers to the long route and the short route of accountability. Both operate in a circular fashion (see Fig. 5.1). Citizens/clients can use voice to signal policy makers/leaders on their needs and problems. The latter in turn can hold service providers accountable for the delivery of services through a compact, much as a contract, with explicit terms and obligations of a mutual kind. Service providers then deliver services through their frontline workers and units that directly interface with citizens. Accountability here is enforced through the use of voice that works through the political process. In the short route, the linkage between citizens and providers is more direct. Here, client voice directly impacts on the provider and accountability is achieved through this direct pressure.

It is not our objective here to delve deep into this framework and its merits. Suffice it to note that it is a departure from the traditional notions of vertical accountability mechanisms. The latter have not been assumed away in this figure. The traditional audit function is presumably built into the right side of the figure. The operation of the compact and the resources deployed for services are subject to audits of various kind. But the new feature here is the mechanism of voice and the manner in which it acts as an aid to accountability.

But, the big question is whether this framework can actually be made to work. The logic is appealing. In a democratic setting, listening to the people or responding to their collective voice seems desirable and feasible. Are there barriers that can derail or weaken these linkages? Figure 5.2 provides some answers.

The figure below illustrates the kinds of barriers that can break the neat relationships and influences implied in Fig. 5.1. It highlights two sets of barriers, one that could weaken the power of voice and the other that can render the compact ineffective. Voice, for example, will not work when citizens/clients do not have the necessary information or knowledge to make it effective. This can happen when people have limited knowledge in a specific area and are, therefore, unable to digest new information and make use of it. Even if they are educated, but have no access to information, then again the outcome will be no different. Thus, governments can create barriers to voice by denying people knowledge about their rights and entitlements and standards and norms pertaining to services. Even when such information is available, if citizens do not have a sufficient background for understanding this information, it can

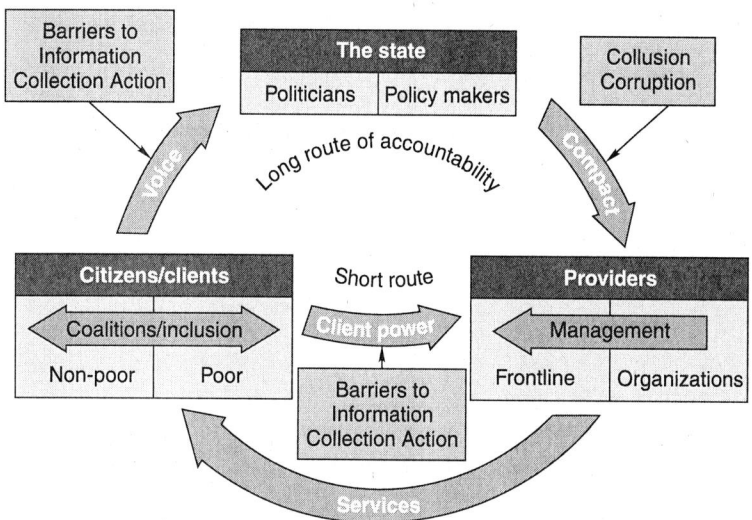

FIGURE 5.2   Barriers to Accountability

Source: Adapted from Chapter 5, *World Development Report*, 2004.

potentially act as a barrier to voice. The poor often tend to suffer from this handicap.

There are equally important barriers to collective action as a form of voice. Collective action calls for time, organizational skills, and resources. It requires capacity to identify key issues and knowledge about possible remedies. The poor, typically, are weak in terms of these capabilities. When they are struggling to survive, they may not have the ability nor the incentives to invest in collective action. It is the reason why intermediary organizations (such as NGOs) enter the scene and organize the poor and marginalized communities. Collective action is easier to organise for the better-off sections of society. Nevertheless, it is an uphill task even for them because of the 'free rider' problem and the indifference characteristic of many middle-class citizens who seek easy exits. It is not uncommon, for example, for people to pay a bribe to get their work done.

There is a similar set of barriers on the right hand side of the figure that can turn the compact between policy makers and providers into a hollow ritual. There may be a nominal compact, but, in reality, both parties may agree to ignore its provisions and collude to follow their own interests rather than the public good. When those who are meant to enforce the compact dilute or ignore it, there is no one left to demand accountability, and the casualty is the service provider's performance. In a country where citizens' access to information is limited, the latter will be unable to challenge collusive conduct. More often than not, corruption and political patronage are at the heart of this phenomenon. Extreme cases of this kind signal the existence of a predatory state that citizens are unable to break.

What is described above applies to both the long and short routes of accountability depicted in the figure. Barriers to information and collective action could render voice ineffective when citizens try to influence service providers directly (the short route). Delivery of services to the poor and the accountability of the providers to the people will not improve under these conditions. To conclude, unless the barriers to information and collective action are somehow eliminated, and citizens' voice is strengthened enough to weaken the grip of collusion and corruption in the machinery of government, it is unrealistic to expect that public accountability will improve.

ACCOUNTABILITY INITIATIVES BY CITIZENS

Despite the barriers discussed above, there have been numerous efforts by individual citizens, civil society groups, and NGOs in several countries to improve the accountability of governments and service providers. Their interventions have taken different forms, depending on the context, the problems involved, and the skills and resources of the participants in these movements. Whether they have made any lasting impact or led to systemic changes within governments is difficult to say. Some of the interventions have been documented and assessed, and their lessons have been widely disseminated. In all cases, they have exerted pressure from outside the system. And some of them have resulted in models and approaches that have been replicated or adapted in other settings and even countries.

The civil society initiatives for accountability presented below fall into five categories: (1) community management of local services, (2) independent budget analysis and tracking, (3) public hearings, (4) public interest litigation, and (5) citizen report cards on services. A brief description of each follows.

COMMUNITY MANAGEMENT OF LOCAL SERVICES

There are many public services which lend themselves to direct monitoring and supervision by local communities.[5] In many cases, citizens and users of the services could participate in aspects of managing and monitoring such services. A good example is the local school where the parent-teacher association could actively participate in planning and supervising the school programmes. Similarly, the maintenance of drinking-water facilities, and community toilets has benefited from the participation of user groups. A recent case from the slums of Mumbai, India, has shown how local communities have pitched in to manage and maintain the newly built toilet facilities. NGOs and local communities have played a lead role in this project and the government has funded it through a World Bank project.

The initiative for community management has come largely from NGOs working in the field in local communities. Their primary interest is in promoting community participation in local development programmes and services so as to make them more relevant to the people and more sustainable. But, it turns out that such participation is also a powerful means to hold the government or service provider accountable to the people. When the latter influence the design of a service and monitor its delivery or contribute to the maintenance of public facilities, they have a strong interest in ensuring that the agencies involved are responsive to their problems and needs. Being closer to the scene and with a seat at the table, they can observe and challenge abuses and poor performance. Community management of local services can thus act as an aid to accountability, and, to a large extent, compensate for the inherent problems in monitoring local activities that higher-level officials encounter. In several countries, governments and international donors are now encouraging and facilitating community management of public services and facilities.

INDEPENDENT BUDGET ANALYSIS AND TRACKING

Budgets are the basic instrument of governments to mobilize, allocate, and monitor scarce resources (money and personnel). By bringing government budgets under public scrutiny, civil society groups are able to raise important questions about taxation, public expenditure, and the distribution of benefits to different groups of people. This initiative, of course, calls for special skills in terms of analysis and evaluation. Examples of civil society groups engaging in budget analysis and using the findings for advocacy are, therefore, not many. But wherever it has been attempted, the process has resulted in informing and educating both the people and the authorities (legislators and officials) on the implications of the allocations and on the need to modify them to achieve the stated policy objectives. Budget analysis can also be used to advocate reforms, especially with reference to the poor, as their interests are seldom adequately addressed in the complex bargaining processes behind the budgetary allocations.

A classic case of such budget analysis where citizens are actively involved comes from Porto Allegre, Brazil. Here, communities participate by articulating their needs and priorities. This is an open process that helps the government to listen to the people's voice and arrive at allocations that take into account public concerns. Needless to say, the process presupposes a government that is inclined to listen and seek ideas from the people. It is also a time-consuming process that calls for a great deal of involvement by community groups. Broad-based budget analysis has been carried out in South Africa under the auspices of a local NGO. The International Centre on Budget and Policy Priorities in Washington, DC, is engaged in strengthening civil society capabilities to undertake budget analysis in developing countries.[6]

A more limited form of budget analysis has been attempted by DISHA, an NGO in Gujarat State, India. The focus here has been on analysis of the budget from the standpoint of the poor, especially the tribal population. The findings are used by the NGO to engage in dialogues with elected representatives and officials. The findings are publicized through the media in order to create public support for the proposals made by the NGO.

A third example is from Africa where public expenditure tracking has been attempted to monitor the effectiveness of the public spending on the services for the poor. The World Bank has led this effort in Uganda and other countries, but the approach lends itself to be used as an initiative to increase accountability. Budget analysis, of course, is primarily a means to improve the process of resource allocation by governments and to nudge them to be effective. But when civil society groups engage governments in this exercise, it can act as a force for greater public accountability.

PUBLIC HEARINGS

Public hearings are a well-known mechanism for eliciting the views and concerns of the people on a variety of issues. Regulatory agencies use this approach in the determination of tariff rates and other policies. In recent years, NGOs and other civil society groups have organized public hearings as a means to demand increased public accountability towards the poor and marginalized communities. Being an open process, it attracts the attention of the media and lends itself to being used as an aid to advocacy to improve the conditions of the poor. NGOs act as intermediaries in the process, as the poor are not equipped with the skills and organization necessary to make a success of public hearings. When people face highly localized problems, it is possible to stimulate the poor to participate in public hearings.

A documented case from India narrates how MKSS, an NGO based in Rajasthan, India, used public hearings in rural areas to publicize the abuses in public employment programmes. This adverse publicity led to the authorities taking corrective action that benefited the local communities. It also gave a strong push to the right to information movement that was gaining momentum in the country in the early 1990s. Public hearings were used in this case to demand accountability in the programmes that are supposed to benefit the poor. In the absence of the resultant pressure, abuses in the employment programme might have continued unabated.

PUBLIC INTEREST LITIGATION (PIL)

Public interest litigation refers to legal action taken in a court of law for enforcing the public interest or to protect the legal rights and liabilities of the public or a community of people. The term, PIL, was first used in the USA in the 1960s to describe a legal development that sought to widen civic participation in governance. In some developing countries like India, PIL has been widely used to get the courts to direct governments to take corrective steps to restore the rights and entitlements of the poor. An independent judiciary and a democratic constitution are essential prerequisites for PIL to succeed.

PIL is a potent accountability mechanism when the executive and legislative branches of government are unable or unwilling to protect the rights and entitlements of the poor.

Individual citizens, especially the poor, will find it difficult to resort to PIL to hold the government accountable for the denial of their rights simply because of the time and costs involved. As in public hearings, it is NGOs and organized civic groups that make use of PIL in most countries.

CITIZEN REPORT CARDS—AN ACCOUNTABILITY TOOL

A citizen report card (CRC) is a new way to rate different service providers from a user perspective and to utilise this information to make the providers more accountable to the people. User feedback is a cost-effective way for a government to find out whether its services are reaching the people, especially the poor. Users of a public service can tell the government a lot about the quality and value of a service. Surprisingly, this is not a method that is known to or used by most developing-country governments. The continuing neglect of the quality of services is in part a consequence of this gap. This is in sharp contrast to the practice of seeking 'customer feedback' that is common in the competitive marketplace.

A CRC on public services is not just one more opinion poll. Report cards reflect the actual experience of people with respect to a wide range of public services. The survey on which a report card is based covers only those who have had experiences in the use of specific services and interactions with the relevant public agencies or other aspects of public services. Users possess fairly accurate information, for example, on whether a public agency actually solved their problems or whether they had to pay bribes to officials. Of course, errors of recall cannot be ruled out. But the large numbers of responses that sample surveys generate lend credibility to the findings.

Stratified random sample surveys using well-structured questionnaires are the basis on which report cards are prepared. It is generally assumed that people from similar backgrounds, in terms of education, culture, etc., are likely to use comparable standards in their assessments. But, these standards may be higher for higher-income groups than for the poor, whose expectations about public services tend to be much lower. Dividing households into relatively homogenous categories is one way to minimise the biases that differing expectations can cause.

Since this author played a modest role in launching the first CRC in Bangalore, India, a brief case study of this experiment will be presented. Public Affairs Centre (PAC), founded in Bangalore, has taken this initiative much further over the past decade. The first report card on Bangalore's public agencies in 1994 covered municipal services, water supply, electricity, telecom, and transport. Since then, PAC has brought out report cards on several other cities, rural services, and also on specific sectoral services such as health care. But since it has tracked services for a longer period in Bangalore, this experiment shall be referred to in detail below.[7]

The findings of the first CRC on Bangalore were most striking. Almost all of the public-service providers received low ratings from the people. Agencies were rated and compared in terms of public satisfaction, corruption, and responsiveness. The media publicity that the findings received and the public discussions that followed brought the issue of public services out in the open. Civil society groups began to organize themselves to voice their demands for better performance. Some of the public agencies responded to these demands and took steps to improve their services. The interagency comparisons and the associated public glare seem to have contributed to this outcome. When the second report card on Bangalore came out in 1999, these improvements were reflected in the somewhat better ratings that the agencies received. Still, several agencies remained indifferent and corruption levels continued to be high.

The third CRC on Bangalore, in 2003, has shown a surprising turnaround in the city's services. It noted a remarkable rise in the citizen ratings of almost all the agencies.[8] Not only did public satisfaction improve across the board, but problem incidence and corruption seem to have declined perceptibly in the routine transactions between the public and the agencies (see Figures 5.3–5.5). It is clear that more decisive steps have been taken by the agencies to improve services between 1999 and 2003.

What accounts for this distinct turnaround in Bangalore's public services? What lessons can we learn from this experiment? Needless to say, without deliberate interventions by the government and the service providers, no improvement would have taken place in the services. But, the key question is, what made them act? A whole complex of factors seems to have been at work. The new Chief Minister of the state, who took over in 1999, was very much concerned about the public dissatisfaction with the city's services. He set in motion new mechanisms such as the 'Bangalore Agenda Task Force,' a forum for public–private partnership that helped energize the agencies and assist in the upgradation of services. Civil society groups and the media supported and monitored these efforts. What is significant is that the initial trigger for these actions came largely from the civil society initiative that we call 'citizen report cards.'

TABLE 5.1   Agencies Covered by CRC 3

BMP	The City Municipal Corporation
BESCOM	The Electricity Authority
BWSSB	The Water & Sanitation Board
BDA	Land Development Authority
BSNL	Telecom Department
BMTC	City Transport Company
POLICE	City Police
RTO	Motor Vehicle Office
Govt. Hospital	Government Hospital

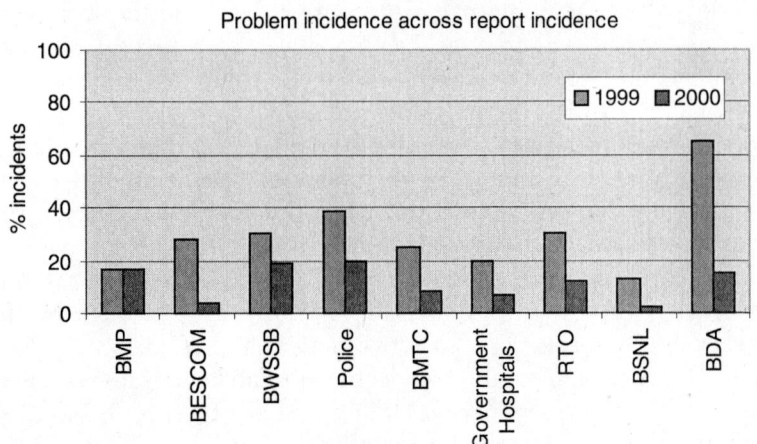

FIGURE 5.3   Decline in Problem Incidence

Source: Drawn on the survey data of 1999 and 2003.

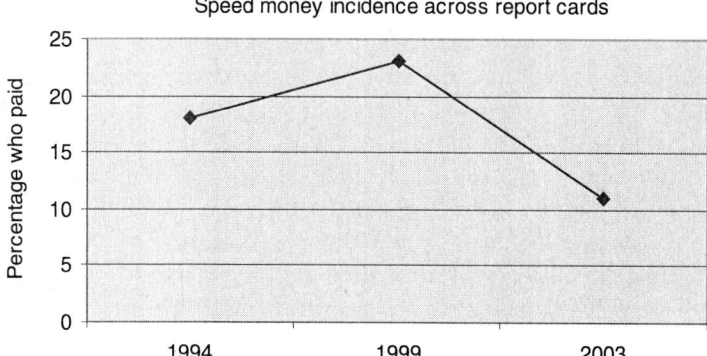

FIGURE 5.4   Decline in Corruption Levels (routine transactions)
Source: Drawn on the survey data of 1999 and 2003.

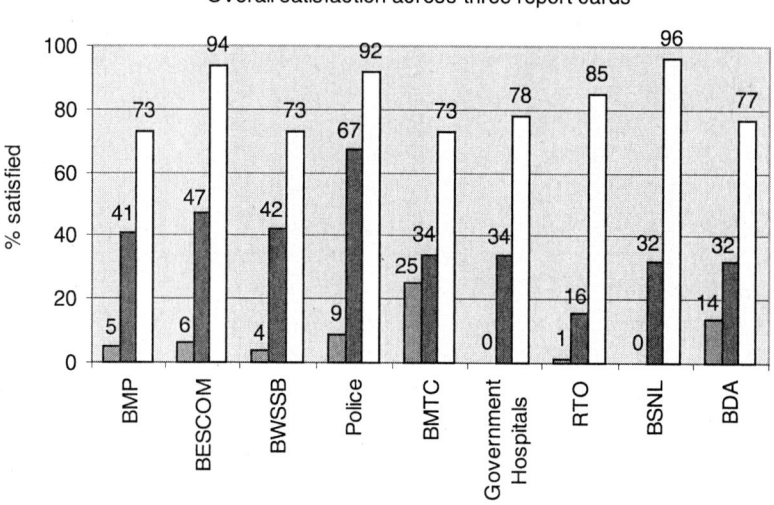

Figure 5.5   Rise in Satisfaction Levels
Source: Drawn on the survey data of 1999 and 2003.

What are the preconditions for such civil society initiatives to work? It is obvious that these initiatives are more likely to succeed in a democratic and open society. Without adequate space for participation, CRCs are unlikely to make an impact. A tradition of activism within the civil society also can help. People should be willing to organize themselves to engage in advocacy and seek reforms supported by credible information. Political and bureaucratic leaders must have the will and resources to respond to such information and the call for improved governance by the people. Last, but not least, the credibility of those who craft CRCs is equally important. The initiators of the exercise should be seen as non-partisan and independent. They need to maintain high professional standards. The conduct of the survey and the interpretation of the findings should be done with utmost professional integrity.

When service providers and governments on their own improve their services and accountability, initiatives such as CRCs may not be necessary. Even under these conditions, a report card can be an effective means for civil society groups to monitor the performance of government and its service providers. Public agencies can on their own initiate report cards on their performance as indeed some in Bangalore have done. But when a government is indifferent to these concerns, advocacy based on a CRC can act as an accountability tool to challenge the government to perform better.

POLICY IMPLICATIONS FOR
SUPREME AUDIT INSTITUTIONS (SAIs)

The range of accountability initiatives described above tells us the story of how civil society has responded to the weak public accountability that prevails in many developing countries. In a real sense, they represent a form of audit by the people on the effectiveness and outcomes of what government does. Note that it does not focus on the internal processes of government. A common thread that runs through these diverse experiments is the manner in which they have empowered citizens with new information and knowledge that could be used to hold a government or service provider accountable. These initiatives emerged in different countries and contexts and in response to different problems. That some of these concepts and tools are being replicated in other countries and sectors testify to their wide applicability.

Despite the potential power and impact of these civil society initiatives, it is difficult to imagine that they are the answer to the accountability deficit in developing countries. They do inspire us and provide models for others to follow. In critical situations, their pressure may make service providers and public agencies more accountable. And such initiatives will continue to emerge in different places. But they cannot assume the role of the institutions of government that have been assigned the responsibility of making accountability mechanisms work. In the final analysis, it is the governments and their SAIs that have a duty to make public accountability a reality.

What are the policy implications of the civil society initiatives for SAIs? Do they offer new ideas or practices that can be incorporated into the agenda of SAIs? Are there ways to tap into the energies and insights of civil society that can be an aid to the work of SAIs? Admittedly, all of the civil society initiatives discussed above are not equally relevant to SAIs. PIL is clearly not an approach that an audit institution can adopt. It cannot get involved in community management. Not can it be in the business of budget analysis. But, there are several other things that SAIs can do. Let me offer some tentative ideas for consideration.

INCORPORATE CITIZEN FEEDBACK INTO PERFORMANCE AUDITS

The audit function in developing countries is, for the most part, compliance oriented. Compliance is certainly a legitimate concern. But in the context of MDG goals and poverty reduction, concern for effectiveness needs to receive far more attention from auditors than at present. Performance audits and value-for-money audits represent moves in this direction. These practices are beginning to be adopted by developing countries. But the methodology used in these new types of audits may benefit greatly by incorporating the findings of user feedback. Performance audits should go beyond output measures to get an assessment of the quality and effectiveness dimensions of services. This is what user feedback can provide to the auditor. Performance audits that focus only on physical outputs and costs may miss this insight. In a drinking-water supply programme, a performance audit may count the number of water taps installed or the volume of water supplied. But the regularity of water supply or the maintenance of the facility that matter a lot to citizens may still leave much to be desired. Corruption may add to users' costs, but do not get reported anywhere. These aspects of effectiveness can be captured only through systematic user feedback.

Figure 5.6 below shows the value added that user feedback can offer when taken together with compliance audit.

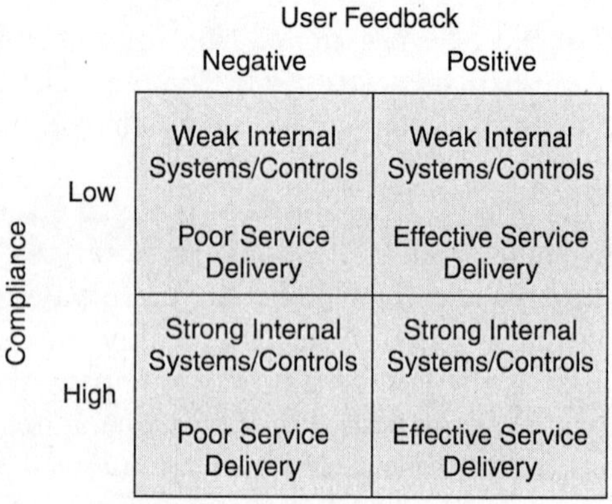

User Feedback

		Negative	Positive
Compliance	Low	Weak Internal Systems/Controls Poor Service Delivery	Weak Internal Systems/Controls Effective Service Delivery
	High	Strong Internal Systems/Controls Poor Service Delivery	Strong Internal Systems/Controls Effective Service Delivery

FIGURE 5.6   Compliance vs User Feedback

In this 2×2 matrix, the findings of compliance audit are graded vertically, while the user feedback results are graded horizontally. The quality of compliance in a programme or department may be rated low or high. Similarly, user feedback may turn out to be negative or positive.[9] Four combinations of these two variables can be seen in the figure (A, B, C, and D). Insights from user feedback will now enable the SAI to see that some departments/programmes may be weak in compliance and yet are more effective in their services (cell B). Cell A refers to departments/programmes that are weak on both counts. Cell C shows that a department/programme may be high on compliance, yet fail to deliver services effectively. Cell D is the only case where the performance is good on both counts. It is clear from this analysis that a more complete picture of how well a department/programme is managed can be generated when information on both variables is taken together. This approach may help SAIs to make more balanced and well-focused recommendations to the government.

CRC FOR MONITORING MDGs

Using the CRC approach to assess the effectiveness of all government functions and programmes may be unrealistic. CRCs do call for extensive field surveys, and the time and cost involved can entail a heavy burden on SAIs. But, it should not be difficult for SAIs to use this approach in programmes and departments that provide essential services for the people. MDGs are a case in point. The long-term targets implied by MDGs will be achieved only through the interventions and service delivery over the years for which the state is responsible. If the delivery is not reaching the people as planned, it is unlikely that MDGs will be achieved. SAIs will be able to give advance warnings to governments on whether they are on track with MDGs, if they can tap into the power of user feedback. The message may stimulate governments to take mid-course corrections.

User feedback is already a component in the performance audits being done by SAIs in some of the more developed countries. USA, UK, and Canada have shown that this approach has merit. India's SAI has sought user feedback in its audit of the public distribution of food programme. CRC's feasibility is thus not in doubt. But it is not known or widely used by SAIs. The challenge is to deploy it on a scale that can make a difference.

AUDIT OF GOVERNMENT'S INFORMATION DISCLOSURE

A key lesson from the civil society initiatives for accountability discussed in this chapter is that empowerment through new knowledge and information can motivate citizens to demand accountability. Governments are not always proactive in informing and educating citizens on their rights, entitlements, and what they should know in order to access public services and programmes. This is an aspect of government that needs a systematic audit. Just as SAIs audit public expenditure, they should also assess the adequacy and quality of the information being provided to citizens to access services. There is much talk of citizen charters, the right to information, e-governance, etc. They lend themselves to be audited in terms of their relevance, implementation, and effectiveness. If citizens can be empowered through information, they will complement and reinforce the efforts of SAI.

EDUCATE CITIZENS ON SAI AUDITS

In many countries, SAIs's reports and recommendations are not widely known to the public. Audit reports may go to the government and legislature, but may or may not get much attention in the press or other public fora. It is also possible that governments and SAIs restrict their public dissemination. Some of the reports that pertain to the inner workings of the government may not, in any case, interest the average citizen. If these reports do not get acted on by governments, nothing more will be heard of them. But, this is not the case with reports and recommendations on programmes that directly impact citizens. If SAIs can increase citizen access to such reports, it is possible to generate public support for the changes and reforms being proposed. In many countries there are public interest groups and NGOs that may help initiate public debates on their implications. Stimulating informed debates on audit findings can be a powerful way to facilitate increased participation by citizens in governance processes and to strengthen the constituency for accountability.

Notes

[1] The views expressed in this paper are those of the author and do not necessarily represent those of the United Nations or its Member States.

[2] For a fuller discussion, see Samuel Paul, 'Accountability in Public Services: Exit, Voice and Control', *World Development Report*, Washington, DC: World Bank, July 1992.

[3] See *World Development Report*, Washington, DC: World Bank, 2004; Manjunath and Balakrishnan, *Civic Engagement for Better Governance*, Public Affairs Centre, Bangalore, 2004.

[4] The figure is taken from chapter 5 of *WDR*, 2004.

[5] See *Development Outreach*, World Bank Institute, January 2004, for a number of applications of this nature.

[6] See 'International Budget Project', Centre on Budget and Policy Priorities, Washington, DC, 2003.

[7] See Samuel Paul, *Holding the State to Account: Citizen Monitoring in Action*, Bangalore: Books for Change, 2002; Paul and Shekhar, *Benchmarking Urban Services*, Public Affairs Centre, Bangalore, 2000; A. Ravindra, *An Assessment of the Impact of Bangalore Citizen Report Cards on the Performance of Public Agencies*, OED Working Paper no: 12, Washington, DC, 2004.

[8] For details, see Samuel Paul, *Citizen Report Cards in Bangalore: A Case Study in Accountability*, mimeo, PAC, Bangalore, 2005.

[9] Grading can be refined further by creating more categories. A 2×2 matrix is being used for the sake of simplicity.

6

The Governmentality of Globalizing Managerial Discourses

The Case of New Public Management in Local Government Practices

Dorte Salskov-Iversen, Hans Krause Hansen, and Sven Bislev

INTRODUCTION

This chapter explores the creation, dissemination, and local appropriation of the highly influential global discourse of public sector reform, new public management (NPM). What we present is an abridged and edited version of an article that came out in 2000.[1] In 2006, NPM's influence remains unquestioned, only, today, the broad thrust of public sector reform in the OECD world and beyond is subsumed under the overarching concept of modernization,[2] a wide but diffuse project aiming at improving public sector performance and making government more efficient, open, and responsive, much like new public management, but less openly ideologically invested and blended with other discourses on how best to manage the public sector.

Drawing on theories of discourse and governmentality and on constructivist theories of governance and globalization, this chapter focuses on changes in governmentality—the way ruling is conceived of and practised. Against the backdrop of (1) an empirical analysis of how NPM was developed within and disseminated from transnational discourse communities linked to the OECD and the World Bank, and on the basis of (2) an exploration of the local appropriation in the 1980s and 1990s of NPM in two OECD municipalities in Mexico and Britain, it is argued that globalization does not *per se* foster harmonization of previous national and regional systems under one conceptual model. On the contrary, the discursive moments of governance and globalization bring out the subtleties of the then hegemony of management thinking in the public sector: at the local level, interpretations of the globally dominant NPM discourse follow contextually defined logics, latching it onto local discourses and harnessing it for local projects that need not be grounded in the political and ideological inclinations widely believed inherent in NPM.

How are the administrative practices of local governments being reshaped by globalizing forces, while maintaining their profoundly contextual embeddedness and character? To answer this question, we have sought inspiration in studies of governmentality. While much of the governmentality literature initially confined itself to the study of ruling within nation-states, that is, as a macrolevel conceptualization of the states' regulation of their inhabitants, and as a meso- or microlevel conceptualization of governance in large- and small-scale organizational forms,[3] there is now a growing interest in analysing patterns of ruling in the international, transnational, and global domains through the lenses of governmentality. The concept of global governmentality is indicative of this interest and reveals a particular concern with understanding how the governance of spaces above, beyond, between, and across states is constituted and shaped by particular beliefs and practices of ruling.[4]

Evolved from modest beginnings among international administrative experts working for the UN, taken up by the Carter administration, and then processed and refined by the OECD, NPM arguably acquired the status of a dominant governmentality at some point during the 1980s. This was when most contemporary discourses in the field of public administration and management began to position themselves in relation to elements of NPM. Also sub-national government could be seen, to varying degrees, to introduce or appropriate (selected aspects of) NPM, not seldom moulding them for specific purposes in the process. Though not a coherent set of values and notions and, therefore, not readily definable, NPM—in its multiple guises and applications—can be distinguished by (1) its clear emphasis on business management practices, and by (2) its reliance on individual rationalities and market mechanisms in the restructuring and operation of the public sector. In this way, NPM implied a break with a century-old tradition of distinguishing sharply between the values and practices of the public and private sectors.

The rise of NPM to pre-eminence coincided with societal changes sometimes theorized as a shift from government to governance in a context of globalization: from coordinated, hierarchical structures and processes of societal steering to a network-based process of exchange and negotiation. We extend the governance perspective to include a view of the public sector as being discursively regulated. Our chapter is about a change in governmentality. Globalization and the knowledge of it bring about this change, not as a unidirectional force, but as a set of complex processes, some of which are essentially discursive and, therefore, require a particular lens to be captured and analysed.

The existence, even necessity, of a process whereby universal regulations are modified at the local level is no novelty in policy research, where it has long occupied the minds of implementation researchers. According to this perspective, the limits to rationalism can be found in information problems and political interests. While these aspects remain highly relevant, we prefer to approach our investigation of the limits to rationalism through the lens of constructivism, that is, the discursive construction of local interpretations.

The theories that have inspired us have two things in common. One is that they emphasize the connection between discourse, knowledge, and power: the practice of government is very much a question of mastering a language that draws on the socially valued expertise present in networks characterized and shaped by power differentials. Another similarity is attention to the discursive moment[5] of globalization. Not only are distant localities being linked together by very real and rapidly increasing flows of capital, flexible production processes, and people in motion, they are also becoming connected through networks of expertise that develop new ways of approaching and defining the problems of government in a context of globalization, that is, problems of regulating society, of understanding it and of developing democratic dialogues. By emphasizing globalization's relational character and complexity, its reliance on discourse and local mediation, as well as its production of hybridity, we privilege heterogenizing over homogenizing understandings of globalization.[6]

Our approach focuses on communication, but not in the Habermasian sense of rational communication.[7] We assume that all communication has implications of power and hegemony.[8] Looking for those implications and exploring their nature are, therefore, central to any study of communication. We also focus on functional reforms, on the improvement of efficiency and transparency in public administration. But, unlike studies concerned with assessing the practical vices and virtues of different variations of NPM,[9] we merely assume that intended as well as unintended effects flow from these different initiatives. Our main concern, however, is to study why they are defined as they are, and how they are transmitted and adapted.

In the first part of the chapter, we unfold and explicate our conceptual framework. In the second part, we present a genealogy of NPM, focusing on how NPM acquired the position of a hegemonic discourse, in part through the development of transnational discourse communities. In the third part, we connect the discussion to the study of two OECD municipalities that entered the global fray, embracing the NPM discourse while appropriating it in a creative fashion. This part is based on visits to and semi-structured interviews with the two municipalities from 1998–2000 and on official documents, internal papers, and local media reports during the same period. A thorough examination of the historical, economic, and socio-political background for introducing managerial reforms in the two municipalities is, however, beyond the scope of this chapter— what we present are vignettes.

THE DISCURSIVE MOMENTS OF GOVERNANCE AND GLOBALIZATION

The transition from government theories to governance theories implies a more processual view of politics and the state: the assumption of a hierarchical structure capable of panoptically overviewing society, somewhat implicit in a government perspective, is abandoned. Governance—like NPM—defies simple definitions,[10] but indicates the emergence of a more plural political world, a declining role of the nation-state, and a more complex set of societal problems. Society is seen as a network of negotiating units, whose compositions vary, as do their positions in the power structure, over time and across subjects. From a government perspective, a logical structure is presupposed: thus, in this line of thinking, it is possible to identify relatively clear distinctions and connections, implications and derivations between policies and programmes. Seen from a governance point of view, the policy process involves constant negotiating of logics and rationalities.

In the political science literature on policy implementation and evaluation, it has long been recognized that steering societies is less a matter of the hierarchical operation of a rational structure, and more a matter of negotiation, experimentation, and iteration. Commands are rough and imprecise instruments, dialogue and feedback are necessary. Societies or sectors that have tried the command may have encountered increasing degrees of chaos and/ or double standards. In their seminal work, Pressman and Wildawsky demonstrated how conceptual misalignments, ideological contra-dictions, and contextual changes created a gulf between federal policy statements and local implementation. Michael Lipsky showed how frontline staff form their own practical interpretations of policies—interpretations that contrast with the text of the law but express the experienced reality of their own daily lives.[11]

These works were empirical accounts with preliminary conceptualizations of a complex and fluid world; for Pressman and Wildawsky, a world of limited rationalism, and for Lipsky, a world of social construction. A recent spate of Foucauldian-inspired re-search has elaborated the theoretical underpinning, theorizing the process whereby several rationalities are constructed into one com-plex structure, a confluence of knowledge, discourse, and power.[12] In this literature, the conceptual construction of reality is seen as part of the practices of power. In a governance perspective, the work of construction happens in the networks that negotiate societal discourses, including those on globalization. Governmentality is formed as a perception of the good society and the means to attain it: a construction of rationalities and a range of political technolo-gies, constantly negotiated among actors in a network.

Professionals play a specific role in the formulation and negotiation of the political rationalities and technologies that underpin governmentality. It is the professionals' discourse of expertise that mandates the ordering and reordering of things, and they have a special brief to create visions and practical procedures of public administration. In doing this, state professionals, academics, and private managers are drawing on particular domains of knowledge, fusing them into the discourse of public authorities. The domains of knowledge are formed into conceptual maps that denote the broader means and aims of public sector activities. Of importance here are the specific organizational forms—organizations, networks and alliances—through which the conceptual maps of expertise are articulated, distributed, and appropriated. The authorization of a specific conceptual map of how the public sector should be run is contingent upon the professionals' ascription of social and political authority to organizations—the kind of authority varies with different organizations.

The concept of power acquires a particular meaning from this perspective. As with the formulation and implementation of policies, power does not provide a capacity for rational ordering. Societies have no unitary locus of sovereignty, but a ubiquitous network of power, exercised from multiple points and taking a 'capillary form of existence' which 'reaches into the very grain of individuals, touches their bodies and inserts itself into their actions and attitudes, their discourses, learning processes and everyday lives'.[13] Governmentality, formed and negotiated among political actors and professionals, also means the formation of logics that govern individuals' lives. Morality is a public affair, adaptable to shifting political rationalities: one's dedication to work, one's health and general lifestyle, are all relevant parts of governmentality. Every individual partakes in the exercise of power through her reproduction of rationalities, political and organizational.[14]

Power, though far from evenly distributed, floats around in networks and alliances, inside and around which conflicts and points of resistance are articulated. This is in line with a Gramscian perspective: domination—hegemony—results not from an all-controlling centre, but from processes of contestation and change in multiple arenas, including locations outside, or at the margins, of national centres and formal politics.[15] In this picture, what we know as the state—whether national or sub-national—appears not as a coherent, autonomous, and calculating political subject but as a loosely coordinated complex of organizational forms, practices, and networks. Some governance and network theorists simply equal the state with other actors.[16] Foucault can be seen both to deconstruct the state, in his early writings on power from a micro-perspective, and to elevate the state in his later macro-oriented work.[17] We suggest that the state-as-organization, a state apparatus, may well need deconstruction, to be reformulated as a complex of interacting networks, political rationalities, and technologies. On the other hand, the state-as-identity, as a representation of the national collectivity, remains very important, not least in a discussion of the mentalities and discourses of rule. In this sense, the state retains a special prerogative to appoint and authorize, to subsidize and tax, and to try to shape the conduct of individuals and groups, both within and outside state organizations.

All these considerations about governance, policy, networks, and implementation are now becoming relevant also in the international arena. Nationally, the traditional governance process with the state as supreme actor is now heavily influenced by international organizations, with a growing number of regulations formulated at the supranational level. Internationally, a number of policies are being made in order to regulate the conduct of international actors— states, businesses, and organizations. These policies and regulations are subject to the same constraints and conditions as national ones— and more, because there are no supranational states to police them. But, supranational professional discourses are travelling across languages, institutions, and cultures, framing and positioning local discourses and being translated by the local configurations of resources and ideas.

TRANSNATIONAL DISCOURSE COMMUNITIES AND GLOBALIZATION

Public administration is a social field where different discourses vie for hegemony. The totality of these discourses—which includes, for example, lay discourses about governmental mismanagement—make up an order of discourse (or discourse order).[18] Regarded as one element in the discourse order of public administration, discourses such as NPM are socially constitutive, infusing the field of public administration with values and ideas. Compared with the discourses of public administration that preceded it—and those that have emerged in recent years, not replacing it but adding new layers— NPM has a certain character and plays a particular role.

Professional discourses of public administration are constructed and disseminated through a range of discourse communities, consisting of numerous networks of expertise, state professionals, academics, and managers. Each community has a broadly agreed set of common public goals, mechanisms, and genres for communication among their members, as well as a specific lexis. In other words, members will have an appropriate degree of relevant content and discursive expertise.[19] Recent decades have seen a dramatic rise in what we have termed transnational discourse communities (TDC). TDCs are inhabited by experts from a wide range of countries, and they tend to have a global rather than national or local outlook on key issues. In the field of public administration, most TDCs aim at stimulating comparisons and learning processes, in order to define and implement best practices.[20] TDCs involved in the development and dissemination of a discourse such as NPM include particular divisions of the OECD (PUMA and DAC), the CLAD (a Latin American network), the World Bank, the UN Public Administrative Division, electronic networks such as LOGOV, and multiple less conspicuous transnational fora for sporting and developing best practice such as the then Bertelsmann Cities of Tomorrow Nework (now disbanded). To the extent that it is possible to identify separate TDCs, they will probably overlap or be interconnected; many professionals participate in more than one TDC. It should be noted that TDCs are often linked to national discourse communities. But a given TDC may be more linked to some national discourse communities than to others.

TDCs and globalization are closely related.[21] On the one hand, TDCs seem to emerge and spread as a consequence of globalization. Increasingly rapid global flows of material and cultural products have multiplied the number of organizational forms worldwide, contributing to the complexity of governance: formal political and administrative levels, from the local to the transnational, are being criss-crossed by ever expanding networks of corporations, international organizations, and non-governmental organizations. To further complicate the picture, these organizational structures, levels, and networks, can be seen as overlapped or penetrated by 'scapes', in which people, money, images, ideas, and technology flow. Flows of ideas and people may contribute to a de-territorialization of identities, to the production of cosmopolitans.[22] On the other hand, TDCs are themselves creators and promoters of globalization, and, thus, a particular apt example of the discursive moment of globalization. Since the 1980s, TDCs have used globalization and related terms as discursive devices 'to render the world manageable, to define the range of individual and collective policy choice, to clarify external threats and constraints and to imagine the repertoire of available strategic opportunities'.[23] The point that we want to make here is that the truth effects of such discourses of globalization are relatively independent of the reality that the discourses seek to depict and transform. In addition to its material features, then, globalization is a discourse of power that frames ways of thinking and acting. Articulated in and through TDCs, this discourse of power makes it possible to connect calculations at one place with action at another, enabling action at distance; as the technological dimension of globalization has facilitated the ceaseless travelling across the globe of certain people—notably the symbolic analysts—and their ideas and concepts, discourses become appropriated in places distant from where they were initially developed. Shared understandings arise in processes of negotiation in which professionals 'have come to construe their problems in allied ways and their fate as in some way bound up with one another. Hence persons, organisations, entities and locales which remain differentiated by space, time and formal boundaries can be brought into a loose and approximate, and always mobile and indeterminate alignment'.[24] Facts about globalization and related phenomena become framed and presented in standardized ways, making it possible to retell them, if necessary,[25] far beyond the reach of the members of the TDC in question.

The translation of the shared ideas of a TDC into action in a concrete locality, such as a municipality, should not be viewed as taking the form of an imposition of ideas from above. Globalization does not denote a new hierarchy, positioning supranational organizations on top of national and local ones. Globalization is both relational and contextual. Through a relational 'intermingling of global and distant logics', the geography of territorial states, economies, identities, and localities becomes redefined and to some extent undermined. In concrete local contexts, this intersection of different spatial realities is translated into an increasing 'hybridisation and perforation of social, economic and political life'.[26] The local, which we view as the place of translation and hybridization, should not be conceived as a spatial fixity of tradition and continuity. We suggest that it is more analytically fruitful to see it as a generating site; generating because locality appears as something relational and open-ended as it interacts with global dynamics, rather than as unchangeable, closed, and passive context. However, from the point of view of any locality, interaction with the global is impossible without activity and practice, including resistance, generated in the locality. Thus a locality is also a generating site in the sense of being a place where particular practices and events are unfolding and getting mixed with global dynamics, producing new types of social and spatial differentiation.

GOVERNMENTALITY, POLITICAL RATIONALITY, AND TECHNOLOGIES OF GOVERNMENT

According to Foucault, the expansion of populations in the seventeenth and eighteenth centuries forced governments in Europe to enhance and refine the state's regulation of its inhabitants. Whereas states previously had been almost entirely focused on the management of boundaries to protect their territories, they now had to address more systematically the regulation of their internal affairs. In order to label and organize people, new objects of knowledge and intervention were explored and defined—example, 'society', 'economy', 'population', and 'poverty'—as well as modern techniques of calculation, surveillance, and administration. In describing this change, Foucault coined the concept of governmentality and the associated notions of political rationales and techniques.

Governmentality is a way of thinking about how populations—that is, societies—can be regulated. It becomes the basis of modern forms of political thought and intervention, emphasizing governance through individual self-regulation—that is, through particular types of human subjectivity with high levels of autonomy and self-management, which complement or replace the sovereign power of traditional top-down managerial control.

There are two important dimensions of governmentality: on the one hand, the thoughts and representations involved, as problems and authorities define fields of intervention (that is, a set of political rationalities). Political rationalities are embedded in governmental discourse, for example, in programmes, plans, working papers, and other external and internal documents. On the other hand, governmentality has to do with the ways authorities can and should deal with the problems and fields defined by political rationality (that is, a set of technologies of government). These technologies encompass systems of numbering, accounting and computing, forms of surveillance, methods of timing and spacing of activities in particular locales, methods of organization of work, forms of administration, types of schooling and training, bodies of expertise, and so on.[27]

There is a close relationship between political rationalities and technologies of government. But analytically, it makes sense to distinguish between representation of and intervention into specific domains: between transforming reality into the domain of thought and making it governable and to translate these thoughts into the domain of reality in order to shape and normalize conduct.[28] In sum, if one is to govern a social field, it is necessary to represent and conceptualize the object of management. It is through this manoeuvre of representation and conceptualization that reality becomes inscribed in oral and written language.[29]

The next section looks at the historical and societal conditioning of NPM from such a perspective, sketching the genealogy of NPM, with a particular focus on the new, radical, and very generalized representations of public administration that emerged within transnational discourse communities centred in the OECD, the UN, and the World Bank. We explore the political rationalities and technologies of NPM as perceived from the position of the experts involved in these transnational discourse communities.

NPM HYPERLINKS: TRANSNATIONAL DISCOURSE COMMUNITIES

NPM's rise to general prominence in the 1980s and 1990s as a quasi-paradigm for contemporary reform efforts in the public sector rests on the historical development and transformation of political rationalities, which created and shaped social fields, generating and deploying a variety of technologies of government. In this process, the relations between expertise, authorities, and populations were gradually redefined and changed.[30] The very existence of a separate public sector—which fostered the need for public administration—emerges from the political rationality of liberalism. Without retelling the history of liberalism and its development into the welfare state, we can say that the fundamental constructs of liberalism were modified by the more ambitious governmentality of welfare. Those ambitions came up against the constriction of the market forces, limiting the ambitions of politics, and producing, what Rose calls, the new rationality of 'advanced liberalism', with which NPM is associated. It lies, on the one hand, in its articulation of criticisms of the rationality and technologies of welfare—its bureaucracy, inefficiency, distortion of the market, and so on. On the other hand, it is able to turn these criticisms into new technologies of government. For one thing, neo-liberalism has made economists the fastest growing group of professionals in bureaucracies, giving rise to 'the calculative regimes of accounting and financial management...a range of new techniques for exercising critical scrutiny over authority—budget disciplines, accountancy, and audit being three of the most salient.'[31]

In addition to this new relation between expertise and government, the rationality of neo-liberalism emphasizes pluralization, autonomization, self-help, and the role of personal choice. It incorporates a sort of de-governmentalization of the state through which the state detaches itself from many of the regulatory mechanisms it used to have. These mechanisms are delegated to individuals, and to a network of decentralized agencies, associations, and alliances. New subjects of government are specified—the customer and the self-helping citizen—both are 'entrepreneurs of the self' and rely on the 'expertise of the market'.[32]

THE EMERGENCE OF A PARADIGM: THE NPM DISCOURSE OF THE OECD

Despite its debt to the rationality of advanced liberalism, some NPM discourses, however, explicitly state that the basic values of the welfare state are worth retaining, and what is needed is a better technology for implementing them. Thus, our perspective suggests the existence of competing and, quite often, interlaced public sector discourses.

When the economists formulated a crisis of the rationale of welfare, an economic co-operation organization took the lead in developing new technologies of government. The discourse of public management was based on orthodox economic thinking, with its doctrines of free markets and maximizing individuals. As an ideal, it referred to private sector experiences and practices. NPM expresses an organized effort to accomplish certain ends, applying resources that are considered scarce and must be used efficiently. It contrasts with bureaucratic rationalities that prioritize legal and political correctness. For example: in a bureaucracy, hierarchical organization and a competence-based division of labour are indispensable tools to ensure consistency in decision premises; management thinking sees those features as just one possible organizational structure among several others. Using management tools in the public sector implies both organizational and processual flexibility, and a much higher priority is given to economic considerations. The discourse of public management is not a product of academic research or internal administrative thinking, but emerged out of the discussions taking place in TDCs, providing an important basis for policy recommendations promulgated by international organizations. In this way, NPM became elevated to programmatic status in prominent organizations such as the World Bank and the UN Development Programme, and not least in the OECD. Throughout the 1990s, the concept of 'Good Governance' was woven into the World Bank's rhetorics and lending policies towards Third World countries, addressing not only issues of political legitimacy and democracy, but also the need for administrative efficiency by means of marketization and competition.[33] Interestingly, the notions of political legitimacy and democratization were taken up explicitly by the OECD's special task force in the field of development: the Development Assistance Committee[34] (DAC), while much of the management orientation in the NPM paradigm promoted by the OECD was maintained and further developed in the World Bank documents. Traces of the NPM discourse can thus be found in the WB's *World Development Report 1997*, which stresses the necessity of reinvigorating the state's institutional capability by subjecting the state to more competition, internally by boosting competition within the civil service, and externally by introducing more competition in the provision of public goods and services.[35]

In other words, the OECD was not lone in formulating ideas of administrative reform, but it was probably the most important vehicle for the development of the various reform concepts, ideas, and campaigns subsumed under the NPM label. The first major initiative came with a 1979 conference in Madrid, Managing Change in Public Administration.[36] A sense of public sector crisis had put the need for improving public administration on the agenda of this organization otherwise devoted to economic progress. In 1979, an international conference on 'improving public management and performance' had been held in Washington, DC, with the International Institute of Administrative Services as co-sponsor. It was the first occasion where managerial reform was seen as relevant for countries not classified as 'developing'.[37] The Madrid conference marked the emergence of the OECD as the leader in developing concepts and theories.

In Madrid, conceptual innovation came from the Carter Administration in the USA. The National Productivity Council of 1978 had produced the Civil Service Reform Act (1979), through the Office of Personnel Management. Focused on public efficiency— in the interest of improving public services[38]—this act introduced some important and significant managerial perspectives that broke with traditional public administration norms: an emphasis on managerial flexibility—as opposed to the norm of strengthening political control of the 'bureaucracy'; and monetary and status rewards based on effective performance—contrary to the classical rewarding of loyalty.[39] The ideas of decentralized flexibility and operational incentives proved to be crucial for the development of NPM.

NPM discourse was only slowly emerging. Great care was taken to signal respect for national specificity: *'there cannot only be a single solution of these problems* [underlining in original]...different cultures, constitutions and administrative traditions...'.[40] It was repeated in the Synthesis Report[41] and in the opening addresses. Nonetheless, managerialism had come to stay and expand, not least through the influence of the OECD.

In developing the NPM discourse, the OECD launched a number of new concepts, expressing the movement from administration to management, from politics to market. In a 1987 pamphlet entitled 'Administration as service, the user as client', one guiding notion is 'client-orientation': The public sector is there for those who use its services; also citizens with a need or demand for help from the public sector deserve a respectful and sympathetic response, rather than being disciplined by an insensitive authority. Later, a more direct loan from management has changed the notion to 'customer orientation'.

A second concept, 'service-orientation', used in the same pamphlet, took the parallel further: seeing public administration as 'service production' implies a more pragmatic, goal-oriented view of public sector practices than the tradition of legal correctness. To produce is to use resources efficiently—the choice of structural and processual forms becomes subservient to the need to economize.

The two concepts together constitute the notion of responsiveness, an ideal of a public administration that is responsive to its users and doing its best to meet their expectations: 'Making administration more responsive means changing individual behaviours and organisations so that clients will experience a more responsive service'.[42] In this conception, political ideals have disappeared from view. Public 'services' are delivered, efficiently and with a smile, to individual customers. Politics lies in choosing what services to deliver, but implies nothing about how to deliver it.

'Efficiency' as an all-embracing ideal was (and is) of course the nucleus of the NPM discourse. It took on a new meaning—both broader than the managerial one of 'performance standards' and more precise than the old administrative one of 'effectiveness', meaning the accomplishment of the right goals. In the preface to PUMA's 1990 *Report on Public Management Developments*, the authors wrote that 'productivity and responsiveness to the public are becoming the new standards for measuring performance, both for individuals and the organisations in which they work'.[43]

The same 1990 survey launched the concept of 'results-orientation'. Defining results in operational terms is a tool in the definition and management of productivity, and management by results (MbR) became an important method for public administrators in the following years. The survey described it as a development away from the old Programme-Planning-Budgeting system, in a vaguely conceived direction: 'management-oriented and focus on what organisations do and produce and on the means for holding them accountable for performance'.[44]

The 1990 report described several other trends in the conceptual and practical development of public administration/management—privatization, human resource management, service quality management, decentralization, and deregulation are the most pertinent ones. The register of technologies kept expanding, and every new item was drawn from the discourses of private sector management and economic efficiency.

In the 1993 survey of public management developments, the national specificity mantra gave way to a normative concept of One Best Way to Reform. This way was still very broadly conceived, and many of the concepts were vague and open to different interpretations, but the survey left no doubt about the eventual rewards of travelling down the road of reform, and the general direction was consistently given as going from political administration to service management.[45]

Finally, in 1995, in a report taking stock of public management reform efforts in OECD countries, the OECD confidently declared that 'A new paradigm for public management has emerged, aimed at fostering a performance-oriented culture in a less centralised public sector'.[46] Intended as an overview of 'the dynamic changes in strategies of governance' taking place at the time—and as a synthesis of past work carried out in the PUMA since the first manifestations of this project in the mid-1970s—this report not only repeated the need for reform expressed in earlier publications, it announced the arrival of a new paradigm capable of tackling the new context of governance, that is, an 'increasingly dynamic, open, and internationally competitive' world economy. The new paradigm was meant to make public administration more efficient and adapt it to new societal realities. Among those realities, this 'dynamic, open, and internationally competitive economy' played an important role—the discourse of globalization was often invoked as part of the new NPM discourse.

THE NPM PARADIGM

Defining NPM remains a challenge, but, for the purpose of the present discussion, we suggest viewing it as a powerful orientation in the public sector order of discourse, giving priority to responsiveness and efficiency in a context of globalization.[47] It represents a turn away from communitarian conceptions of the state towards contractual relations between individuals and agencies. The political technologies implied are derived from the necessity to meet citizens' expectations and to deliver optimal results in terms of legitimacy and efficiency. Responsiveness implies flexibility, change orientation, and openness. Efficiency implies performance orientation, active management, and systematic evaluation. Globalization implies that administering public functions and institutions as if they were unique and alone in the world makes no sense. Importantly, though, the political rationality implied in NPM is not one of consistent and unidirectional neo-liberalism.

Although certain applications have been more programmatic than others, NPM has never been a political programme proper. It has been used both by neo-liberals for diminishing government and by New Labourites for directing social change. The core of NPM remains the import of management thinking—and management is different things to different people. Among current management fads one finds concepts that are narrowly oriented towards 'shareholder value' and focus on material incentives and physical restrictions. On the other hand, other trends include emphases on human relations, ethics, and values. Any NPM scheme may choose its own selections from the management menu: privatization and monetary bonus systems, or user involvement and value-based management, on the other.

The openness and lack of finality is partly a strength of NPM, making it more broadly palatable and enabling it to survive changes of political regimes. But the same openness means that a strong and specific process of authorization is needed, in order to establish that NPM is the correct way of doing things.

An important aspect of this authorization happens in TDCs, and, in particular, through members of an authoritative status like the OECD. While not being a supranational organization, the OECD wields considerable influence in terms of preparing the political ground for a whole raft of different policies, articulating and disseminating a certain view of the world. Its power rests on the acceptance of its discourse; its research-based opinions provide it with expert status and enable it to canvass support for its 'objective', universally applicable knowledge, which transcends time and space. From a Giddensian point of view, the OECD's systematic use of knowledge about social life for organizing it and transforming it makes it a distinctively contemporary institution: its production—its discourse—is designed to ensure its entrance in a myriad of textual chains, providing policy makers and the media with a framework of action, an order of representation.

A number of other TDCs are also highly active in the on-going processes of authorizing specific ideas and discourses. Some of them are traditional—the international associations of public administration practitioners, organized by sector, profession, level, nation, region, etc. In these traditional networks, NPM enlivened a sometimes slightly worn atmosphere of partly scientific insight, partly anecdotal wisdom. In the case of NPM, a discourse of imminence and impact breathed new life in old networks. A number of new networks were formed in the process—notably a number of excellence networks, with a missionary purpose and with prizes to bestow on those government agencies and localities that best followed the prescriptions.

NPM discourse was—and, in new guises, continues to be—reproduced in these TDCs and associated with authority: the status of state institutions, international, scientific, and professional organizations. It is discursively connected with eminence, prominence, and inevitability. Much NPM discourse is concerned with the naturalization of changes—portraying developments as following from natural causes like organic growth or historic progress, and establishing deductive relationships between international and regional developments and those things that must happen at lower levels. What is implied is subsumption—from the global down to the local, a string of necessities determine and delimit the possible action space for both business and government.[48]

The relationship constructed in this kind of logic between the global, the nation-state, and sub-national economies, and, by implication, different layers of government and (members of) the public is a one-way relationship. It contains a specific, unquestionable logic descending from the global economy (origins unknown, no owners) to national governments and economies, which in turn are expected to translate the acquired wisdom about the global economic regularities into local action, in part via territorial authorities.

This technique is an example of how power relationships work in discursive processes. Imposing new rules from above is not possible, but discourses can be changed through what Clarke and Newman call 'the cascade of change'—the establishment of globalization as a metanarrative, framing all other orders of discourse. The cascade of change technique

accomplishes a range of narrative closures. The first is at the global level where change tends to read as uni-directional or non-contradictory and as such resulting in clear imperatives or directions for lower level changes. Such lower level changes are represented as the natural or logical reflection of global or universal tendencies. Global and national changes are then constituted as the necessary conditions of organisational projects for change.[49]

GLOBALIZED MUNICIPALITIES: NPM MADE TO MEASURE

In the remainder of the chapter we will look at how this naturalization of change was assimilated and transformed[50] into programmatic representations by two OECD municipalities: Tijuana in northern Mexico and Newham in East London, UK. Both municipalities described in their programmes a rapidly increasing need for responsiveness and efficiency in the public sector, applying in this way the conceptual map of the new managerialism. They also justified the adoption of specific managerial technologies of government with reference to the logics of globalization. As examples of professional representations and constructions of 'reality', these programmatic claims were building on previous analyses from which more concrete policy aims are established and technologies of government outlined.

However, when we take a closer look at the local programmatic representations produced and distributed by the two municipalities, it soon becomes clear that the suggested need for changes in the administrations were represented as the logical consequence of not only globalization and other 'universal' tendencies—as suggested in Clarke and Newman's 'cascade of change' metaphor—but also of 'local' and rather unique phenomena. This observation—to be unfolded below—can add some nuances to the figure of descending isomorphic effects [51]which seems to underpin the 'cascade of change' metaphor. A first reading of the programmatic representations may confirm the picture of a thundering waterfall of unavoidable innovations, forcibly introducing managerialism to local and national authorities—herein lies the effect of isomorphism. The cascade appears to construct a unity of identities. However, a second reading suggests a capability of using the message to generate differences.

The adoption of managerial discourse in our two municipalities happened about the same time—about a decade ago. But it had different backgrounds: the British example started as a series of centrally directed reforms introducing textbook neo-liberalism: privatization, deregulation, and individualization. The 1980s were the era of neo-liberalism, and neo-conservative governments took over in most of western Europe, to stay for a decade or more. Britain, with the US, was the prime example. In Mexico, the de la Madrid (1982–8) and Salinas (1988–94) governments also spoke the language of freer markets. Federal reforms to reorganize and grant municipalities greater autonomy from federal and state control were introduced already in 1983, but unlike the Thatcher governments, these and later reform attempts had no specified NPM agenda for local government. So the Mexican example is almost the opposite: an expression of political dissent by a local government won by the opposition party at the time (Partido Acción Nacional, PAN), underlining the virtues of decentralization, efficiency, responsiveness, honesty, and democratic participation—virtues which had been incessantly emphasized by the federal government for decades, yet not translated into practice. Both municipalities offer evidence of creative appropriation of the NPM discourse to further their local agendas.

In order to make sense of their local environment and to act upon it, municipal officials create representations of the challenges that they perceive their locality to be facing. In this process of construction they draw on already existing linguistic resources, knowledge, and expertise. In drawing on the conceptual map of NPM, which foregrounds the narrative of responsiveness and efficiency in a context of globalization, the representations appear to be influenced by similar contextual developments, in part inspired from the same sources but adapting local inputs to achieve unique effects.

TIJUANA: 'COMPETITIVE POSITIONING'

In the case of Tijuana the main actors of the new managerialism were PANista politicians, representing local businesses interested in improving the social and economic environment. NPM was adopted with the purpose of expressing a wish and a need for a public sector with less corruption and better performance—to get out of a vicious circle of poverty, corruption, and inefficiency. In this sense, the local discourse of public management emerged against the backdrop of the local and national discourse on corruption and mismanagement.[52] The version of NPM that Tijuana adopted carried an emphasis on economic positioning, competitiveness, identity and image management, and, not least, participation. Pervasive corruption could only be eradicated by drawing citizens into political and administrative decisions and by introducing a variety of business-inspired technologies in the municipal organization, revolving around the image of 'active', 'entrepreneurial', and 'responsible' individuals. Tijuana's heavy concern with the city's spatial and economic position in a world of globalization was consistent with another core feature of the new public managerialism—the significance of responsiveness and efficiency. By emphasizing responsiveness and efficiency, and by coupling these notions with technologies of managing reputation, image and identity—both at the levels of internal municipal organization and of territorial municipal space—a vocabulary of distinctions was constructed and projected: it enabled 'outsiders' (example, investors) to measure the achievements of Tijuana with its potential 'competitors' (example, other municipalities or regions, that is, sites in Mexico as well as abroad), and it made it possible for 'insiders' (that is, the local population) to generate a positive feeling of living in an active and entrepreneurial site.

It is clear that the municipal officers in charge were inspired not only about the local and national discourse of mismanagement, but also by TDCs, in particular those connected to the World Bank, to Anderson Consulting, and to other cities, especially Bilbao and San Diego, each carrying slightly different versions of the discourse of the new managerialism. One example of the fuzziness of NPM was the concept of participation so important in Tijuana's reform process. The dimension of participation has not always been part of NPM, but clearly an element to be found in some versions.[53] In the case of Tijuana, there seemed to be a quite important influence from the World Bank's conceptualization of 'good governance', which blends the entrepreneurial core of NPM with the advocacy of liberal democracy.

NEWHAM: 'BEST VALUE'

Newham was—and still is—an economically and socially strained eastern London borough. Starting in the early 1990s, the borough embarked on an ambitious plan to reconstruct the identity, image, and reputation of the area, and, by implication, also of the Council, in order to retain and attract the right kind of citizens, businesses, and employees. It set out to map the borough's destiny onto a very different conceptualization of the future and a very different idea of the kind of technologies that could take the borough and the Council to that future.[54] At a very general level, the Council rested its bid for a new beginning on managerialism and notions of entrepreneurialism, which were rolled out across the Council's discourse. Interestingly, Newham's conversion to NPM-inspired thinking pre-dated New Labour by several years. In other words, it picked up the gauntlet of managerialism in the John Major era and set out to beat the then neo-liberal regime at its own game. However, the eventual translation of this thinking into programmes and specific initiatives owed a lot to the New Labour government in 1997 and the continued pressure from above. A good example of the Council's appropriation of a centrally devised instrument—or programme—for local change was its successful bid to become a so-called Best Value pilot authority in 1997, testing the incoming Labour government's ideas about public service provision. The Council's reform vision hinged to a large extent on its faith in the capacity of its new discourse to provide its various audiences with a set of ideas capable of instigating a virtuous circle of identity and social engineering whereby (1) Newham Council and its employees would come to see themselves as agents of change with internal organizational reform as the means to an end, transformation of the local; (2) the world outside, notably commercial interests, would come to view Newham as an attractive and strategically positioned location; and (3) local people, responding to the new discourse from the local leadership and its new legitimacy, would become prepared to commit themselves to the area as citizens.

The Council's discourse was teeming with references to external recognition and verification of its achievements, whether in the form of awards, academic comments, quotes from mention in the media. Newham, moreover, began to articulate a view of the world, which stretched far beyond its boundaries, enthusiastically sporting its strategic location in Greater London 'effectively the major business location, communications hub and cultural forum for the whole European bloc, which with 370 million people is also the world's biggest single market'.[55] Finally, the Council stressed the importance of shaping a 'New Politics', which was about increasing public participation and empowerment of citizens. By raising local people's expectations and local engagement, both in their capacity as citizens and as users of the Council's services, there was clearly a sense in which many of the NPM inspired practices—discursive as well as real—became the vehicle for a somewhat different project than the OECD efficiency and responsiveness vision.

In sum, in Newham's case, the very strategic embrace of NPM was not initially imposed from above. However, at the local level, it was very much a tightly steered top-down affair. However, the sheer level of ambition—radical socio-economic reengineering—suggested that even in the best of cases, it would take a long time for any conclusive effects to materialize from the initiatives.[56] The Council's systematic image, reputation, and identity work was nevertheless impressive just as its shrewd use of NPM testified to its careful reading of contemporary cultural values and political games.

CONCLUSIONS

The history of the discourse of NPM shows a development from scattered ideas and pluralistic rhetoric, to a more focused, normative discourse about the necessity of change and the correct way to create better public services, favouring managerial technologies over more traditional bureaucratic measures. By shaping the claims and declarations of prestigious organizations such as the OECD and the World Bank, TDCs are incessantly reproducing NPM discourse globally, with a specific view to local application in all places and at all levels.

In this sense, NPM is sufficiently influential to be viewed as a hegemonic discourse: its rationality and technologies of change, responsiveness and efficiency frame and direct public administration reforms almost everywhere, contributing to a new sense of what 'ruling' is about—a new governmentality. Our cases show how public administration reforms in locations as different as Tijuana and Newham self-consciously apply core elements from NPM. We have studied other cases in other countries, not reported here, and seen other applications.[57] One can always use the word 'hegemony' in a loose sense, merely indicating some form of dominance and ubiquitousness—the simple transmission of a pattern of dominance. With the above observations in mind, therefore, the discourse of NPM is certainly hegemonic: NPM does reflect a certain political rationality. It points in the direction of less state, more market, less order and more choice, implying less equality, more differentiation. But, we believe that the interests in liberalization are complicated and widely distributed. Thus NPM is not hegemonic if we by hegemony understand an ideology reflecting the perspectives of a ruling class and justifying class domination. It is possible to identify a clear direction of the development of international economic regimes—liberalizing the international movements of capital. But it would be difficult to identify a 'class' of international capital-owners directing the liberalization and reaping the benefits.[58] In line with our perspective on governance, the advantages as well as the disadvantages of neo-liberalism are negotiated and distributed unevenly across categories of people, states, and societies through a loosely coupled and highly complex network of economic and political power.

But, our cases also show a different aspect of the process of dissemination and application, and, consequently, of the dynamics of hegemony: the translation that NPM discourse undergoes locally, the contextual contingency of the reproduction of a global discourse. Following our conceptualization of the local as a 'generating site', this comes hardly as a surprise. For one thing, Tijuana and Newham are examples of how municipal authorities relate to and engage with national and global developments, through the production of new political rationalities and technologies of government. It would be wrong, in other words, to view the municipal authorities as passive organizational forms that *are 'being "suited to" some already pre-existing stable space'*. This is the typical perspective applied in studies of bureaucratic organizations[59] as well as in many studies of globalization in which the capacity or agency of the local is underconceptualized or entirely left out. In contrast to such a perspective, the municipalities in question appear as highly productive organizations that shape the local environment, as well as national and global discourse. This is in fact not only a prime example of what Robertson has coined 'glocalization'.[60] It also pinpoints a core dimension of hegemony: In a truly Gramscian view, hegemony is never stable nor solid, but always a *process* that involves a constant renegotiation of interpretations and incorporates subordinate perspectives.[61]

By adapting a globally hegemonic discourse for local purposes, the municipalities may end up producing new types of social and spatial differentiation, not only externally but also internally: as territorial political and administrative units, the municipalities can now promote themselves as more responsive and efficient—as true 'entrepreneurs of themselves'. At present, this appears to be a prime quality not only in the worlds of government and business, but also more generally because managerialism reflects wider societal changes whereby, increasingly, human life is conceived of in entrepreneurial terms. In this way, they may expect to attract investments and the 'right' people from the outside. And they can project a new and different picture of themselves in the local context. In doing this, they contribute to a modification of the relations between local authorities and citizens; the former is turned into a partner and promoter, the later into a self-helping and co-responsible citizen.

In sum, our identification of a 'hegemonic' NPM discourse implies the view of hegemony as a process, an on-going reinterpretation of the field of public administration. At present, this process is headed by and articulated through TDCs, but it also takes place at the local level. NPM discourse is used for political projects, but those projects are defined in local contexts and translate the global discourse into configurations that are contingent upon the lived world of local people. The political interests served through these processes depend upon local power configurations. With NPM managerialist and liberalist, managers and business owners feel at home in the NPM discourse, while trade unions and public professionals feel that their influence is diminishing, and their established positions crumbling. No one hegemonic class, however, corresponds to the hegemony of NPM, and in today's complex world of multi-level business and governance, a number of different political projects can apply the discourse of New Public Management.

Notes

[1] For the 2000 version, see D. Salskov-Iversen, H.K. Hansen, and S. Bislev, 'Governmentality, Globalization and Local Practice: Transformations of a Hegemonic Discourse', *Alternatives* 25 (2), 2000, pp. 183–222.

[2] OECD *Modernizing Government: The Way Forward*, Paris: OECD, 2005.

[3] Clegg, 1998; Gordon Burchell, and Miller (eds), *The Foucault Effect: Studies in Governmentality*, London: Harvester, Wheatsheaf 1991; Deetz, 1998.

[4] See W. Larner, and W. Walthers (eds), *Global Governmentality: Governing International Spaces*, London: Routledge 2004; H.K. Hansen, and D.Salskov-Iversen, 'Remodelling the Transnational Political Realm: Partnerships, Benchmarking Schemes and the Digitalization of Governance', *Alternatives*, 30 (2), 2005; H.K. Hansen, and D. Salskov-Iversen, 'Globalizing Webs: Translation of Public Sector e-Modernization', *in Global Ideas*, Barbara Czarniawska, and Guje Sévon, (eds), (Malmö: Liber), 2005, and H.K. Hansen, and D. Salskov-Iversen, (eds), *Critical Perspectives on Private Authority in Politics,* London: Palgrave Macmillan, 2008.

[5] D. Harvey, *Justice, Nature & the Geography of Difference*, Oxford: Blackwell,1996, pp. 77–95.

[6] M. Featherstone, S. Lash, and R. Robertson, *Global Modernities*, London: Sage, 1995, pp. 1–7. M. Kearney, 'The Local and the Global: The Anthropology of Globalization and Transnationalism', *Annual Review of Anthropology* 24 (547), 1995, p. 65.

[7] T. Richardson, 'Foucauldian Discourse: Power and Truth in Urban and Regional Policy Making', *European Planning Studies*, 4 (3), 1996, pp. 279–92. C.J.Fox, *Postmodern Public Administration—Towards Discourse*, London: Sage, 1995.

[8] S. Deetz, 'Discursive Formations, Strategized Subordination and Self-surveillance', in *Foucault, Management and Organization Theory*, A. McKinlay, and K. Starkey (eds), London: Sage, 1998, pp. 151–72; B. Flyvbjerg, 'Habermas and Foucault: Thinkers for Civil Society?' *British Journal of Sociology*, 49 (2), 1998, pp. 210–33.

[9] Marga Pröhl, (ed.), *International Strategies and Techniques for Future Local Government*, Gütersloh: Bertlesmann Foundation Publishers, 1997, and *The Evolving Organization: Building Trust in Local Government*, Gütersloh: Bertelsmann Foundation Publishers, 1997.

[10] R.A.W. Rhodes, 'Governance and Public Administration' in *Debating Governance,* J. Pierre (ed.), Oxford: Oxford University Press, 1999. P. Miller, and N. Rose, 'Governing Economic Life', *Economy and Society* vol. 19, 1990, pp. 1–31.

[11] J.L. Pressmann, and A. Wildawsky, *Implementation: How Great Expectations in Washington are Dashed in Oakland*, Berkeley: University

of California Press, 1983 [1973] and M. Lipsky, *Street-Level Bureaucracy: Dilemmas of the Individual in Public Services*, N.Y.: Russell Sage, 1980.

[12] N. Fairclough, *Discourse and Social Change*, Cambridge: Polity Press, 1992; M. Dean, *Critical and Effective Histories. Foucault's Methods and Historical Sociology*, Routledge: London,1994; M. Foucault, 'Governmentality', in *The Foucault Effect. Studies in Governmentality*, Gordon Burchell, and Miller (eds), 1991 [1978], pp. 87–104; Deetz, 1998; A. McKinley, and K. Starkey (eds), *Foucault, Management and Organization Theory*, London: Sage, 1999; Miller and Rose, 1990, op.cit.; D. Smith, *Text, Facts, and Feminity. Exploring the Relations of Ruling*, London: Routledge 1990; N. Rose, 'The Death of the Social? Re-figuring the Territory of Government', *Economy and Society*, 25 (3), 1996, pp. 327–56; Richardson, 1996, op.cit; S. Clegg, 'Foucault, Power and Organizations', in *Foucault, Management and Organization Theory*, Mckinlay and Starkey (eds), London: Sage, 1998, pp. 29–48

[13] M. Foucault, *Power/Knowledge. Selected Interviews and Other Writings 1972–77*, New York: Pantheon Books, 1980, p. 39.

[14] N. Rose, and P. Miller, 'Political Power beyond the State: Problematics of Government', *British Journal of Sociology*, 43 (2), 1992, pp. 171–205; Deetz, 1998.

[15] C. Buci-Glucksman, *Gramsci and the State,* London: Lawrence and Wishart, 1980; J. Rubin, *Decentering the Regime: Ethnicity, Radicalism and Democracy in Juchitán, México*, Durham: Duke University Press, 1997.

[16] W.J.M. Kickert, E.A. Klijn, and J.F.M. Koppenjahn (eds), *Managing Complex Networks: Strategies for the Public Sector.* London: Sage, 1997, p. 9.

[17] Dean, 1994, pp. 179ff.

[18] A. Gupta, 'Blurred Boundaries: The Discourse of Corruption, the Culture of Politics, and the Imagined State', *American Ethnologist*, 22 (2), 1995; H.K Hansen, 'Small Happenings and Scandalous Events: Corruption and Scandal in Contemporary Yucatán', *Folk Journal of the Danish Ethnographic Society*, 37, 1995, pp. 75–101; and H.K. Hansen, 'Governmental Mismanagement and Symbolic Violence: Discourses on Corruption in the Yucatán of the 1990s', *Bulletin of Latin American Research* 17 (3), 1998, pp. 367–86. See Fairclough, 1992 on the concept of 'discourse order'.

[19] K-H. Pogner, *Schreiben im Beruf als Handeln im Fach*, Tübingen: Gunter Narr Verlag Tübingen, 1999, pp. 54–5.

[20] As in the Bertelsmann Reports—See Pröhl 1997a and 1997b.

[21] We take 'globalization' to refer to the growing number of chains of economic, social, cultural, and political activity that are worldwide in scope. It also has to do with the intensification of relations between the agents that participate in these chains. Finally, it refers to reflexivity, i.e., the expanding use of all forms of expertise and knowledge to reflect on social

practices, including globalization itself. In other words, 'globalization' refers both to some material and cultural transformations of the global environment and to the representations of these transformations. It should be noted, however, that our constructivist approach puts more emphasis on exploring the character and the role of the latter than on analyzing and documenting global material transformation. See, for example, A. Amin, 'Placing Globalization', in *Theory, Culture & Society*, 14, 1997, pp. 123–37; A. Appadurai, *Modernity at Large: Cultural Dimensions of Globalization*, Minneapolis: University of Minnesota Press, 1996; J. Nederveen Pieterse, 'Globalization as Hybridization', in *Global Modernities*, M., Featherstone, S. Lash, and R. Robertson, London: Sage, 1995; R. Robertson, and H.H. Khonder, 'Discourses of Globalization: Preliminary Considerations', *International Sociology*, 13 (1), 1998, pp. 25–40; A. Hoogvelt, *Globalisation and the Postclonial World: The New Political Economy of Development*, London: Macmillan, 1997; B. Rosamond, 'Discourses on Globalization and the Social Construction of European Identities', *Journal of European Public Policy*, 6, 1999, pp. 652–68.

[22] U. Hannerz, *Transnational Connections. Culture, People, Places*, London: Routledge, 1996; Appadurai, 1996, op.cit.

[23] Rosamond, 1999, p. 657.

[24] Rose and Miller, 1990, p. 10.

[25] A. Escobar, *Encountering Development. The Making and Unmaking of the Third World*. New Jersey: Princeton University Press, 1995.

[26] A. Amin, 1997, p. 133.

[27] Miller and Rose, 1990; Dean 1994, pp. 187–8.

[28] This interpretation of the distinction between representation and intervention does not imply a 'move' from rationality to technology, but rather a circular process in which rationality and technology are inscribed in one another. Where political rationality contributes to the conceptualization of specific technologies, the technologies themselves are a condition for that specific rationality, and forms of rationality are inscribed in these technologies (Dean 1994,188).

[29] Smith 1990.

[30] N. Rose, 'Government, Authority and Expertise in Advanced Liberalism', in *Economy and Society*, 22 (3), 1993, pp. 283–99; Rose 1996.

[31] Rose 1993, p. 295.

[32] P. Du Gay, 'In the Name of 'Globalization': Enterprising Up Nations, Organizations and Individuals', in *Globalisation and Labour Relations*, P. Leisink (ed.), Edward Elgar Publishing Limited, 1999.

[33] World Bank, *Governance and Development*. Washington, D.C.: World Bank, 1992; World Bank, *World Development Report. The State in a Changing World*, Washington, D.C.: World Bank, 1997.

[34] For an example, see OECD *Participatory Development and Good Governance*, Paris: OECD, 1995, p. 14.

[35] World Bank, 1997.

[36] OECD *Strategies for Change and Reform in Public Management*, Paris: OECD, 1980.

[37] G.E. Caiden, *Administrative Reform Comes of Age*, Berlin: De Gruyter, 1991, p. 64.

[38] In the words of the successful presidential candidate during the campaign of 1976: 'waste and inefficiency never fed a hungry child'.

[39] Alan Campbell, Keynote Paper in OECD, 1980, pp. 49–56.

[40] G. Eldin, 'Opening Address', in *Strategies for Change and Reform in Public Management*, OECD, 1980, p. 46.

[41] D. Ink, 'Synthesis Report', in OECD, 1980, pp. 7–34.

[42] OECD *Administration as Service. The Public as Client*, Paris: OECD, 1987, p. 97.

[43] PUMA is OECD's Public Management unit, established in 1990. The quote is from OECD, *Public Management Developments. Survey 1990*, Paris, 1990, p. 7.

[44] Ibid., p. 11.

[45] OECD, *Public Management Developments. Survey 1993*, Paris, 1993.

[46] PUMA, *Governance in Transition. Public Management Reforms in OECD Countries. Conclusions of the Public Management Committee*, Paris: OECD, 1995.

[47] See, for example, P. Dunleavy, 'The Globalization of Public Services Production: Can Government be "Best in World"?' in *Globalization and Marketization of Government Services*, A. Massey (ed.), Macmillan: London, 1997; E. Ferlie *et al.*, *The New Public Management in Action*, Oxford: Oxford University Press, 1996; C. Hood, *Beyond the Public Bureaucratic State? Public Administration in the 1990s*, London: LSPS, 1990; K.K. Klausen, and K. Ståhlberg, 'New Public Management', in *New Public Management in Norden*, K.K. Klausen, and K. Ståhlberg (eds), Odense: Odense Universitetsforlag, 1998; and F. Naschold, *The Dialectics of Modernizing Local Government—An Assessment for the Mid 90s and an Agenda for the 21st Century (Agenda 21)*, Wissenshaftzentrum Berlin für Sozialforschung, 1997.

[48] D. Salskov-Iversen, 'Clients, Consumers or Citizens? Cascading Discourses on the Users of Welfare' in *Professions, New Public Management and the European Welfare State*, Dent O'Neil, and Bagley (eds), Staffordshire: Staffordshire University Press, 1999.

[49] J. Clarke, and J. Newman, 1997, p. 48.

[50] In this sense, our point is the opposite of what is implied in the Clark and Newman volume, op. cit.

[51] Ibid., p. 47.

[52] H.K. Hansen, 1995, 1998.

[53] In the typology of Ferlie *et al.*, especially NPM version 4 emphasizes this (Ferlie *et al.* 1996)

[54] Newham Council, *New millenium. New opportunities. Newham,* June 1999.

[55] London Lee Valley, *Space to Grow near the Heart of London,* 1997.

[56] In an interesting twist of events, Newham was not awarded 'Beacon' status in the latest stage of New Labour NPM. The Council leader, in a November 1999 interview, ascribed it to Newham's very radicalism: the attempt at reforming not just one sector or function but across the totality of local government activities.

[57] For example, Bislev, 'New Public Management and Municipal Organization: Danish and German Employment Programmes' in *Professions, New Public Management and the European Welfare State.* Pröhl 1997a, 1997b.

[58] L. Sklair, 'The Maquilas in Mexico: a Global Perspective', *Bulletin of Latin American Research,* 11 (1), 1992, pp. 91–107.

[59] Du Gay, 1999, p. 22.

[60] R. Robertson, 'Glocalization: Time-Space and Homogeneity-Heterogeneity', in *Global Modernities.*

[61] Buci-Glucksman, 1980, pp. 56ff; Rubin, 1997; F. Mallón, 'Reflections on the Ruins: Everyday Forms of State Formation in Nineteenth-Century Mexico', *Everyday Forms of State Formation. Revolution and the Negotiation of Rule in Modern Mexico,* G.M. Joseph, and D. Nugent (eds), Durham: Duke University Press, 1994, pp. 69–106.

PART II

EMPIRICAL MANIFESTATIONS
OF GOVERNANCE

7

Administrative Reforms and the Demand of Good Governance

Kuldeep Mathur

The shift from government to governance represents a new focus on the role of public administration. The new focus has emerged because the role of state itself has undergone a change. From the time of the beginning of the Plan period in India in 1951–2, public administration was looked upon as the main instrument of implementation of development policies. The Five Year Plans laid much store by the capability of bureaucracy to achieve development goals. Until the advent of economic reforms in 1991, bureaucracy bore the main burden of the failure of development policies but also attracted relentless efforts to reform it and transform it as a suitable instrument of Plan implementation. These efforts have not yielded results, and the country has entered the era of economic liberalization, with governance carrying the refrain of administrative reforms but in a different mould.

This time round, the context of reforms is different. The period beginning from 1991 is marked by the emergence of a liberal economic regime that is attempting to dismantle the centrally directed framework of economic development. It is also the beginning of the period when international multilateral agencies have begun attaching conditionalities while giving aid. These conditionalities initially were limited to prescriptions on how the aid would be administered but have gradually broadened their scope by suggesting reforms in the overall framework of governance itself. This is happening the world over. Reform is in the air and no country is left out of this global discourse. Changes in the intellectual climate that provided a new understanding of the role and scope of public administration propels this discourse while 'reinventing government' summarizes and celebrates this new understanding.

The purpose of this chapter is to examine the conceptual basis of administrative reform efforts undertaken in India and attempt to unravel their complexity. The argument is that there is more to the technical aspect of reform, and one has to take into account the ideological imperatives embedded in the reform effort. The first section attempts to locate public administration in the governance discourse and attempts to identify the kinds of models that are being employed to think of administration of the future. The second section is concerned with assessing the reform efforts in the past, and the final section critically explores the direction of current efforts and investigates the ideological underpinnings that lead to the acceptance or rejection of reforms.

PUBLIC ADMINISTRATION AND THE AGENDA OF GOVERNANCE

Much of the discussion of the new agenda of governance is set within the broader understanding of the previous activities of the state and the neo-liberal critique of it. The early liberal theorists took the feudal order, which was grounded in impositional claims about natural hierarchies and the organic whole, and recast it as a 'world of walls'. Church was divided from the state so that the latter could be shaped and governed according to the principles of liberalism and later democracy. The state was separated from the economy so that market could develop according to its laws of supply and demand. Such division helped develop rules and practices of state or public terrain different from those of the private. But as Bowles and Gintis (1986, 66) point out, the public-private partition is neither fixed, natural, nor obvious. Historically the boundaries have been drawn and redrawn. The Keynesian State asserted the primacy of the public over the 'invisible' hand of the market and engendered expectations that the state was responsible for meeting the basic needs of the citizens (Brodie 1996, 386). The current attempt tends to reverse this formulation and seeks to rearrange the public and private by shrinking the state and expanding the autonomy of the market. Civil society is seen as filling the gap of the withdrawal of the state, in promoting market as well as democracy.

The World Bank's construction of good governance starts from the rejection of the development models of the past. 'The post-independence development efforts failed', the World Bank (1989, 3) tells us, 'because the strategy was misconceived.' According to the bank, there is now 'a growing consensus' that these strategies 'pinned too much hope on rapid state-led industrialization.' State failures compounded development failures; private sector and individual initiatives were stifled, and institutions were set up that did not reflect a society's characteristics and culture. Good governance agenda, then, underlines the curbing of the role of state and expanding the space for market and competition. Competition is accepted as a powerful tool and essential dimension of economic, political, and social life. Competing for the efficient exploitation of natural resources and generation of new means to satisfy individual and collective needs at lower costs and higher quality is seen to have contributed greatly to the improvement of material and non-material levels of well-being. It is seen as the driving force behind technological innovation.

In extolling the virtues of the market and competition and in laying stress on past failures of the state, a good governance agenda virtually condemns the state for having suppressed the energies of a society. Because the state is an alien oppressor, the curtailment of state activities becomes a people-friendly, democratic venture, almost to the extent that state contraction or dissatisfaction is presented as synonymous with democratization (Abrahamsen 2000, 51). Its emphasis on civil society and its institutions have to be seen in this perspective of strengthening democracy and in constructing an informal sector that can harness people's entrepreneurship through community institutions and interpersonal relationships. In the good governance discourse, democracy emerges as the necessary political framework for successful economic development, and within this discourse, democracy and economic liberalism are conceptually linked: bad governance equals state intervention, good governance equals democracy and economic liberalism (Abrahamsen 2000, 51).

Civil society is seen as a source of vitality for both democracy and economic growth. Its institutions are a countervailing force that curbs authoritarian practices and corruption. They also create or strengthen associational organizations that provide such goods and services that can be furnished more efficiently than the state. The space left by a retreating state can be filled by such private initiatives and proliferation of associations that manage local resources or deliver basic services, which will in turn support the trend towards greater participation and democracy. This belief is nurtured by the contention that social organizations succeed because there is collaborative action based on trust, norms, and networks. It is these relationships popularized as social capital that builds capacity for participation and self-government. The argument is that associations help generate social capital that strengthens democracy and improves the efficiency of the markets.

In this agenda of good governance, the conceptualization of civil society proceeds on the assumption that power and exploitation is associated with the state while freedom and liberty fall in the realm of civil society. This leads to a kind of romantic view of civil society where the existence of institutions outside the state becomes a sufficient basis to assume that state power is curbed and greater democratization is taking place. It is in this perspective that the concept of civil society carries with it a notion of something worthy and of value. It is considered good in itself and its creation a worthy goal to be pursued. The ideologues of the Washington consensus helped the international donors and governments of the Third World shape an uncritical view of civil society and persuaded them to believe that it can be created though their aid and policies of support. As Eade (2000, 12) says, the view that 'civil society could do no wrong and there was nothing it could not do' was widely accepted among donor agencies. Non-governmental organizations sprang up like mushrooms, offering to strengthen civil society and as civil organizations in their own right. In many cases they claimed to speak on behalf of civil society at large. In the field of development, the role of NGOs was strengthened through donor aid and policies.

A kind of revolution occurred and the focus shifted from the control of bureaucracy and its pre-eminent role in the delivery of goods and services to increased privatization of government and shaping its role as an entrepreneur competing with other social groups and institutions to provide goods and services to the citizens. The book by Osborne and Gaebler, 'Reinventing Government' was a landmark in the growth of ideas that have sought to build a new public administration. Public administration was admonished to 'steer rather than row' for 'those who steer the boat have far more power than those who row it' (Osborne and Gaebler 1992, 32). Since then, these ideas have swept across the world, and the international/multilateral agencies have used them to influence public management of their economic-aid programmes. The common theme in the myriad applications of these ideas has been the use of market mechanisms and terminology, in which the relationship of public agencies and their customers is understood as based on self-interest, involving transactions similar to those occurring in the marketplace. Public managers are urged to steer not row their organizations and they are challenged to find new and innovative ways to achieve results or to privatize functions previously provided by government (Denhardt and Denhardt 2000, 550). In this new world view, the primary role of government is not merely to direct the actions of the public through regulation and decree, nor is it merely to establish a set of rules and incentives through which people will be guided in the proper direction. Rather, government becomes another player in the process of moving society in one direction or another. Where traditionally government has responded to needs by saying, 'yes, we can provide service' or 'no, we cannot', the new public service suggests that elected officials and public managers should respond to the requests of the citizens by saying, 'let us work together to figure out what we are going to do, and then make it happen' (Denhardt and Denhardt 2000, 554).

Operationally these ideas have advocated, (1) managerially oriented administration, (2) reducing public budgets, (3) downsizing the government, (4) selective privatization of public enterprises, (5) contracting-out of services, (6) decentralization, (7) transparency and accountability, and (8) emphasis on civil society institutions and non-governmental organizations to deliver goods and services. The discipline of public administration adopted these ideas in what has come to be known as new public management. Much of the distinction between the public and private sectors is being narrowed and multiple institutions are being forged to 'steer' society. The academic attention is shifting from a state-centric approach; the main research problem is to what extent the state has the capacity to 'steer', and how it relates to the interests of other influential actors. Within the discourse of governance, what were seen as indisputable roles of government are now increasingly seen as more common, generic, societal problems which can be resolved by not only political institutions but also by other actors (Pierre 2000).

THE EFFORT AT ADMINISTRATIVE
REFORM DURING THE PLAN PERIOD

The inability of national leadership to bring about change in the early 1950s set the old system of administration firmly in the saddle. Nehru, writing much before independence, had said, 'I am quite sure that no new order can be built up in India so long as the spirit of the ICS pervades our administration and our public services. That spirit of authoritarianism...cannot exist with freedom....Therefore, it seems essential that the ICS and similar services must disappear completely as such before we can start real work on a new order.' (Nehru 1953, 8). In the spring of 1964, Nehru was asked at a private meeting with some friends what he considered to be his greatest failure as India's first Prime Minister. He reportedly replied, 'I could not change the administration, it is still colonial administration' (quoted in Potter 1986, 2).

The emphasis on the schism between the old colonial administration and the new plan administration gained scholarly attention really after Paul Appleby, a Professor at Syracuse University, was invited by the Government of India to report on Indian administration. He expressed the view that there was a dichotomy between bureaucratic dispositions and development needs in India (Appleby 1953). Some Ford Foundation experts reinforced this view when they recalled their work in community development programmes, and commented that '...the inadequacies of the Indian bureaucracy are not due to the fact that it is bureaucracy but due to considerable fact that it carries too much baggage from the past.'(Taylor *et al.* 1966, 579) This view gained further support when scholars like La Palombara (1963, 1) wrote, 'Public Administration steeped in the tradition of the Indian Civil Service may be less useful as developmental administrators than those who are not so rigidly tied to the notions of bureaucratic status, hierarchy and impartiality'.

Simultaneously, the development administration movement was gaining momentum within the discipline of public administration. This thrust had several dimensions among which at least two dominated. One was of professionalization of administration through the acceptance of a management orientation. It was argued that management techniques and tools could be used successfully to improve the implementation of development programmes, and administrators must spend significant time and effort in learning these techniques and applying them. Improved education and training became the core efforts at professionalization.

Another dimension of this movement had to do with a change in the behavioural orientation of public administrators. This focus was aptly summed up by a leading contributor when he suggested that only by becoming less oligarchic, less technocratic, less stratified, closer to the administered and the managed, more deeply rooted in the aspirations and needs of the ordinary people, only by such changes can public service become a force with which the people of a developing country may identify and may have justified confidence (Gross 1974).

It was this message that the academics and consultants from the West, particularly the United States, brought to India, and through financial and technical aid influenced the theory and practice of public administration in the country. The Ford Foundation alone spent US $360,400 in grants to institutions and US $76,000 in providing consultants and specialists to improve public administration in India during 1951–62 (Braibanti 1965, 148). An important consequence of this financial and technical aid as well as the intellectual thrust of development administration was that it began to be believed that change in the colonial administrative system lies in changing the behaviour and the professional capacity of the individual bureaucrat. This was possible through education and training programmes. Training institutions proliferated and studies that supported this broad argument multiplied. A large number of scholars was attracted to the field of development administration, motivated not only by scholarly reasons but also by the belief that administration was the instrument of change and that administrative behaviour could be transformed without structural changes in the colonial administrative structure and procedure.

During the period from 1952–66, policies of administrative reform were heavily influenced by developments in the disciplinary understanding of public administration in the United States, and the perceptions of these academics and consultants of the problems of administration in developing countries like India. It was at the request of the Government of India that the Ford Foundation readily made available Professor Paul Appleby of Syracuse University to suggest changes in the administrative system in the country. He presented a report in 1953 that set the tone of much of what was done later. What is important to note is that until 1966, no other committee was appointed to have a broad look at administration. As a consequence of the Appleby report, Organization and Methods divisions were established in each government department to take care of the everyday issues of procedural efficiency. Another recommendation of Paul Appleby's to establish an Indian Institute of Public Administration was also accepted. This institute was supposed to take up reform measures on a continuous basis but based on research studies.

In operational terms, the effort at administrative reform during this period was based on education and training programmes for civil servants. The international aid was extensively utilized for this purpose. A large number of training institutions was established at both the central and state levels. The pattern of recruitment to the higher civil services was changed, and the training system was also reformed.

A comprehensive examination of the Indian administrative system was undertaken with the appointment of the Administrative Reforms Commission in 1966. It was patterned after the Hoover Commission of the US, having a political and civil servant membership with experts coming in to write reports after study and research. The commission worked over a period of four years making a total of 581 recommendations (Maheshwari 1993, 116). The impact of the commission was little felt, for no recommendations of consequence were accepted. The politicians who became members did not command prestige and influence with the government of the day. As a matter of fact, the government itself was in flux. Lal Bahadur Shastri, the Prime Minister, who had appointed the commission in 1965, suddenly died and Indira Gandhi took over. For the years up to 1971, she was fighting for her political survival, attending to crises and did not find time to reflect on administrative change. When the commission finished its tasks, the country was facing a war for the liberation of Bangladesh and subsequently was caught in the turmoil of national emergency. The ruling party was comfortable working with the existing administrative system and reforming it was not on the agenda of the political parties in opposition. The Administrative Reforms Commission just faded away, leaving behind a pile of reports and frustration at the national inability to reform a colonial administrative system.

If, during the early period of India's independence, administration was seen as an instrument of change, during the period after the Third Plan, 1961–6, it began to be seen as an impediment to development. Plan performance had been poor and the policy makers saw the lack of effective administration as a major contributing factor. As a matter of fact, in 1969, the Congress Party itself raised the issue of the inability of a neutral civil service to implement goals of development. It pleaded for a committed civil service. The question 'committed to what?' was left open. A fierce debate followed in which retired and serving bureaucrats participated freely (see Dubhashi 1971; Chaturvedi 1971; *Seminar* 1973). No formal change took place, but the practice of shifting bureaucrats on the demands of political leadership became a characteristic that is, even today, widely prevalent. During the period of emergency, loyalty became an important criterion for holding a pivotal position in government, and this was replicated when the Janata Party came to power defeating the Congress and Mrs Gandhi. The return of the Congress and defeat of the Janata Party in 1980 signalled the beginning of the process again. The practice has spawned what is colloquially known as the 'transfer industry', and the central government has begun to reflect what was confined to only the states. (Banik 2001). Formal acceptance of this idea would have transformed the role of the civil service, but this did not happen. What could not be formalized was openly accepted in practice.

FAILURE OF REFORM EFFORT

One possible reason that administrative reform failed to make a dent in the inherited administrative system was the weakness on the conceptual front. No alternative was offered. What was offered was ways to improve the existing system. And, these ways were too inconsequential. Intellectually, adherence to the Weberian model and Taylorian norms of work considerably constrained the generation of alternatives. Overwhelming academic response to administrative problems was through analyses of structural attributes that caused bottlenecks in coordination or communication, or of the behavioural irritants that led to friction either in a team of bureaucrats only or one of bureaucrats and politicians. The prescription was already decided and not questioned, and, therefore, when the problems persisted, the solution was to increase the dosage of further division of labour and specialization or tighten controls through improved lines of communication and authority.

The problem was that empirical insights did not reflect the dominant concerns in the intellectual study of public administration, where Weberian influences held the attention of most scholars who explained variations in administrative performance by examining issues of neutrality, training, and professionalism, structure of hierarchies and processes of work, and behavioural orientations. Another source of explanation was the emphasis on the abilities and qualities of an individual and the belief that it was an individual who made the difference whatever be the structural constraints. A development-oriented bureaucrat implemented programmes well in spite of the prevailing administrative system. The memoirs of the civil servants are replete with illustrations that show how they as individuals dealt with new political issue (see for a recent example, Dar 1999).

Little concern for administrative reform was expressed in the 1970s and later. The declaration of emergency pushed out concerns for long-term perspectives on reform, and made the bureaucracy subservient to political concerns. Severe indictment of the civil service was made by the Shah Commission of Inquiry, which reported that it carried out instructions from politicians and administrative heads on personal and political considerations. There were many instances where officers curried favour with politicians by doing what they thought the people in authority desired. In short, the evidence showed, as a journalist remarked, that '[the Emergency was] the high water-mark of the politicians' victory in the long-drawn-out struggle against the civil service' (quoted in Potter 1986, 157).

Over the decades, bureaucrats have emerged as a powerful component of the decision-making process in the country, as the political establishment was only too happy to abdicate its responsibility to concentrate more on matters that were political. In providing continuity to civil administration despite political turbulence, the civil service accumulated bureaucratic capital that it could use to stall changes that could make it more accountable to the public. However, it must be realised that the government writes the rulebook, which is only interpreted and applied by the bureaucrats. How much effort has gone into revising the rulebook? The rulebook provides the checks and balances in administration and lays down the administrative processes of decision making. It lays down, for example, how the departmental accounts and treasury accounts have to be matched so that discrepancies can be detected early; it lays down its frequency and identifies who has to do it. The ill-famous fodder scam is probably partly a product of the malfunctioning of this system. In spite of audit reports, little action is taken in this regard. For, the rulebook comes handy to the bureaucrat for stopping politicians in their tracks, and to the politicians for blaming the bureaucrats when not pliable. Handing over the responsibility of initiating administrative reform to the very people who stand to lose by it jeopardises the search for innovative solutions.

ADMINISTRATIVE REFORM IN THE ERA
OF ECONOMIC LIBERALIZATION

When India embarked upon an ambitious programme of economic reform in 1991, the ideas about public administration reform had already entered the package of aid that was promised by the World Bank and the IMF. It will be fair to say that they were reflecting a change in the disciplinary thrusts of public administration too. Country after country was deciding to change and reform their governments. There is little doubt that this change was being triggered off by the wave of policies of structural adjustment and liberalization prompted by a new globalization, which set in after the collapse of the Soviet Union. Thus, while administrative reforms are profoundly domestic issues, the fact that they are being seen as part of a package of the 'new deal' makes them open to external pressures and influences. Reform is stylish today. And for more than one reason. Technological changes are calling for managerial changes. Information technology with its computer base has caught the imagination of both administrators and politicians. Demands for greater decentralization are being met because of change in the political scenario. People's groups are becoming more aware of their rights and demanding improved government services that are transparent and accountable to them. This is apart from the influence that international financial agencies are exercising on government to reform to be eligible for more loan/aid and their directly funding NGOs to implement development programmes.

The effort at reducing the size of government began with successive budgets presented by the union finance minister from 1992. The imperative was to reduce fiscal deficit and cut down on unproductive expenditure. In a bid to bring about fiscal prudence and austerity, the centre imposed a 10 per cent cut across the board in the number of sanctioned posts as on 1 January 1992. The Fifth Pay Commission report contained a recommendation for a whopping one-third cut in government size in ten years. The downsizing exercise was later taken up by the Expenditure Commission, which further recommended a cut in the number of sanctioned posts as on 1 January 2000. As a matter of fact, instructions for cutting sanctioned posts were renewed in 2000, directing a 10 per cent reduction in the posts created between 1992–9 (Raina 2002). Statistics maintained by the Ministry of Finance show that the pay and allowances bill of the central government was Rs 33,977.79 crores for the year 1999–2000, showing a hike of Rs 31,560.19 crores over the previous year. The number of central government civilian regular employees was 38.55 lakhs on 1 March 2000, down from 39.07 lakhs on 31 March 1999. There had been a decrease of 51,605 posts, that is, just 1.32 per cent (Mishra 2002). As one can see, there has been very little impact from these efforts.

In 1996, a Chief Secretaries Conference reiterated the popular policy prescriptions for a responsive and effective administration. The conference recognised that the public image of the bureaucracy was one of inaccessibility, indifference, procedure orientation, poor quality and sluggishness, corruption proneness, and non-accountability for results (Government of India 1996, 1). The Fifth Pay Commission (Government of India 1997) took the concerns of the chief secretaries and listed, among many of its recommendations, the need to downsize the government and to bring about greater transparency and openness in government. In 1997, the Chief Ministers Conference endorsed measures for (1) making administration friendly and accountable, (2) ensuring transparency and right to information, and (3) improving the performance and integrity of the civil service.

A people's organization in Rajasthan, known as the Mazdoor Kisan Shakti Sangathan (MKSS) has been in the vanguard of this struggle and has forced the government to respond to the demands of information and accountability. As documented in Roy *et al.* (2001), the people began to understand that their livelihood, wages, and employment depended a great deal on the investments made by the government as a development agency. If these benefits were not coming, then they had the right to know where the investment had been made, and how much of it was actually spent. The right to economic well-being got translated into the right to information. As Roy *et al.* (1996) point out, the struggle became an issue of *'hamara paisa hamara hisab'*. In other words, accountability became a critical issue in the public hearings organized in five blocks of four districts. Four demands were made: transparency of development spending, accountability, sanctity of social audit, and redressal. This campaign began in 1994 and gradually gained momentum spreading to most parts of the state. It reached the level where assurances had to be provided by the Chief Minister.

The essence of the campaign that steamrollered into a movement for right to information was the *jan sunwai* (public hearing), where villagers assembled to testify whether the public works that had been met out of the expenditures certified by the government actually existed or not. The first jan sunwai was held in a village of Kot Kirana in 1994. Since then, they have caught the imagination of the MKSS, which has held them at several places. Beawar was the scene of a major event in April 1996. It was followed by a forty-day *dharna* in which activists were fed and sheltered by the public. Another fifty-three-day dharna was organized at Jaipur (see Bunker Roy, the *Asian Age* 30 May 2001). The Rajasthan government responded reluctantly but the Chief Minister ultimately announced that the people had the right to demand and receive details of expenditure on development works in their villages.

Three months after the event in Beawar, politicians, jurists, former bureaucrats, academics, and others joined in, demanding a right to information legislation at a conference in New Delhi. A committee under the chairmanship of Justice P.B. Sawant was authorized to draft a model bill. The central government, too, came under pressure to introduce the legislation in parliament, which could be followed by the states.

The Government of India set up a Working Group on Right to Information and Promotion of Open and Transparent Government in 1997. The terms of reference of the group included the examination of feasibility and need to introduce a full-fledged Right to Information Act so as to meet the needs of an open and responsive government. The working group placed its tasks within the broad framework of democracy and accountability and emphasized, 'democracy means choice and a sound and informed choice is possible only on the basis of knowledge'(*Working Group Report* 1997, 3). It also argued that transparency and openness in functioning have a cleansing effect on the operations of public agencies and approvingly quoted the saying that sunlight is the best disinfectant.

The working group accepted the following broad principles to the formulation of the legislation:

1. disclosure of information should be the rule and secrecy the exception; and the exceptions should be clearly defined; and
2. there should be an independent mechanism for adjudication of disputes between the citizens and public authorities.

With considerable public pressure but with reluctance from the government, the parliament finally enacted a Right to Information Act in 2005. But, the controversy about its scope and reach has not yet died down. The major contestation is about what can be revealed. The bureaucrats and the political leadership have been reluctant to make the file notings public. File notings are crucial information on the government's decision-making process, because these help track responses, identify who did what, when and why. While interpreting the act, the Department of Personnel and Training inferred that the file noting should not be made available to the public to maintain the sanctity of the decision-making process. The Ministry of Home Affairs issued an office memorandum on 25 November 2005 asking all its central information officers and the appellate authorities to comply with this interpretation. However, in a statement issued from the Prime Minister's Office, a distinction has now been made between notings that cannot be disclosed and 'substantive notings' that can be revealed. Substantive notings that can be disclosed include those on plans, schemes, programmes, and projects of the government related to development and social issues except those protected by certain exemption clauses. However, the Principal Information Officer appointed under the act, may withhold the individual identity of the functionary who has made the file noting (*The Hindu,* 2 December 2005, 1). The PM's office statement has come after the representation and protest of several citizen groups. The distinction in notings has not gone down well with the citizen groups, and the Commonwealth Human Rights Initiative, at the forefront of the RTI Act, was quick to criticize the PM's action on file notings (*The Times of India,* 2 December 2005, 1). The Convenor of the National campaign for People's Right to Information has also gone on record to say that this kind of distinction cannot be made by the PMO (*The Hindu,* 2 December 2005, 1).

In another assault on the spirit of the act, all the twelve chief information commissioners appointed so far under the act, whether at the centre or in the states, have turned out to be IAS officers, serving or retired (*The Times of India,* 5 December 2005, 1). In the bill introduced in December 2004 the eligibility was limited to experts of administration and governance. But, this category was expanded at the insistence of the National Advisory Council to eminent persons from fields beyond these specializations. The rationale behind this change was that an information commission packed with bureaucrats was unlikely to help change the mindset of bureaucracy and make it transparent in its functioning.

It is clear from the above that this dimension of administrative reform that stresses transparency and right to information is an issue that has been spearheaded by the people. It is not a change attempted by a well-meaning and benign government. However, the struggle is not enough yet to give teeth to the legislation passed by the parliament or the state legislatures. There has been resistance not only from political leaders, who swear by the name of democracy, but also from bureaucrats, whose norms of work had been dictated by secrecy and confidentiality. The Rajasthan experience has shown that even local-level administrators have found ways to thwart attempts at opening the administration closet to the people for scrutiny.

The citizen's right to information has been coupled with the idea of a citizen's charter. The aim of the charter is to make available to the citizen the information to demand accountability, transparency, quality, and choice of services by government departments. It was first introduced in Britain in 1991 to streamline administration and make it citizen-friendly. A core group has been set up under the Chairmanship of Secretary (Personnel) for monitoring the progress of initiatives taken by ministries/departments with a substantial public interface. So far, sixty-one charters have been formulated which include twenty-seven charters for public sector banks and four charters for hospitals (Agnihotri 2000, 126). For lack of effective monitoring, this has remained a paper exercise.

Another dimension of administrative reforms being undertaken is induced by information technology. The government has initiated a 'Minimum Agenda for Governance' for the use of information technology along with reengineering processes in government towards greater transparency, accountability, and speed (Singh 2005, 54–6) In the year 2002–3, a composite plan scheme to pilot projects in the following areas has been formulated:

1. Evaluation and benchmarking.
2. Application of information technology.
3. Research projects in administrative reforms.
4. Development of knowledge-management systems.
5. Assessment of quality in government.

The latest in the string of good intentions is the report of a core group on administrative reforms headed by the Cabinet Secretary and consisting of other top-level bureaucrats. Lowering the age of recruitment, weeding out of corrupt civil servants after a number of years of service, and rewarding meritorious officers are some of the suggestions that have been made. Tinkering with the age of recruitment has been a political problem and not an administrative question. There was little administrative justification in the change that occurred earlier. If identification of corrupt officers could be so easy as to be done through a cabinet fiat, it could have been done many seasons ago. It must be recalled that even the rationalization of the transfer process has not taken place in spite of proposals for establishing civil service boards, etc. In many cases the ruling politicians have wrested the authoritative initiative from the official hierarchy to stall changes; in other cases the official hierarchy has acted as a barrier to any political initiative to bring about reform. What has happened is that change is expected from the same group that has much to lose if the change occurs.

CHALLENGES AHEAD

In the last two decades, the story of administration as an impediment to development has taken a drastic turn. If the beginning of the Plan period saw an effort to strengthen state intervention as a recipe for triggering development, the 1980s ended with disastrous accounts of failures of regulatory and interventionist states and with strong pleas to dismantle state machinery and its roles. Neo-liberal economic theory tended to build its case on how rulers extract resources and invest them. It argued that rulers in interventionist states tend to use resources for their own benefit to the detriment of the development of their societies. The argument of state failure was based on how monopoly rents are created through the imposition of regulation and control of the economy. Political pressures dominate economic policy formulation and execution. A consequence of this system is that government machinery is used for personal interests. The policy recommendation that follows from this diagnosis is to minimize state intervention and to rely increasingly on markets for resource-use and allocation.

Weber had contended that bureaucratic organization was the manifestation of rationality and a powerful mechanism to bring about efficiency. Well-laid-down formal rules, hierarchy, and obedience to rule of law ensured that individual bureaucrats would respond with rational behaviour and work for public interest. It is this formulation that is not being accepted in the new agenda of administrative reforms. Administrative reform is becoming an exploration of alternative strategies for privatizing the public sector. However, the ideological argument of privatization leading to efficiency has not necessarily captured the Indian public opinion. Modern capitalists in India have to contend with prejudices and images that portray them as heartless moneylenders, or greedy merchants, or powerful social exploiters. Profit is perceived as an ill-gotten gain at the expense of the consumer, or the labourer, or society and not as a source of capital accumulation for investment. The celebration of entrepreneurship and that of creating private wealth is a recent phenomenon associated with economic reforms and globalization.

What this illustrates is that the role of the state has to be defined in a way that reflects Indian realities. In a society that has a multiplicity of inequalities and disparities, institutions that can work for inclusion not for exclusion have to be identified and made effective. In this endeavour, the role of the state cannot be put in the same perspective as the new dogma of new public management puts it. There is no one single answer for all countries.

The reforms that have been initiated in the form of right to information are an attempt to make the ruling classes more accountable and not an indictment of the administration per se. The demand is for an effective administration. Thus, if government schools do not perform well, the demand is to make them perform better and not for privatization of education. This is the crux of the problem. Within the neo-liberal agenda, administrative reforms are being undertaken on the assumption that privatization is the only method of bringing about efficiency and effectiveness in the delivery of public services. However, most market-based solutions to public sector dysfunction are very controversial and not politically possible in most jurisdictions (Fukuyama 2004, 80). It is one thing to talk about the privatization of public sector activities like state-owned airlines, telecommunication, or oil business, and another of education, health, or municipal services. The performance of public services has varied in India. Those services that are urban based and responsive to the needs of the rich and the powerful seem to perform better. Within the education sector, primary schools or primary health-care centres have been losers for lack of funds, professionals, and accountability. Privatization is not necessarily the answer to the dysfunction in providing primary education and health services to the rural poor and the marginalized.

In the present endeavour of administrative reforms, little attention is being paid to the ways of improving delivery services: attention is on changing ownership. The central problem that many public services face is that of over-centralization. Discretion is not delegated; school decisions are taken far removed from the scene of activity. Monitoring systems are not in place and resources are not available for even the minimum activities to be performed.

Administrative reform in India finds an echo in the formulation that public service reform is highly complicated and emotional. It is bound up with ideology and values, not with just techniques and processes, and includes not mere detail but key societal issues. (Caiden and Sundaram 2004). In this sense administrative reform is politics and requires political action.

Select References

Abrahamsen, Rita, *Disciplining Democracy Development Discourse and Good Governance in Africa*, London: Zed Books, 2000.

Agnihotri, Vivek K. 'Government of India's Measures for Administrative Reforms', in *Reforming Administration in India*, Vinod Mehta (ed.), New Delhi: Indian Council of Social Science Research and Har Anand Publications, 2000.

Banik, 'The Transfer Raj: Indian Civil Servants on the Move', the *European Journal Development Research*, 13 (1), June 2001, pp.106–34.

Bowles, S. and Gintis Bowles, *Democracy and Capitalism* London: Routledge and Kegan Paul, 1986.

Braibanti, Ralph, 'Transnational Inducement of Administrative Reform', in *Approaches to Development, Politics and Change*, J.D. Montgomery, and W.J. Siffin (eds), New York: McGraw-Hill, 1965.

Brodie, Janine, 'New State Forms New Political Spaces', in *States Against Markets: The Limits of Globalisation*, Robert Boyer, and Daniel Drache (eds), London: Routledge and Kegan Paul, 1996.

Caiden, Gerald E., and P. Sundaram, 'The Specificity of Public Service Reform', *Public Administration and Development*, 24, 2004, pp. 373–83.

Chaturvedi, M.K. 'Commitment in Civil Service', *Indian Journal of Public Administration*, xvii (1), 1971, pp. 40–6.

Dar, R.K. (ed.), *Governance and the IAS In Search of Resilience*, New Delhi: Tata McGraw Hill, 1999.

Denhardt, Robert B., and J.V. Denhardt 'The New Public Service: Serving rather than Steering', *Public Administration Review*, 60 (6) November/December, 2000.

Dubhashi, P.R., 'Committed Bureaucracy', *Indian Journal of Public Administration*, xvii (1), 1971, pp. 33–9.

Eade, Deborah, Preface in *Development, NGOs, and Civil Society Selected Essays from Development in Practice*, Oxford: An Oxfam Publication, 2000.

Fukuyama, Francis, *State Building Governance and World Order in the Twenty-First Century*, London: Profile Books, 2004.

Government of India, Chief Secretatries Conference on Administration, ' *Action Plan for Effective and Responsive Administration*', statement issued at the Chief Ministers Conference, New Delhi, 1996.

———, *Report of the Working Group on Right to Information and Promotion of Open and Transparent*, New Delhi: GOI, 1997.

Gross, P.M. 'The Limits of Development Administration', in *United Nations, Proceedings of the Inter-Regional Seminar on Organization and Administration of Development and Planning Agencies*, New York: United Nations, 1974.

La Palombara, J. (ed.), *Bureaucracy and Political Development,* Princeton: Princeton University Press, 1963.

Maheshwari, S.R., *Administrative Reform in India,* Delhi: Jawahar Publishers, 1993.

Mishra, D., 'Quality Government for Sound Economy', *Hindustan Times,* 8 February 2002.

Nehru, Jawaharlal, *An Autobiography,* Oxford: Oxford University Press, 1953.

Osborne, D. and T. Gaebler, *Reinventing Government: How the Entrepreneurial Spirit is Transforming the Public Sector,* New York: Penguin, 1992.

Pierre, Jon (ed.), *Debating Governance: Authority, Steering, and Democracy,* Oxford: Oxford University Press, 2000.

Potter, David C., *India's Political Administrators 1919–1983,* Oxford: Clarendon Press, 1986.

Raina, Jay, 'Downsizing May be Uphill Task', the *Hindustan Times,* New Delhi, 2002.

Roy, Aruna, Nikhil Dey, and Shanker Singh, 'Demanding Accountability', *Seminar* April 2001.

Seminar 1973 July, whole issue.

Taylor, Carl, *et al., India's Roots of Democracy* New York: Praeger, 1966.

World Bank, *Sub-Saharan Africa: From Crisis to Sustainable Growth,* Washington, DC: World Bank, 1989.

8

Good Governance and Administrative Reforms in India

Bidyut Chakrabarty

Discussion on administrative reform is generally confined to changes in bureaucracy. Administrative theories are therefore attempts at conceptually grappling with the phenomenon of change in civil service. In the Wilsonian theoretical construct, administration is a technical task that is separate from politics. The promise of a 'science' of administration has been premised on the autonomous nature of administration as a tool or means for translating political objectives into practical reality. Purity of administration as differentiated functions received great intellectual support from Weber's concept of rational bureaucracy. The structural features and the behavioural norms implicit in a bureaucratic form of organization, as conceived by Weber, contributed to the growth of public administration as a fairly autonomous institution bound by rigorous rules and uncontaminated by irrational forces. The idealized concept of bureaucracy as it came to be accepted in the West has, according to La Palombara, a number of 'behavioural and attitudinal norms that can be added to what has already been said about Weberian bureaucracy'.[1] These can be identified as: (1) limited instrumental role in rule making, (2) free and open interaction with a plurality of voluntary associations, (3) maintenance of separate identity and position while dealing with organized voluntary associations, (4) acceptance of electoral sovereignty and recognition of the legitimate role of the elected leaders to specify what is or is not in the public interests, (5) honesty and integrity of public administrators in the performance of their functions, and

(6) acceptance of and loyalty to the administrative and political system of which administrators constitute an integral part. These characteristics are contrary to the Weberian norms of anonymity, impartiality, and neutrality. Anonymity means that the civil servant advises the politicians from behind the scenes and will never be exposed to the din and fury of politics. Impartiality stands for the quality of the civil servant to act without bias irrespective of the social pressures and variations in the nature of clients. Neutrality is a kind of political sterilization, the bureaucracy remaining unaffected by the changes in the flow of politics. The civil servant has been axiomatically considered as politically neutral. By implication, there might be changes in political leadership but the civil servants will be unfailingly offering technical advice to the political master keeping himself/herself aloof from the politics of the day. The bureaucracy has thus been portrayed as a universal and permanent institution uncontaminated by the frailties and frivolities of politics. Such an image of bureaucracy is, however, far from true. As a recent study of British bureaucracy has shown, civil servants in Britain tend to substitute the politician's role in preparing legislation. This is attributed to the fact that ministers typically know relatively little about the law even if they are interested. Perhaps the biggest danger for democracy, Page therefore argues, is not a civil service putting forward a proposal which a minister feels forced to accept, 'but rather that ministers do not notice or fully appreciate what is being proposed in their name despite having political authority to change it'.[2] Hence, despite the proclaimed non-political characteristics of bureaucracy, the role of civil servants in preparing legislation is far more important than is generally assumed.

The appointment of the Fifth Pay Commission in 1994 by the Government of India is significant for two important reasons: (1) this is a pay commission which undertakes the exercise when globalization seems to have influenced, if not shaped, human life to a significant extent; and (2) there is no doubt that the governance paradigm (which is clearly an antithesis to the state-directed development model) provides a critical reference point to civil service reform in most of the developing countries seeking loans from international agencies. The primary goal of civil service is, as the commission identifies, to 'understand customer needs'. Based on this basic concern, the mission statement [3] of the commission thus runs as follows:

1. clarify the goals of the organization in the mind of the management,
2. clarify for staff the purpose of their jobs in meeting the organizational goals,
3. make clear the policy of the government to ensure that it is interpreted accurately by staff,
4. engender pride in belonging to the organization, and
5. provide targets to aim for, against which results can be assessed.

The aim of this chapter is twofold: first, the focus is to identify the sociological roots of the Fifth Pay Commission that came into existence following the adoption of the 1991 New Economic Policy in India, and second, to evaluate whether the recommendations are merely contextual, independent of the neo-liberal directions of the global forces, or are clearly dictated by the so-called international actors devoid, largely, if not entirely, of national roots.

GLOBALIZATION AND ADMINISTRATIVE CHANGE

Issues arising out of globalization have dramatically changed the nature and scope of public administration. No longer confined to the analysis of the structure of administration, the government has to respond to the challenges of the 'new economic order' that appeared to have decisively influenced, if not determined, public administration. In the context of globalization, national economies are becoming more and more 'open' and subject to supranational economic influences. As economies lose their discrete, self-contained character and become enmeshed in global networks and processes, they become less and less amenable to national control and management. In a nutshell, the ideology and practice of globalization privileges voluntarism and the market as the underpinnings of the new economic order.[4] The role of the state as the sole responsible agent for providing welfare services is being challenged. The state, it is believed, should be a facilitator rather than a provider because 'any attempt to combine Government with "doing" on a large scale paralyses the decision-making capacity. Any attempt to have decision making organs actually do, also means very poor doing. They are not focused on doing. They are not equipped for it. They are not fundamentally concerned with it'.[5] Government is thus to steer and not row. Hence, government is not required to get involved in delivering services which amounts to rowing. This is a foundational assumption on which the governance paradigm rests, as a World Bank note stipulates by underlining that

civil service reform involves revamping government functions and organizational structures, improving human resource policies in central, local and sector governments, revising the legal and regulatory framework for public administration, providing institutional support for government decentralization, and managing the process through which these changes are implemented.[6]

Unlike the traditional public administration that focuses on bureaucracy and delivery of 'public' services, the governance model envisages public managers as 'entrepreneurs' of a new, leaner, and increasingly privatized government adapting to the practices and values of private businesses. Seeking to transform civil services, the neo-liberal governance ideology underlines reforms to (1) reorganize and downsize the government, (2) set up performance-based organization, (3) adopt private sector management practices, and (4) promote customer-orientation of administration.[7] The governance approach emphasizes 'three dimensions of civil service reform: institutional environment, economic management and pay/incentive systems' as they affect performance'.[8] These three dimensions are interlinked. Institutional environment is indicative of 'the mission of the state', especially its ideological preferences, whereby the state defines its relationship with the private sectors, non-governmental organizations, and other professional and community associations. Economic management dwells on 'the quality of the core economic management functions' of the polity such as budget and financial management and policy management. The importance of pay/incentive system is obvious because of two valid reasons: (1) by providing attractive pay packages, one can make the civil service a most sought-after profession; and (2) a satisfied civil service is perhaps the best guarantee for the better delivery of services. There is no doubt that these three dimensional characteristics of civil service reform are drawn on a realistic assessment of the processes of administrative reform in any concrete situation. The reform package needs to take into account the administrative profile of the country in question, which means both the institutional and economic environments. A patrimonial bureaucracy is, for instance, always partisan and thus resistant to Weberian normative values. Ignorant of this dimension, no reform package will yield results and the exercise *à la* civil service reform will remain merely academic. Therefore, better pay and incentives may not be an effective device unless the institutional environment is also tuned to appreciate 'the neutral' character of civil service.

Public administration today reflects, in large part, the changing nature of the practice of governments especially in the developed world. The practices of traditional public administration have been increasingly under attack from neo-liberal economists, interest-group theorists, and rational-choice scholars, who have provided the intellectual inputs to the politicians determined to reduce the size and scope of the public sector. This is scarcely surprising since the theoretical changes have tended to emphasize the significant extent to which public administration is political and is part of the overall process of determining 'who gets what'. Approaches to administration are also embedded in wider conceptions of the state, the relationship between state and market and of citizenship. Changes in the ideological climate are, therefore, likely to have a decisive impact on public administration. Management in the public domain should rather be, as the argument goes, 'designed to support and express the political processes that govern that domain'.[9] Within such a theoretical conceptualization, civil society—as a sphere of association between state, on the one hand, and family and kin groups, on the other—acquires massive significance. Not only has civil society become integral to good governance, it has also replaced the centrality of state in governance. This fits in perfectly well with the growing popularity of neo-liberal ideas where 'states are identified as inherently predatory, bureaucrats inevitably rent-seekers, and politicians always venal pursuers of power-in-order-to-secure-profits. [T]hen the notion that "citizens" could so much better look after themselves through association in civil society, was of course immensely attractive'.[10]

ADMINISTRATIVE REFORMS IN INDIA

Turning to the 'reforms' scenario in India, one has to run through a long period of bureaucratic ups and downs since the advent of colonial rule. During imperial rule, the core purpose of administration was to bolster up colonialism where people's interests were absolutely peripheral if not entirely absent.[11] Hence administrative reforms had, for obvious reason, a single priority of perpetuating British rule.[12] With independence, the nature and spirit of administration were bound to be radically different, since its moral foundation had undergone dramatic changes. Indian historical experience, both during the British period and its immediate aftermath, has led to the emergence of a public administration that was ill-suited to the needs and aspirations of the people. The reasons are not difficult to seek, as studies have shown that the bureaucrats who have been brought up and trained in the colonial administrative culture are wedded to the Weberian characteristics of hierarchy, status, and rigidity of rules and regulations and concerned mainly with the enforcement of and order and collection of revenues. For the colonial regime, this structure was most appropriate, but it is completely unfit to discharge the functions in the changed environment of an administration geared to the task of development. As the government becomes the main institution for development in the democratic set-up that India adopted following independence, the role of the officials has undergone changes. Their sole objective is to 'emphasize results, rather than procedures, teamwork rather than hierarchy and status, [and] flexibility and decentralization rather control and authority'.[13] Seen as 'the development administrator', the bureaucrat is therefore characterized by 'tact, pragmatism, dynamism, flexibility, adaptability to any situation and willingness to take rapid, ad-hoc decisions without worrying too much about procedures and protocol'.[14]

Following independence, government functions have also expanded in scope and content. With the introduction of the parliamentary form of government and the setting up of people's institutions right down to the village level, there has been an inevitable rise in the level of expectations and performance. People's institutions were set up with the objective of creating self-governing institutions at the village level. A true democracy as advocated by Mahatma Gandhi ensures that local, state, and national representatives are accountable to the people for local, state, and national matters, respectively, through effective transparency. Such one-to-one accountability may promote responsible politics and attract competent professionals and social workers to politics. The objective remains distant. Our present system based on diffused accountability, as mentioned in the consultation paper of the National Commission for Review of the Working of the Constitution, 'breeds corruption and attracts self-seekers to politics'. For this breed, the paper further underlines, 'interests of national development, welfare of the people and needs of good governance take lower priorities, if any'.[15] Similarly, independence and Five Year Plans were perceived by people as synonymous with economic and social equity and well-being, and freedom from want and oppression. In the early days of the planning era people did not crib much about shortages, which they confronted with fortitude, because the future held hope and promise for them. With the passage of time, they felt their hopes were 'belied' and they were 'no where near the promised land of honesty, plenty and happiness'. The ethos of self-governance, decentralization, and community development were flagged off with considerable élan and fanfare. For example, the three-tier panchayati raj system and the urban local bodies were conceived of as a properly meshed network of institutions to accelerate the development process.[16] The recent Seventy-Third and Seventy-Fourth Amendments (1992) to the Constitution seek to advance the concept of 'self-governance' by providing for, (1) regular elections, (2) minimal suppression of panchayati raj bodies through an administrative fiat, and (3) regular finances through statutory distribution by state finance commissions. The aim, argues Kuldeep Mathur, 'is to reduce the margin of political and administrative discretion and to allow the decentralised institutions to gather strength on the basis of people's involvement'.[17] But, owing to various reasons, the political process became what may be termed as 'reversed' and highly centralized and personalized systems of government developed both at the central and state levels. There has been a massive erosion of institutions, whether they are the parliament and parliamentary institutions, or the party system and democratic procedures in the running of parties, or the judiciary, or indeed the press. Describing the crisis and erosion of institutions as 'the natural and expected consequences of a political process that has undermined both the role and authority of basic institutions',[18] Rajni Kothari has sought to grapple with this peculiar reality in which public administration appears to be largely de-linked from the basic institutions of a democratic system that has flourished in India following Independence.[19]

It is obvious that even before the onset of liberalization, several measures were adopted to revitalize the administration that owe its origin to completely different socio-economic concerns where reforms were largely internally generated while post-liberalization efforts are mostly externally driven. There has been a clear shift towards a reduced role for the government in all countries. In the words of the Fifth Pay Commission, 'Thatcherism in UK and Reaganomics in USA tried to pull out the State from the morass of over-involvement. The decline of Communism in Eastern Europe has furthered the trend towards economic liberalization and disinvestment in public sector enterprises'.[20] Thus, the impetus for reducing the role of government came from outside, as the commission admits by mentioning that 'India could not have remained unaffected by these global trends'.[21] What was however most critical in the entire process was 'the deep economic crisis of 1991 which pushed [India] on to a new path of development, [which meant that] Government should confine itself primarily to the core functions that cannot be performed by the market. Everything else must be left to the private initiative'.[22] As evident, the Fifth Pay Commission clearly articulates 'a new path of development', underlining the reduced role of the government. Critical of 'the over-involvement' of government, the commission demarcates certain 'core functions' for the government, keeping aside a wide range of functions for private enterprises. Conceptualizing government within the governance paradigm, the commission also seeks to negotiate with the neo-liberal thrust in public administration and accordingly suggests 'reform packages' to adapt civil services in India to the changed milieu. The government retreats giving space to private operators for discharging functions which it performed traditionally for 'public well-being'. By redefining the role of government, the commission seems to have equipped the state to keep pace with the changes in an interdependent world.

In view of the above well-directed designs for civil service reform, the recommendations of the Fifth Pay Commission are another milestone in this direction. True to the spirit, expressed in the 1996 Chief Secretaries Conference, the Fifth Pay Commission has recommended: (1) downsizing the government through corporatization of activities which involves 'manufacturing of goods or the provision of commercial services'; (2) transparency, openness and economy in government operation through 'privatization of activities where government does not need to play a direct role' and also 'contracting-out of services which can be conveniently outsourced to the private sector';[23] and (3) contractual appointment in selected areas of operations 'for the purpose of maintaining a certain flexibility in staffing both for lateral entry of experts, moderating the numbers deployed depending on the exigencies of work and ensuring availability of most competent and committed personnel for certain sensitive/specialized jobs.'[24]

The central government has been advised to go for a 30 per cent reduction in the strength of the civil services, as the pay commission felt that it would be unwise to let the government sector continue as 'an island of inefficiency' and 'inertia'. The normal procedure of voluntary retirement after completing twenty years should be continued. Alongside this, the commission recommended a special scheme of voluntary retirement in the departments where surplus manpower has been identified. In such cases, there should be a provision for selective retirement of persons, the initiative always resting with the government and for 'a golden handshake'.

The other significant recommendation of the commission is concerned with 'openness' in administration. Defending the repeal of 'the Official Secrets Act of the old colonial days', the commission insists on openness which 'means giving everyone the right to have access to information about the various decisions taken by the Government and the reasoning behind them'.[25] Except for what is detrimental to the interests of the nation, the security of the state, or its commercial, economic, and other strategic interests, which may not be made public, 'nothing should be held back just to subserve the interests of individual bureaucrats and politicians'.[26] Every important government decision involving 'a shift in policy' should invariably be accompanied by a White Paper 'in the nature of an explanatory memorandum'. As an integral part of civil service reform, the commission insisted on the formation of an efficient grievance redressal machinery '[that] has to be effective, speedy, objective, readily accessible and easy to operate'.[27] Drawing upon the examples of Canada, UK, and Malaysia where effective grievance redressal cells have been functioning efficiently, the idea of a citizen's charter—defining the rights of the customers of government schemes and services—was mooted by the commission. The recognition by the commission of the citizen's right to information and the procedures suggested in this connection are of seminal importance from the point of de-bureaucratizing government and making it citizen-friendly. The issues, raised by the pay commission figured prominently in the 1997 Conference of Chief Ministers where an action plan was adopted to, (1) make the administration accountable and citizen-friendly, (2) ensure transparency and right to information, and (3) adopt measures to cleanse and motivate civil services.[28]

CONCLUDING OBSERVATIONS

The Fifth Pay Commission is a watershed in the evolution of India's civil service for a variety of reasons. This is not a pay commission in the ordinary sense of the term since it has also sought to reshape the bureaucracy in the light of the emerging global trends, especially after the collapse of the Soviet system. By suggesting significant changes in the administrative hierarchy, the commission translates into reality the drive towards 'de-bureaucratization'. There are two immediate consequences: (1) it draws our attention away from the 'steel-frame' to other agencies which are equally crucial in 'public service', but have not been recognized so far formally. In this sense, the commission provides a powerful critique of Weberian bureaucracy that is strictly hierarchical and largely 'status-quoist'; (2) by recognizing the importance of civil society organizations in public administration, the commission provides a formal recognition to a space of cooperation between governmental bureaucracy and these organizations. Such cooperation was discouraged presumably because of 'the sanctity' of the governmental domain in which the state bureaucracy appears to be 'the only legitimate agency' in discharging responsibilities on behalf of the state. Underlining the importance of agencies, not exactly linked with government and its peripheral organizations, the Fifth Pay Commission has not only redefined Indian bureaucracy but has also expanded its sphere of influence by seeking to involve various non-governmental agencies, the role of which was never recognized under traditional theories of public administration.

The Fifth Pay Commission is also a significant comment on the nature of Indian administration that has a clear colonial hangover. Critical of hierarchical Weberian administration, the commission is, clearly, favourably disposed towards 'decentralized' administration that provides room for organizations which are not exactly within the government. In structural terms, decentralized administration underlines the importance of various layers of the decision-making process. What cripples public administration in postcolonial India is, as the World Bank document underlines, 'overregulation', which is both 'a cause and an effect of bloated public employment and the surest route to corruption'.[29] Apart from 'contracting-out of the state', the World Bank suggests several specific measures to 'motivate' the civil servants 'through a combination of mechanisms to encourage internal competition'.[30] That the pay commission's recommendations have not been accepted *in toto* by the Government of India clearly suggests that the Indian response to the governance-initiated civil service reforms is a guarded one. In India's planned economy, the role that the civil service has discharged is that of 'a regulator' and not 'a facilitator'. And, yet, civil service was not severely challenged presumably because of its structural requirement in governance. The mood does not appear to have changed radically in the context of an interconnected global order. This can perhaps be linked with India's response to globalization, which is equally tempered by her peculiar socio-economic and political circumstances. Hence two contrasting scenes are visible: on the one hand, there are evidences of a growing free market in India though the Indian state is, on the other hand, still very interventionist and the Indian economy is still relatively closed to external goods, finance, and investors. The policy trend is thus 'better interpreted as a rightward drift in which the embrace of the state and business continues to grow warmer, leaving many others out in the cold'.[31]

Irrespective of whether the recommendations of the Fifth Pay Commission are rightward drifts or not, the fact remains that it has drawn on the neo-liberal theoretical thrust towards globalization. Accepting that bureaucracy in the developing countries tends to be 'rent-seekers', the commission has raised issues which are pertinent in redefining its role in the changed environment of governance. What is sadly missing is the context in which the recommendations are to be implemented. India is perhaps a unique example showing a peculiar combination of roles in public bureaucracy that has a distinct colonial flavour due to its obvious historical roots. Structured in the Weberian mould, Indian bureaucracy, however, reinvented its role and character following the adoption of the state-directed planned economy. Now, governance offers new challenges and the Fifth Pay Commission, by seeking to reorient the Indian civil service, is responding to these challenges. Given the historical nature of Indian bureaucracy, most of the recommendations of the commission may not be appropriate and thus not worthwhile. Nonetheless, there is no doubt that the commission has played a historical role in the sense that its has drawn our attention to the weaknesses of a well-entrenched bureaucracy and also the advantages of critically assessing its utility in the globalization-inspired social, economic, and political circumstances. In some sense, the Fifth Pay Commission brings back the Wilsonian dichotomy between politics and administration in which administration is defined as an unalloyed technical exercise. Whether there is a conclusive resolution of this debate which had its roots in the 1887 article by Woodrow Wilson[32] is debatable. However, one can confidently argue that administration without politics (denoting values or ideologies) is like a fish without water. Administration is a guided action. Hence values seem to be critical in its articulation and manifestation. The Fifth Pay Commission does not seem to have paid adequate attention to this dimension of civil service reform. Instead, it has generally endorsed the ideal of governance in its recommendations. There is no doubt that the recommendations of the pay commission are historical in the sense that they approximate the neo-liberal values; they are ahistorical as well, because they are non-contextual responses to an environment where globalization continues to remain, for valid socio-economic and political reasons, an anathema.

Notes

[1] Joseph La Palombara, 'Bureaucracy and Political Development: Notes, Queries and Dilemmas', in *Bureaucracy and Political Development*, Joseph La Palombara (ed.), Princeton: Princeton University Press: 1963, p. 17.

[2] Edward Page, 'The Civil Servant as Legislators: Law Making in British Administration', *Public Administration*, 81 (4), 2003, pp. 651–79.

[3] Government of India, *The Report of the Fifth Central Pay Commission*, vol. 1, New Delhi: Government of India, 1997, p. 117.

[4] For details, see Gerald Caiden, 'Globalizing the Theory and Practice of Public Administration', in *Public Administration in the Global Village*, Jean-Claude Gracia-Zemor, and Renu Khator (eds), West Port, CT: Praeger, 1994, pp. 49–59.

[5] David Osborne, and Ted Gaebler, *Reinventing Government: How the Entrepreneurial Spirit is Transforming the Public Sector*, New Delhi: Prentice Hall of India, 1992, p. 32.

[6] The World Bank, *PREM (Poverty Reduction and Economic Management) Notes on Public Sector*, October 1999, no. 31, p. 1.

[7] I have drawn on Namrata Singh, *The Salary Structure of Higher Civil Servants in India—an Empirical Study of Fifth Pay Commission*, unpublished PhD dissertation, University of Mumbai, 2003, pp. 128–31.

[8] S. K. Das, *Civil Service Reform and Structural Adjustment*, Delhi: Oxford University Press, 1998, p. 49.

[9] Stewart Ranson and John Stewart, *Management for the Public Domain: Enabling the Learning Society*, New York: St. Martin Press, 1994, p. ix. Critical of privatization, Stewart and Stewart argue that 'the distortion that could result from inappropriate application of the private sector model was the introduction of marketing approaches which treated the public solely as customer, ignoring the public as citizen and the reality that many services in the public domain are rationed according to criteria of need rather than supplied according to demand at a given price'.

[10] John Harriss, *Depoliticizing Development: The World Bank and Social Capital*, New Delhi: Leftworld Books, 2001, p. 114.

[11] Despite its obvious anti-people character, the British rule is, as an insider views, significant in creating 'an incomparable instrument for government, a civil service, minutely just, inflexible upright, well enough paid to be above corruption, independent and confident because assured of a career that could only be interrupted by gross misconduct. This instrument was forged by the East India Company long before Whitehall possessed anything of the kind....The administration in India...was controlled by a cadre of district officers, rigorously picked, but trained almost wholly by doing what in fact they are learning to do. What was most creditable was the fact that few administrations can have ruled so many with so slight use of force. Everything was done through Indians and by Indians to whom power was delegated'. Philip Mason, *The Men who Ruled India*, Calcutta: Rupa, 1997, pp. 345–6.

[12] For a critical discussion of administrative reform under the British rule, see Sumit Sarkar, *Modern India, 1885–1947*, New Delhi: Macmillan, 1983, pp. 102–4. While commenting on Curzon's administration, Sarkar

argues that what made Curzon's administration ultimately so significant was in fact 'his consistent hostility towards the educated Indian aspirations as represented by the Congress, along with a not unrelented determination to strengthen, streamline and enforce the authority of the Raj', p. 104.

[13] Anil Bhatt, 'Colonial Bureaucratic Culture and Development Administration: Portrait of an Old-Fashioned Indian Bureaucrat', *Journal of Commonwealth and Comparative Politics*, 17 (3), 1979, p. 259.

[14] Ibid., p. 281.

[15] *Review of Election Law, Processes and Reform Options* (a consultation paper), 'National Commission to Review the Working of the Constitution', New Delhi, (no date), p. 19. There is no way in which this defect can be done away with within the system of indirect democracy, as practised in India. As this consultation paper further states, 'the elected representative is too far removed from the people as there are an average of one million voters for each Lok Sabha constituency spread over a large geographical area. To influence the choice of such a large and geographically dispersed number of voters, social action on the part of the candidate is totally inadequate. And, this creates space and scope for using both money and muscle power. It is no surprise therefore that the candidates have to spend huge amounts of money at the time of campaigns to "purchase" the votes of these distant voters. And, this is done mostly through a host of intermediary brokers who became the link in this transaction. These huge election expenses breed huge corruption. This also means that the electors are in no position to hold the candidate accountable nor does the candidate consider himself/herself accountable to the people'....To counter this, Gandhi had, for instance, 'advocated a low-expense election system linked with watchdog councils and separate elected chief executives at each local level' (19–20).

[16] For an interesting, though slightly dated account of the panchayati system in West Bengal, Uttar Pradesh, and Karnataka, see Atul Kohli, *The State and Poverty in India; the Politics of Reform*, Cambridge: Cambridge University Press, 1987; and for studies of urban government of Delhi, see Ajoy K. Mehra, *The Politics of Urban Development: A Study of Old Delhi*, New Delhi: Sage, 1991.

[17] Kuldeep Mathur, 'Strengthening Bureaucracy: State and Development in India', *Indian Social Science Review*, 1 (1), January–June 1999, p. 22. According to Mathur, '[t]he success of the Seventy-Third and Seventy-Fourth Amendments making decentralised structures part of the Constitution has yet to be seen-not only because they were only instituted in 1993, but also because the states have shown little evidence of implementing the requirement through their own statutes'.

[18] Rajni Kothari, *State Against Democracy: In Search of Human Governance*, Delhi: Ajanta, 1988, p. 287.

[19] The process, known as 'deinstitutionalization' invariably leads to a non-policy government that 'operates by means of spoils and preferments that take into account the particular situations of persons and communities'. Very common in Sub-Saharan Africa, 'such government tends to be "private government" both in the sense that government offices are treated as private property and in the sense that spoils, unlike policies, must be managed in a discreet and even clandestine fashion. They cannot be advertised, nor can they be publicly debated'. See Goran Hyden, 'Democratization and Administration' in *Democracy's Victory and Crisis* (Nobel symposium no. 93), Axel Hadenius (ed.), Cambridge: Cambridge UniversityPress, 1997, p. 252.

[20] Government of India, *Report of the Fifth Central Pay Commission*, vol. 1, New Delhi: Government of India Press, January 1997, p. 95.

[21] Ibid.

[22] Ibid., pp. 95–6.

[23] Ibid., pp. 122–3.

[24] Ibid., p. 175.

[25] Ibid., p. 150.

[26] Ibid., p. 151.

[27] Ibid., p. 157.

[28] *The Times of India,* 25 May 1997. For details of the recommendations, see *Annual Reports, 1997–98*, Ministry of Personnel, Public Grievances and Pensions, New Delhi, 1998, pp. 65–9.

[29] World Bank, 'The State in a Changing World', *The World Development Report* (summary), Washington, DC: World Bank, 1997, p. 14.

[30] According to the 1997 *World Development Report* (summary), there are three ways in which civil service can be radically reformed: (1) a recruitment system based on merit, not favouritism; (2) a merit-based internal promotion system, and (3) adequate compensation. 'The State in a Changing World', p. 9.

[31] Atul Kohli, *State-Directed Development: Political Power and Industrialization in the Global Periphery*, Cambridge: Cambridge University Press, 2004, p. 285.

[32] Woodrow Wilson, 'The Study of Administration', *Political Science Quarterly*, June 1887, pp. 197–222.

9

E-Government

Building a SMART Administration for India's States*

Subhash C. Bhatnagar

Everything about information technology in India is characterized by both hype and substance; so is the case with e-government. E-government is at an early stage of implementation, with just three or four Indian states having built a few service delivery applications. However, e-government applications are expected to grow in scope and also to cover more states. E-government represents a win-win situation for all stakeholders: the private sector gets new markets, governments increase efficiency and effectiveness, and the citizens get more convenient services with greater transparency and less corruption. Some states have already reaped these benefits. Andhra Pradesh has successfully sold the idea of building a Simple, Moral, Accountable, Responsive, and Transparent (SMART) government to its employees and citizens. In this chapter, lessons are drawn from Andhra Pradesh's strategy and experience, and a few challenges that lie ahead are outlined.

WHAT IS E-GOVERNMENT?

E-government is about a process of reform in the way governments work, share information, and deliver services to internal and external

* Originally published as 'E-Government: Building a SMART Administration for India's States', in Stephen Howes, Ashok K. Lahiri, and Nicholas Stern (eds), *State-level Reforms in India: Towards More Effective Government*, New Delhi: Macmillan India Ltd., 2003, pp. 256–66.

clients. Specifically, e-government harnesses information and communication technologies (ICT), such as the internet, the web, and mobile phones, to deliver information and services to citizens and businesses. As a first step, information about services is published on a website and citizens can interact with the site to download application forms for a variety of services. The next stage involves the use of ICT in the actual delivery of services, such as filing a tax return, or renewing a licence. More sophisticated applications can process on-line payments.

In developed countries, these services are offered in a self-service mode through internet portals that become a single point of interaction for the citizen to receive services from a large number of departments. In developing countries, on-line service counters may operate in a department, offering services related only to that department. In more evolved models, citizen service centres have been created at convenient locations where citizens can access on-line services of several departments. Departmental or private operators operate these counters; citizens do not directly interact with computer screens. Collection of payment is often handled through conventional means. In addition to such service centres, citizens may also be able to access service delivery portals.

Perhaps e-government is different from earlier fads, as one of its foundations is a truly discontinuous innovation in technology: the marriage, polygamous as it were, of the internet, the web, and mobile computing. It rests not only on the vendor/consultant push, as these groups stand to benefit from higher investments in hardware and consultancy, but also on a growing demand for better services from citizens, who now experience vastly improved services from the private sector. The benefits of a changed way of doing things accrue to all stakeholders: citizens businesses, and government employees. The biggest barrier is change management. The developed world continues to be concerned with issues of security and privacy of information; in the developing world these issues are less important. However, the necessary infrastructure is not always in place.

INTEREST IN E-GOVERNMENT: WHY DEVELOPING COUNTRIES SEEK ON-LINE SUCCESS?

Interest in e-government within developing countries is growing. During the last decade, many countries have gone through a process of economic liberalization and economic growth. Many large countries like India and China have grown at 6 to 10 per cent over the last decade. This growth has created a large middle class, which has begun to demand improvements in the quality of products and services. In some areas where the private sector has developed e-commerce, citizens are already experiencing a significant improvement in service levels, leading them to expect governments to use the same technologies to achieve systematic improvements in service delivery. Consequently, the citizens are, in fact, asking the government to go on-line.

The spread of the internet in the urban areas of many developing countries is beginning to create a critical mass, not as considerable as in most developed countries, but large enough to lead the government to deliver services on-line. In the large and highly urbanized countries in Latin America or Asia, it has become possible to deliver these services on-line. In some places where e-government has been introduced, it has shown that it can work and have a wide impact on government efficiency and effectiveness. E-government pilots have demonstrated a positive impact on corruption, transparency, and quality of service. In fact, these early successes have spurred competition between states and countries to go on-line.

These successes are also a source of pride. Some countries believe that through early adoption of emerging technologies, they can leapfrog to more effective governance and administration. To illustrate, Brazilians take pride in the fact that their recently launched electronic voting system is better than the existing system in the United States. Another example is from Gujarat in India, where the transport department has pioneered the use of driving licences based on smart cards.

E-GOVERNMENT APPLICATIONS IN INDIA: TAKING STOCK

India is well poised to explore the use of information technology (IT) to improve governanace.[1] The factors that support such an initiative are:

1. its mature IT industry, which had a turnover of $15 billion and growth of 40 per cent in 2001;

2. the federal government's commitment to making India an IT superpower (the centre and most state governments have a minister for IT);
3. a cyber legislation in place; and
4. a growing telecom and networking infrastructure.

Some state governments, such as those of Andhra Pradesh, Karnataka, Kerala, and Gujarat, have built a few applications on an extensive scale, covering the delivery of specific services to a large proportion of their population. Other states are also in the process of experimenting with some pilot applications. Within the central government, certain departments, notably customs and excise, have taken the lead. A very large number of government departments publish information on websites, though, by and large, these sites are neither well designed nor updated and do not own responsibility for the quality of information available on them. Initially, this effort was targeted at attracting foreign investments; however, as internet penetration grows in urban areas, many sites focus on delivering information and services to citizens and businesses.

India is a leader among developing countries in e-government. Amongst the twenty-five cases on e-government on the World Bank website, thirteen are from India. These include those dealing with delivery of services to urban and rural citizens, tax collection from businesses, and websites focusing on promoting transparency and reducing corruption. E-government applications have been used in India for e-procurement, tax collection, processing licence applications, sharing budget/expenditure information, and sharing information across departments. Citizens have benefited in service delivery through convenient service delivery locations and significant reduction in service delivery time. Now a driving licence is issued in two to three hours instead of days, and real-estate-property sale is registered in half a day instead of the two weeks required earlier. Often, so-called 'speed money' to hasten the manual process had to be paid earlier, as the operators could delay the processing of an application. Now, with automation of the processes, there are fewer opportunities for officers to obstruct the process, and corruption has actually been reduced.

Models of service delivery, different to those found in developed countries, are being explored. Unlike the self-service model, where citizens interact with a portal, most applications in India deliver on-line services at public kiosks, where government or private sector employees interact with citizens and computer screens to process transactions.

BENEFITS DELIVERED BY E-GOVERNMENT APPLICATIONS

The types of benefits demonstrated by e-government applications in India are:

1. greater convenience to citizens in transactions dealing with the government;
2. increased transparency in the work of the government, and lower levels of corruptions;
3. a significant increase in the collection of revenue; and
4. the empowerment of rural communities.

Some specific illustrations are discussed below.

ON-LINE DELIVERY SERVICE: INCREASED
TRANSPARENCY AND LESS CORRUPTION

Land registration offices throughout Andhra Pradesh now operate computerized counters to help citizens to complete registration requirements within an hour, instead of the several days needed under the earlier system. The lack of transparency in property valuation in the earlier system resulted in a flourishing business for brokers and middlemen, leading to corruption. Antiquated procedures, such as manual copying and indexing of documents, and storage in paper form in ill-maintained backrooms, have all been replaced.[2]

By computerizing ten interstate checkposts in Gujarat, the state government has trebled the collection of fines from overloaded trucks and taken away from the inspectors the incentive for seeking transfer to 'lucrative' posts. The departmental inspectors at these checkposts were notoriously corrupt and this led to the harassment of truck drivers and loss of revenue to the state. An enlightened political executive and a technology-savvy administrator was able to implement an on-line system in which each truck is weighed on an electronic weighbridge. The base data is retrieved from a database, and fines and taxes due to the government are automatically calculated and printed out. This has reduced corruption and significantly increased revenue.[3] However, a recent evaluation of the project suggests that corruption is back even though the revenue collection continues to be at the increased level.

The Indian customs department has put into operation the Indian Customs Electronic Data Interchange System (ICEDIS) in five air cargo units, eight seaports, and three internal container departments. A cargo-handling agent can now file an electronic bill of entry from his or her own premises or service centres, specifically created for this purpose away from the customs office. The bill of entry is processed on-line at different workstations. Acknowledgement, queries, and status are delivered at the service centre, and responses are also input here. The system provides a check on misrepresentation of data, or wrong interpretation of rules. Under-reporting of value, for example, can be detected through a detailed audit, which compares cost data declared by different companies for the same product across different ports. The system has led to greater transparency, less corruption, and quicker processing of transactions.[4]

As part of its initiative to bring the benefits of IT to citizens, the Andhra Pradesh government has implemented the Twin Cities Network Services (TWINS) project, which provides a one-stop government-to-citizens (G2C) interface for several services to the citizens of Secundrabad-Hyderabad twin cities with a combined population of four million. Department functionaries interact with citizens to deliver a variety of services, such as the payment of utility bills, the issue of birth/death certificates and the issue of driving licences. The centre handles 3,000 transactions a day of which 80 per cent involve the payment of utility bills. The investment on the pilot project was $2 million, including hardware, software, networking, training, and site preparation. The project has been renamed as e-Seva and has been extended to eighteen other locations through partnership with the private sector.[5]

The Vijaywada On-line Information Centre (VOICE) delivers municipal services, such as building approvals and birth and death certificates, and handles the collection of property, water, and sewerage taxes in seven kiosks located close to the citizens in the city of Vijaywada (AP), which has a population of a million. The back-end processes in the municipal corporation were reengineered, computerized, and linked to the kiosks through a wide area network.

The application had reduced corruption, made access to services more convenient, and improved the finances of the municipal corporation.[6]

Independent audits have revealed that in many of the above examples, corruption had been reduced, but not rooted out completely,[7] suggesting that e-governance on its own may not be able to eliminate corruption. In processes where rent is extracted by delaying a process or by denial, complaints can be generated from the aggrieved groups provided there is honesty at the top. Citizens can be encouraged to provide feedback on service, and filing complaints can be made easier through appropriately designed websites. Delivery of services through IT-based systems can reduce the opportunities to cause delay. It is important to automate the complete process to take away any opportunity for a manual override. Less complex and more explicit rules can reduce any wrong interpretation of rules. If the rules are completely unambiguous, a software can apply the rule and a person can authorize it. An automatic system can be developed to formally document any use of judgement or override.

The biggest problem in tackling corruption is its widespread acceptance as a way of life. Corrupt people enjoy social acceptance and even admiration. A huge effort is required to safeguard fundamental values like honesty. In a bold initiative, the Central Vigilance Commission in India has created a website to share with citizens a large amount of information related to corruption, in an effort to propagate the idea of zero tolerance of corruption. The site published the names of officers from the elite administrative and revenue services, against whom investigations had been ordered or penalties imposed in cases of corruption. Here, the web has been used to shame the corrupt officials. The performance of investigating agencies is also presented on the website. The site attempts to raise consciousness and involve citizens in the fight against corruption. Such efforts have to be supported by the media, which needs to tap into such information sources and disseminate the information widely.[8]

EMPOWERMENT AND TACKLING POVERTY

In many developing countries, the poor people are alienated from the government, in part because there is very little contact between the government and them. In two states of India, an experiment is being conducted for using the internet to share development plans with the community: for example, the number of schools that are going to be built in a particular local community, their location, and learning programmes. Initially, rural people are seldom interested in accessing this information, but once the media, the non-government organizations, and grassroots organizations pick up, circulate, and publicize it, a community discussion is generated. When governments begin to involve the people in the process by cross-sharing information with them, delivering services to them, and then having them comment on the development plans proposed for the future, a beginning is made towards e-democracy.

The Gyandoot project in Madhya Pradesh attempts to reach out to citizens through privately run kiosks, where citizens can lodge a complaint, seek information on the prices of agricultural commodities, or apply for some government services. A large number of people have used these services at a cost of Rs 10 per transaction.[9] In an experiment in the Panchmahal district of Gujarat, the district administration has created a portal, which publishes data on rural schemes that can benefit the poor. It also publishes data on the performance of key departments, permits download of about a hundred forms, accepts a few of these on-line, and shares information on developmental projects. Both the above experiments empower the citizens by providing access to information.[10]

Alleviation of poverty through e-government is a difficult goal to achieve, because it would assume that e-government reaches the poor. Telecom infrastructure in rural India is inadequate and the poor do not have access to the net. Nevertheless, e-government still has a huge potential impact. Milk production in India would serve as a befitting example.

India has become the largest milk producer in the world, and that has largely happened because the cooperative sector is now able to collect the milk at the doorstep of the milk producer. Twice a day, 365 days a year, people come and deposit milk at rural collection centres. In 3,000 such locations, where computers are now being used to process the transaction of buying and selling of milk, a great impact has been made. This is because, earlier, people were not paid the proper amount for the milk as payment depends on the fat content of the milk.

Since the fat content could not be measured immediately, there was a great deal of corruption at these collection centres: milk was pooled and tested afterward, and producers were not paid the right amount for the fat content. Now, in the computerized system, a plastic card identifies the seller to the computer, the milk is weighed electronically, and the fat content is measured and displayed in half a minute through a semi-automated system. The weight and fat content information is transferred to a personal computer, which immediately prints out the amount due, and it is paid out. Thus, both efficiency and transparency have been greatly improved, and even the small producers are receiving their due. Moreover, milk producers are not experimenting with some pilot initiatives, by being connected through the internet to a 'dairy portal', where they can access information on how to improve their productivity, or recognize if their cattle suffers from a disease. A dairy unit can interact with its collection centre through the system, providing many services, including veterinary assistance and artificial insemination services.[11]

In this case, knowledge and information have directly benefited the rural communities and have had an impact on poverty alleviation. Another way to impact rural poverty is to enable the rural people to use e-commerce, which can give greater opportunity to smaller producers to sell to distant markets, to know the market prices, have better negotiating power, and sell their products to alternative distribution chains.

PROFILING A PIONEER: ANDHRA PRADESH

The state government in Andhra Pradesh adopted e-government very early. It has a well-documented strategy[12] guiding the entire effort. It has succeeded in selling the idea of building a SMART government to its employees and citizens. The success of some of its large-scale applications have been recognized nationally.

A key element of AP's strategy is to pilot applications that are likely to have high impact through state funding. After implementing the applications successfully at the pilot site, the private sector is invited to participate in the roll-out to other locations. In the case of TWINS, for example, two private sector vendors have bid for the roll-out of the pilot to nineteen other locations. The entire investment in hardware, software, and networking will be borne by the vendors.

The government will provide the sites suitably remodelled to serve as a TWINS centre. All the operational expenses will be borne by the vendor except for the salaries of the counter staff, which will consist of government employees drawn from different departments. The vendor will be reimbursed a fixed transaction-based fee. A bidding process was held to get the lowest quotation of fee.

By creating suitable media coverage of the e-governance applications developed in AP, the AP government has acquired an image of a leader and innovator in IT applications. This image enables them to attract vendors for partnering their future endeavours. The vendors are willing to bend backwards to associate with the AP government in the hope of generating business elsewhere in the country. Thus, the AP government is able to use its first-mover advantage to drive bargains with the vendors, which other state governments may not be in a position to do.

In applications involving interfacing with citizens, the private sector has an opportunity to earn additional revenue streams by providing value-added services to citizens who come to pay utility bills at the TWINS centres. The government encourages its private partners to offer services, such as the collection of insurance premium, bus and train reservations, and so on, for which a transaction fee could be collected from the citizens.

In applications where the above model does not work, the government has invited bids from the private sector to Build, Operate, and Transfer (BOT). Thus, for handling the on-line issue of vehicle registration and driving licences in the Fully Automated Services of Transport (FAST) project, when no private vendor was willing to put up the investment on a transaction-fee model, the alternative BOT model was tried. In this model a fixed fee is provided to the vendor to create the infrastructure and maintain it over a three-year period. At the end of this period the entire infrastructure is bought back by the government at a depreciated price of 5 to 10 per cent. Almost all the applications implemented so far have focused on improving the interface with the citizens. However, with the exception of the computerization of Mandal revenue offices and the rural centres of the Computer-aided Administration of Registration Department (CARD), most of the other applications serve a largely urban population.

The Chenna Reddy Institute, the apex training institution for the state civil service, plays a pivotal role in the government reform process in AP. The institute has created a good computing infrastructure to provide hands-on training to government staff. It hopes to build sophisticated administration applications at the institute. These applications would serve to demonstrate the potential of IT to the trainees who come to the centre. The training centre now focuses on programmes for the highest level of political and civil service executives. These programmes are designed to have a problem solving focus, so that reform ideas are not just discussed but also acted upon. In many ways, the institute is working as a think tank for the process of reforms in the state. Significantly, coupled with the enthusiasm of the central team leading the IT effort, there is the push from the Chief Minister in the form of monthly monitoring of departmental performance. This monitoring not only reviews the IT initiatives but also demands analysis from departments, which can only be provided efficiently through computer systems. Thus, the importance of information and analysis are emphasized.

Early successes in the state were based on aware and enthusiastic civil servants acting as champions of reform. The AP government has recognized the importance of educating its senior civil servants to design and execute e-government projects. It spent Rs 70 million on a four-and-a-half-month training programme designed by the Indian Institute of Management, Ahmedabad, to train twenty officers to function as chief information officers. The programme covered a wide array of interdisciplinary topics, such as technology assessment, process reengineering, change management, information analysis, and project management. The programme was offered as a sandwich of classroom training alternated with hands-on project work.

The successful strategy of AP highlights the importance of:

1. leadership by elected executives;
2. clearly articulated programmes for on-line service delivery, focusing on measurable benefits;
3. developing a mature IT infrastructure and back-office use;
4. building an administrative culture oriented to service; and
5. the presence of strong in-house project management skills.

The AP government understood that it did not have either the finances or the skills to undertake an ambitious e-government programme, and therefore, relied heavily on building a partnership with the private sector.

THE CHALLENGES AHEAD

In the last decades, organizations have tended to try out several management movements to bring in incremental change, such as management by objectives, zero-based budgeting, decentralization, rightsizing, and reinventing government. However, almost all of these movements have failed to deliver their full promise. Will e-government turn out to be yet another buzzword, or can it truly transform governments in their dealings with different stakeholders?

The experience so far has been somewhat encouraging. In isolated pockets, innovative e-government applications have already been implemented. However, the real challenge is for it to have a wide-scale impact. Making e-government widespread entails bridging the digital divide, enabling access to the internet in rural areas and setting up information kiosks. Except for a few political leaders and civil servants who believe in the idea of reform and who have initiated innovative applications, the vast majority is yet to awaken to the potential of e-government for reform. A major task is to build institutional capacity for governance reform. Whereas some of India's state governments have reengineered administrative processes to improve service-delivery time, reduce corruption, and increase transparency, others appear to be more interested in only appearing to be modernizing, while making only half-hearted attempts to reform government functioning.

A large number of sceptics still need to be convinced that investments in IT are as essential as in other forms of infrastructure. What really seems to be missing, in both e-government and e-commerce, is documented research on the impact created by these initiatives on economic development. The information is largely anecdotal, with no clear pointers to whether the benefits are commensurate with the costs.

E-government comprises alignment of IT infrastructures, business processes, and service content towards the provision of high-quality and value-added e-services to citizens and businesses.

Ubiquitous e-government services require the relaxation of time, place, and other accessibility constraints, as well as compliance with architectural principles, such as true one-stop services and life-event orientation. Critical issues arise with respect to:

1. prioritization and pilot scoping of e-government services projects,
2. exploitation of multi-device/multi-channel access technologies,
3. reengineering and security of back-end IT infrastructures, and
4. evaluation of operational schemes.

A significant amount of training inputs would be necessary in all of these areas. Training packages would have to be developed for senior levels of bureaucracy and political executives, on the potential and challenges of implementing e-government. More substantive training programmes will be needed to train the chief information officers and project leaders who will implement specific projects. Also, funding assistance is needed to build internet infrastructure, procure e-government solutions, and get customized software developed to implement e-government applications.

Many of the applications developed in India may not be seen as true e-government applications, as some part of the service delivery (particularly the processing of payments) is not electronic. The delivery model is not self-service, and applications requiring inter-departmental coordination are still not on-line. However, the applications have delivered significant benefits to all stakeholders, and that is what should provide the incentive to go ahead. No developing country is likely to be fully ready to embrace a comprehensive programme of e-government. Still, in many areas, applications can be developed which e-enable a large part of the transactions and deliver significant benefits. Rather than wait for complete readiness, an approach of learning by trial is recommended. Benefits need to be articulated in detailed terms. Finally, the underlying concern for those who implement e-government applications must be the impact of e-government initiatives on transparency, corruption, and poverty.

Notes

[1] 'National Task Force on IT and Software Development'. Available online at: htttp://www.it-taskforce.nic.in.

[2] S.C. Bhatnagar, 'Land/Property Registration in Andhra Pradesh', World Bank, Washington, DC, 2000. Available online at: http://www1.worldbank.org/publicsector/egov/cardcs.htm.

[3] S.C. Bhatnagar, 'Computerized Interstate Check Posts in Gujarat', World Bank, Washington, DC, 2000. Available online at: http://www1.worldbank.org/publicsector/egov/cardcs.htm.

[4] V. Venkata Rao, 'EDI at New Customs House, Indira Gandhi International Airport, New Delhi', Unregistered case, Indian Institute of Management, Ahmedabad.

[5] V. Venkata Rao, K.V. Ramani, and Rajul Asthana, 'TWINS Project, Andhra Pradesh', Registered case (IIMA/CISG-62), Indian Institute of Management, Ahmedabad, 2000.

[6] S.C. Bhatnagar, and Arvind Kumar, 'VOICE: Online Delivery of Municipal Services in Vijaywada, India', World Bank, Washington, DC, 2001.

[7] Suresh Balakrishnan, 'Information Technology in Public Administration: Andhra Pradesh', Public Affairs Centre, Bangalore, 2001.

[8] N. Vittal, 'E-Development Enabling Communities to Shape Their Future: The Indian Perspective', Paper presented in E-Development Symposium, Harvard University, 19–20 October 2000; also, 'Central Vigilance Commission Website: A Bold Anticorruption Experiment', World Bank, Washington, DC, 2001. Available on: http://www1.worldbank.org/publicsector/egov/cvc_cs.htm.

[9] S.C. Bhatnagar, and Nitesh Vyas, 'Gyandoot: Community-Owned Rural Internet Kiosks', World Bank, Washington, DC, 2001. Available on: http://www1.worldbank.org/publicsector/egov/gyandootcs.htm.

[10] 'Citizens Services Portal (2001)', Centre for Electronic Governance, Indian Institute of Management, Ahmedabad. Available on: http://202.41.76.161:8080/godhra/.

[11] S.C. Bhatnagar, 'Empowering Diary Farmers through a Dairy Information and Services Kiosk'. World Bank, Washington, DC, 2000. Available on: http://www1.worldbank.org/publicsector/egov/gyandootcs.htm.

[12] Available on: http://www.andhrapradesh.com/.

10

New Regulatory Institutions in India
White Knights or Trojan Horses?*[1]

Saugata Bhattacharya and Urjit R. Patel

INTRODUCTION

The onset of liberalization in India in the early 1990s was the result of the internal fiscal and balance of payments crises, as much as the on-going process is of international experiences and global competition. The increasing reliance on market forces and price signals have altered the risk profile of economic activity and heightened the prospects of market failures. Independent economic regulators were gradually established to deal with the anticipated abuse of market power by private producers in inherently monopolistic sectors, and to contain the increasingly decentralized and complex transactions in the capital markets leading to risks, which lead to a systemic collapse.

Regulatory institutions have to be understood and evaluated in the context of the market structures prevalent in the industry at the time of their constitution. This section is, therefore, an extension of the previous one. Each segment describes the evolution of markets since the late 1980s and their current state.

There are two segments in India now that have active independent regulators—the financial sector and infrastructure

* Originally prepared for a Conference at Harvard University in February 2001; subsequenty published as 'New Regulatory Institutions in India: White Knights or Trojan Horses?', in Devesh Kapur and Pratap Bhanu Mehta (eds), *Public Institutions in India: Performance and Design*, New Delhi: Oxford University Press, 2005, pp. 406–56.

utilities. Prominent among the former are SEBI and the Insurance Regulatory and Development Authority (IRDA).[2] There are on-going discussions about an Indian Pensions Authority. A number of regulators now oversee infrastructure sectors—Central Electricity Regulatory Commission (CERC), various State Electricity Regulatory Commissions (SERCs), Telecom Regulatory Authority of India (TRAI), and Tariff Authority for Major Ports (TAMP). Other sector regulators, like a proposed Civil Aviation Authority of India (CAAI) and an oil and gas regulator are on the anvil. These institutions have been effective in varying degrees and have transformed the landscape of the sectors under their respective ambits by activist actions or sustained chipping away of the current logjam of institutional barriers and market power of (public sector) incumbents.

The new regulatory commissions are different from those appointed in the past, like the Tariff Commission, Forwards Markets Commission, even the Disinvestment Commission. These were mostly advisory in nature, or restrictive in nature, implementing centrally planned outcomes. There were other statutory bodies like the Company Law Board, Board of Industrial and Financial Reconstruction (BIFR), Debt Recovery Tribunal, and Income Tax Appellate Tribunal, which are quasi-judicial in nature and have the power to enforce their decisions.

The first statutory independent regulatory commission was SEBI, established in January 1992. The first regulator for infrastructure utilities was the Orissa ERC, established in 1996. This was followed by TRAI in 1997 and TAMP. CERC was established in 1998, and, at last count, there are fourteen states with their own ERCs. Before this, publicly owned monopolies operating infrastructure utilities were 'regulated' either by themselves or some other arm of government. The Ministry of Finance, the Department of Company Affairs (DCA), and the RBI, besides the individual stock exchanges, were the regulators in the financial sector. The Department of Telecom (DoT) was the regulator in the telecom sector under the Indian Telegraphic Act (1885) and the India Wireless Telegraphic Act (1933). The State Electricity Boards (SEBs) and the Central Electricity Authority (CEA) were the electricity regulators under the Electricity Supply Act (1948) and the India Electricity Act (1910). The Directorate General (Shipping) at the centre and respective state governments were the port regulators under the Indian Ports Act (1908) and the Major Ports Trusts Act (1963).

Most regulators came into existence after the reform process was underway. SEBI is the only regulator (apart from the fledgling IRDA) that was set-up co-terminously with the restructuring of the market. The scope and functions of the regulators also differ widely across sectors. Independent regulators do not make policy—that is the domain of government—but they do formulate the rules of the game and the conditions for a level playing field for the players in their respective sectors. TRAI has been mandated to regulate the sector as a whole. The CERC has licensing powers for interstate transmission of electricity.[3] The next section summarizes the institutional features of selected regulators.

SELECTED REGULATORY INSTITUTIONS IN INDIA

Telecom Regulatory Authority of India (TRAI)

The most controversial and visible of all infrastructure regulators in India, the current TRAI is the second avatar, the first having been disbanded in January 2000. The TRAI (Amendment) Ordinance came into force on 24 January 2000, ironically the last day of the third year of the first TRAI, splitting the erstwhile institution into a regulator and an adjudicator. The Department of Telecom (DoT) in its erstwhile combined policy-maker-operator-licensor role had created the (previous) independent TRAI in March 1997, when the TRAI Bill was passed, only after its earlier intention to have an administrative-authority regulatory office within the DoT itself was frustrated by the Indian parliament in 1995–6. The DoT took an adversarial stand. Almost every order of the TRAI was questioned and taken to the courts. The TRAI was finally terminated in late 1999 and reconstituted in 2000.

The TRAI Amendment Ordinance 2000 reconstituted the erstwhile regulatory body into two—the regulator TRAI, and a dispute redressal and adjudicatory body, the Telecom Dispute Settlement and Appellate Tribunal (TDSAT). The Amendment separated the functions of the new TRAI into three operationally distinct areas: (1) a set of recommendatory roles, (2) a set of binding roles, and (3) tariff setting functions.

ELECTRICITY REGULATORY COMMISSIONS (ERCs)

There are now fourteen State Electricity Regulatory Commissions (SERCs) besides the Central ERC. The Orissa ERC is the oldest, established in 1996, and the CERC was created in 1998, through the ERC Act. The central commission regulates bulk electricity tariffs up to the boundaries of states and interstate transmission tariffs. The CERC also has powers to license private investment in transmission, with the consent of the public sector, Power Grid Corporation of India Ltd (PGCIL), which is a state monopoly. Tariffs for generation, transmission, distribution within a state, as well as purchase and supply, are regulated by the respective SERC. It is also a mandate for CERC to develop a competitive market for bulk electricity.

TARIFF AUTHORITY FOR MAJOR PORTS (TAMP)

As in the other sectors, an anticipated shortage of capacity in ports and a paucity of public funds was expected to result in severe bottlenecks in an area deemed in the 1990s to be critical to India's growth—exports. Private participation and investment was, therefore, considered essential.

To address the concerns of private operators of discriminatory treatment and charges by the incumbent Port Trusts, a port regulator—TAMP—was established in 1997. With the Port Laws (Amendment) Act in April 1997, which repealed significant portions of the Major Port Trusts Act (1963), TAMP was vested with powers of fixing tariffs. There are now terminals, jetties, and other services being provided by major international port operators in many of the major ports. In the meantime, many private and public industrial enterprises, sensing the difficulty of ensuring timely movement of their freight cargoes through the major ports, decided to set-up their own ports and specialized terminals. Intra- and inter-port competition is expected to increase rapidly (Patel and Bhattacharya 2000).

TAMP's purview is the most limited amongst the infrastructure regulators in India—it only has a tariff-setting role and is not a sector regulator in any sense of the term. Its functions include framing scales of rates and conditions under which services can be provided by the individual port authorities, determine rates of lease of port property, and fix fees for pilotage and other services. It has no jurisdiction over the minor and private ports. TAMP, moreover, has no provision for enforcement of its orders, including powers to summon data or persons and to prescribe time limits for compliance of orders, as well as penal powers. The government (the Ministry of Surface Transport) is the appellate body for TAMP's decisions.

In an environment of increasing competition and market-based pricing, there is a real danger that TAMP's functioning is self-perpetuating, and actually becomes an obstacle to competitive pressures. Tariff fixation, moreover, still continues to be cost-based with an assured rate of return. Recommendations for a statutory levy of fees to be collected from major ports to make TAMP financially autonomous will only serve to increase port charges. An expansion of its role in coordinating the activities of various port-related organizations like the Port Trusts, Customs, Container Corporation of India (CONCOR), and Central Warehousing Corporation (CWC) with a view to reduce charges is redundant and can be achieved more efficiently through market forces.

SECURITIES AND EXCHANGE BOARD OF INDIA (SEBI)

One of the earliest legislations for the securities market in India was the Capital Issues (Control) Act of 1947. The Government of India formulated a draft Bill for Stock Exchanges in 1951, which was submitted to the A.D. Gorwala Committee for further discussions and sharpening. It submitted the Securities Contracts (Regulation) (SC(R)) Bill in 1954. The SC(R) Act was enacted in 1956, followed by a set of SC(R) Rules. The Companies Act was also enacted in 1956 to administer the setting up and composition of commercial firms. First set-up, in April 1988, as an advisory body, SEBI did not have statutory status for three years. Its interim functions were:

1. Collecting information and advising the government on matters relating to stock exchanges and capital markets.
2. Licensing and regulation of merchant banks, mutual funds, etc.
3. Preparing legal drafts for the regulatory and development role of SEBI.
4. Performing any other functions as may be entrusted by the government.

The Pherwani High Level Group on the Establishment of New Stock Exchanges submitted its report in 1991 and recommended the establishment of a unified regulatory body for the stock exchanges. A Presidential Ordinance promulgated on 31 January 1992 accorded SEBI statutory status as an autonomous body. The SEBI Act[4] was passed by parliament on 4 April that year to govern all the stock exchanges and a large part of securities transactions, deemed to come into retrospective effect from 31 January. Almost simultaneously, the 1947 CI(C) Act was repealed in May, and the office of the Controller of Capital Issues (CCI) was abolished. SEBI, as regulator, was. set to take over from the CCI, the restrictor.

The SEBI Board comprises a chairman, two members from the ministries of the Government of India (GoI) dealing with finance and law, one from the RBI, and two other members, appointed by the GoI, who are professionals and have experience or special knowledge relating to securities markets. The GoI has the right to terminate the services of the chairman or any member of the board. The decisions of the board are by majority vote, with the chairman having a tie-breaking second vote.

The board is bound by the directions given by the central government from time to time on questions of policy, and the central government has the right to supersede the board. The board is also obliged to submit a report to the central government every year, giving account of its activities, policies, and programmes. Although the board's decision can be appealed within the courts, given the delays and sloth of the judicial system, the de facto appellate body is the Ministry of Finance.

Section 11 of the SEBI Act provides that '...it shall be the duty of the Board to protect the interest of investors in securities and to promote the development of and to regulate the securities market by such measures, as it thinks fit'. It empowers the board to regulate the business in stock exchanges, to register and regulate the working of stockbrokers, sub-brokers, share transfer agents, bankers to an issue, trustees of trust deeds, registrars to an issue, merchant bankers, underwriters, portfolio managers, investment advisors, and such other intermediaries as may be associated with the securities market, to register and regulate the working of collective investment schemes including mutual funds, to prohibit fraudulent and unfair trade practices and insider trading,[5] to regulate takeovers, to conduct enquiries and audits of the stock exchanges, etc.

Penalties need to he very strict in the securities market.[6] An efficient and transparent securities market is impossible without the confidence instilled by a regulatory process that can swiftly detect irregularities and meet out deterrent punishment in a relatively short time. Contrast the convictions secured against the main accused in the Indian securities scam of 1992 to those of the traders of Barings Bank or Drexel Burnham Lambert.

ASSESSMENT OF REGULATORY INSTITUTIONS IN INDIA: EFFECTIVENESS AND DESIGN

Independent regulatory institutions have now become part of India's language of economic reform. However, in our national enthusiasm for things, there is a danger of overemphasis on regulation, to the detriment of the development of competitive markets. Such markets are now possible in the overwhelming majority of economic activity, thanks both to new technology and information systems and our understanding of the theory of contracts and incentives. The absence of an overt price discovery activity need no longer be a constraint on discovery of value—there are contract mechanisms now available that can extract or mimic this discovery.

There are two sets of issues that will need to be addressed in any such assessment:

1. The performance of the institutions relative to the objectives set out for them.
2. The design of these institutions themselves.

Our focus in this chapter is an assessment of the functioning of the regulators. An assessment of their design is a much more ambitious task, a formal treatment of which will predominantly be delegated to elaboration elsewhere. This chapter contains isolated remarks on the design of the institutions, mainly due to the complex interactions of market structures and the terms of reference of the regulatory institutions.

TELECOM

The process of restructuring and opening the telecom sector to competition began early in the 1990s, and its flawed premises delayed meaningful progress in the sector for almost half a decade. The National Telecom Policy 1994 (NTP 94) expressed the government's intention of introducing competition in various telecom services and increasing the availability of telephones in India. A flawed understanding of telecom markets and a consequently poor sequencing of reforms resulted in a conspicuous lack of any progress of its objectives. Its most damaging impact was in its ignoring trends that were even then becoming quite evident that many telecom services were amenable to competition. The decision to award basic (fixed land-line) licences through auctions failed to foresee the number of potential providers of telephony that would have entered the markets. The government's decision to auction cellular mobile licences in 1995 was a radical departure from its practice hitherto of awarding the rights to service provision through administrative and negotiated routes.[7] The trouble was a totally wrong choice of the auction method that led to interminable litigation and defaults of the licence fees, as well as an inappropriate pricing of the use of (the scarce public property) radio-frequency spectrum (Bhattacharya 2000).

Defaults on the licence fees started right after the completion of auctions. While cellular service providers remained on track on their subscriber targets, revenues were much below expectations. Given the nature of fees imposed on the cellular providers, on the basis of handsets and cellular antennae, there was a built-in disincentive for increasing subscriber base, and concentrating on per-subscriber revenues. Roll-out of basic services were also delayed by an inability to arrange for the substantial investments required after the payment of licence fees.

The first TRAI's actions have been one of the most transparent in India. It set the standards (along with the OERC) of following a systematic procedure of decision making with detailed consultation papers on issues and tariff philosophies, a series of public consultations and hearings and, finally, reasoned and documented orders.

The experience of the telecom sector bolsters the need for a clear division of jurisdictions of the regulator and the government.

The ambiguities in the TRAI Act were compounded by the fact that TRAI had been constituted much after the entry of private players in the telecom sector and the subsequent contracts. Its troubles started with the DoT's adopting an aggressive stance against what it presumed was an arrogation of its powers of policy making by TRAI. The TRAI's interpretation of the TRAI Act deemed it to have a wide range of powers. There were two issues that permeated these differences—interconnection and revenue sharing. The DoT took the position that TRAI had no jurisdiction over the existing contracts and arrangements, which, it held, were in the domain of policy making and hence under its own ambit.

Four cases were filed against TRAI's decisions in the high courts over 1997 through 1999—the stay on DoT's grant of a licence to MTNL for metro cellular operations, disputes regarding licences for Internet Service Providers (ISPs), TRAI's jurisdiction over interconnection regimes and over revenue-sharing 'arrangements'. TRAI's proposal to shift to a Calling Party Pays (CPP) regime for calls from fixed phones to cellular subscribers had been opposed both by DoT and cellular providers, albeit for different reasons. This was a consequence of significant resistance from consumer groups to its tariff order of 1999, where it increased its fixed rental charges while lowering call tariffs, and another NGO challenged the CPP order as well.

There was also the question of TRAI's role in dispute redressal. After the New Telecom Policy 1999 (NTP 99), the government issued a Gazette Notification specifying that TRAI was assigned the role of an 'arbitrator' in disputes between the licensor (DoT) and any licensee (service provider). These proceedings, however, would be governed by the Indian Arbitration and Conciliation Act 1996. TRAI felt that this was inconsistent with the provisions of the TRAI Act which (in their view) empowered TRAI with a range of powers (to adjudicate) that include summons, examination of documents, receipt of evidence, etc., which arbitration powers do not confer. It insisted that the notification required an amendment of the TRAI Act itself.

The final straw was the decision of the Delhi High Court, in January 2000, striking down two TRAI orders—issued in May and September 1999, respectively—on an interconnection regulation overriding existing licence agreements between the government and service providers and then on the revenue-sharing regime between fixed and cellular operators. The Group on Convergence had already begun drafting the reconstitution of TRAI and an ordinance based on the recommendations of the group was promulgated in January 2000.

Recognizing the shortcomings of the NTP 94, both in terms of the slow pace of investments in the sector and the on-going tussle with TRAI, the government formulated the NTP 99. At the same time, the first steps to corporatizing DoT were initiated, and the Department of Telecom Services (DTS) was made a separate entity from the parent (policy making and licensing) DoT.

Assessing the success of TRAI's actions is difficult. Its very public disagreement and litigation with the DoT might well have served to hasten a major reform of a sector in complete disarray, with the formulation of the NTP 99. Media publicity of the differences led to increasing public awareness of the failings of the DoT and its service arms. The NTP 99 acknowledged failure of the process of awards of fixed and cellular licences, and migrated private sector service providers from upfront licence fees to revenue sharing with the government. There is a fairly widespread opinion that TRAI may have been able to leverage its weaker position vis-à-vis the DoT with an aggressive enforcement of quality of service, rather than persisting in defending its rights of regulating interconnection and revenue shares.

ELECTRICITY

One of the remarkable features of the investigations following the collapse of the Northern Grid on 2 January 2001 was the notable absence of the Central Electricity Regulatory Commission in the proceedings. This was symptomatic of the lack of importance attached to the CERC by the public sector enterprises in the electricity business.

Amongst the utilities, the generation segment of electricity was one of the first to be opened to private sector participation, with an Amendment to the 1948 Electricity Supply Act in 1991. A decade after an initial rush of Memoranda of Understanding (MoUs) between Independent Power Producers (IPPs) and the government had failed to translate into any significant investments, the realization has sunk in that augmentation of generation capacity would not occur without reforms in the distribution and supply segments of the industry. The CERC and the various SERCs have complementary roles in increasing the viability of the sectors.

Realizing the unsustainability of the situation arising from the recurring and huge losses of the State Electricity Boards (SEBs) and the political unwillingness to either increase tariffs or reform the existing SEBs, the governments, central and state, hit upon the idea of establishing independent Electricity Regulatory Commissions. An underlying motive was the desire to distance the political executive from the inevitable and unpopular hikes in tariffs, as one of the means of increasing revenue generation.

One of the biggest disappointments about the role of the CERC has been its failure to develop a competitive market for bulk electricity. Bulk (or wholesale) electricity refers to the matching of big suppliers of electricity, like the National Thermal Power Corporation (NTPC), National Hydroelectric Power Corporation (NHPC), etc., to the bulk buyers of electricity, mostly SEBs or their successor entities. The admonition above, undoubtedly, should be amply qualified. The CERC has started the process: its Availability Based Tariff (ABT)[8] Order and Indian Electricity Grid Code is meant to instill a degree of grid discipline in the rampant flouting of norms. A system of merit order despatch, whereby the cheapest producer of electricity is despatched to the grid, was designed to induce SEBs to schedule and dispatch power in a rational manner. High Unscheduled Interchange (VI) charges, imposed on deviations from contracted demand and supply, were meant to reinforce this discipline.

While evidently constrained by the state of the sector, it is likely that it could have adopted a more activist role in influencing policy positions. What are the constraints in the development of bulk markets? A stated power shortage scenario, especially peaking power shortage, is one.[9] Consistent under-investments in transmission systems, and lack of linkages between different grids, rampant grid indiscipline, lack of hard budget constraints on different public sector entities that make them unresponsive to incentives and penalties,[10] and the complete absence of a commercial approach to transactions are formidable hurdles for any regulator. Buyers, too, have no incentives to source the cheapest available power.

Had the CERC been more successful in establishing bulk power markets, its scope of functions would have been significantly reduced, although it would still be tasked with regulating interstate transmission tariff. Many of these changes in the structure of the electricity market had been mandated or enabled in the draft Electricity Bill 2000, which has been passed.

A feature of the ERC Orders that deserves praise is the universal adoption of the public hearings route to decision making despite this not having been mandated in the ERC Act.

CAPITAL MARKET

The technology used in India's capital markets today is some of the best in the world. The establishment over time of the NSE, the National Securities Clearing Corporation of India (NSCCL), the National Securities Depository Ltd (NSDL), the Central Securities Depository Ltd (CDSL), Stock Holding Corporation of India Ltd (SHCIL), etc., has put in place high-quality institutions as well. Although the credit for these institutions must mainly be given to market intermediaries, SEBI played a part in providing the motivation for their establishment by progressively instituting market best practices in trading, delivery, and settlement. The fortuitous development of the National Stock Exchange as a competitor to the Bombay Stock Exchange, Mumbai, aided SEBI immensely in these objectives.

SEBI has moved on a large number of fronts. Its primary concern has, rightly, been the equity markets as this is the operational ambit of a large section of capital-market intermediaries. Electronic screen-based trading, dematerialization of securities, and rolling settlements have made the equities markets more safe and transparent and dramatically reduced the amount of speculative trading and price rigging. Has SEBI been aggressive enough? A chorus of protests from brokers following the drop in turnover in those securities with mandated rolling settlement cycles forced SEBI into delaying the inclusion of other stocks into this format.

SEBI has also progressively increased the requirements of various market intermediaries to disclose information. It has to be noted that proprietary information in the intensely competitive segments of capital markets is what drives innovation and confers an advantage on efficient players. Forcing these institutions to divulge such information may be inimical to the growth of these markets. Balancing disclosure of information with ensuring proprietary ownership of information then becomes the basic challenge of securities regulation. On the whole, market perception is that the availability of the currently disclosed information needs to be disseminated more widely amongst investors.

There are also, quite often, mixed signals that emanate from the regulator and other branches of government. The recent conflicting decisions from SEBI and the Central Board of Direct Taxes (CBDT) of the Ministry of Finance on the tax incentives for venture capital companies was one such instance.

One critical aspect where SEBI has displayed unwarranted timidness is in a more rapid institution of derivatives markets. Part of the hesitation is understandable—prudence in the handling of instruments that involve significant leveraging.

Despite the institution of best practices, SEBI is widely perceived to be a relatively toothless regulator. The nature of securities transactions makes credible deterrence a key weapon against fraud. The number and magnitudes of the SEC's fines, as well as its active coordination with the US Department of Justice, is a pointer to the need for such punitive action even in a mature and (more) transparent market. The securities scandal in India in 1991–2 was an example. The gravity of its effect is still being felt with retail investors not having regained their confidence in the securities markets despite the strengthening of the regulator, SEBI, in the intervening period and the framework of prudential safeguards and information disclosure requirements now in place. Not a single major perpetrator has been punished. Relatively trivial fines let several involved institutions off the hook. More such fraudulent schemes have emerged since, and none has attracted harsh deterrent penalties. The unwillingness of retail investors to subscribe to securities issues is a major impediment for companies in raising capital.

CONCLUSION

Have independent regulators in India been white knights that came to the rescue of sectors that were being mismanaged by public sector monopolies? Or have they functioned as insidious de facto agents of government, perpetuating public sector control under a veneer of competitive forces?

It is difficult to pass a sweeping judgement on their effectiveness. Overall, they have not been fully effective—their performance has been varied. While this is due in part to the faulty design of these institutions, where they have not been conferred the required powers and given the appropriate instruments to enable them to fulfil their objectives, the primary failure has been the lack of attention to the reform of the market structure and an inadequate understanding of the nature of interaction between the market structure and the effectiveness of the regulatory process.

There was inadequate appreciation of the technological changes that were already driving changes in other countries and a lack of understanding of the possibility of competition inherent in these changes. The design of regulation was mostly conceived in terms of intrusive, cost-based behavioural models rather than incentive based. The costs of regulation were not appreciated. The regulators are not likely to attain their objectives of efficient delivery of services given their current resources.

Even in terms of their own (limited) objectives, the performance of regulators has been mixed. An important barrier for effective regulation has been the pervasive presence of public institutions which have used their incumbent advantages to delay the progress of competition in many sectors. They have nudged, at varying rates, their respective sectors towards greater competition. The legislations that set-up the individual regulatory institutions have also provided variable leeway in fulfilling this objective.

It is obvious that the government has been reluctant to let go and relinquish its control. It has also drafted most of the legislations establishing the regulators with sufficient ambiguity to enable reversal or contest of regulatory decisions that it deems inimical to its interests. The qualifications prescribed for membership of the regulatory commissions almost uniformly include an administrative background, and this has been taken full advantage of, given the numbers of retired and serving civil servants in these commissions. Moreover, there is some evidence that a lack of suitable aggressive-ness in their approach might prolong their existence more than is warranted by advances in competition.

The Securities and Exchange Board of India has been a notable success, partially owing to its supervision of a sector where the government recognized the correct structure and devised, more or less, the right policies to foster competition and efficiency. Securities markets in India have been transformed beyond recognition. However, much more could have been achieved by more stringent punitive action. So far, the Central Electricity Regulatory Commission has still not been able to make substantive progress on the establishment of a competitive bulk electricity supply market. The continued existence of the Tariff Authority for Major Ports is the least justifiable, given the current state of inter- and intra-port competition.

Notes

[1] The views expressed in this paper are the authors' and not necessarily those of the institution to which they are affiliated.

[2] There are also other regulators, like Reserve Bank of India (RBI) and, in a more indirect manner, the Department of Company Affairs (DCA) and Ministry of Finance (MoF). These, however, are institutions that are part of the executive branch of government, and are not considered independent regulators.

[3] Albeit with the concurrence of the Central Transmission Utility, Power Grid Corporation of India Ltd (PGCIL).

[4] A relatively brief one with only 35 sections.

[5] One of Securities and Exchange Commission's (SEC) biggest tools is its power to reward informants with a bounty of up to 10 per cent of the monetary penalty of an insider trading action which is successful. This is an important incentive for people to speak up against colleagues and senior officials. It also allows the SEC to spread its dragnet wide enough to nab a curious assortment of insiders.

[6] Prudential Insurance Company of America has been convicted in the USA of deliberately training its agents to mislead, misrepresent, and defraud insurance policyholders. It was accused of unjust enrichment to the tune of US$ 2 billion by duping 10.7 million policyholders over 13 years. It also paid up a fine of $ 35 million for misleading policyholders, to return $ 410 million collected unlawfully from them and to pay $ 1 million as a fine for destroying documents.

[7] Memoranda of Understanding (MoUs) as they are called.

[8] The ABT is a two-part tariff that consists of a capacity charge and an energy charge. The SEB plants are considered as sunk costs and electricity scheduling was purely on the basis of costs of generation, which led to inefficient plants being dispatched first.

[9] The strong caveat, of course, is that there are no firm commercial estimates of power demand, given the excessively skewed tariffs for different segments of power purchasers.

[10] The public ownership of both generators and buyers of power make penalties meaningless and merely transfers between various organs of government.

Select References

Armstrong, M., S. Cowan, and J. Vickers, *Regulatory Reform: A Economic Analysis and British Experience*, Cambridge: MIT Press, 1994.

Berra, Yogi with Tom Horton, *Yogi ... It Ain't Over*, New York: McGraw-Hill, 1989.

Bhattacharya, S., 'Competitive Bidding for Infrastructure Services', mimeograph, Infrastructure Development Finance Company Limited, Mumbai, 2000.

Bhattacharya, S. and U.R. Patel, 'Transport Pricing and Financing: Issues and Lessons for India', in Proceedings of UNESCAP-AITD Conference on *Transport Pricing and Charges for Promoting Sustainable Development*, New Delhi, 2000.

Datta-Chaudhury, M., 'Market Failures and Government Failures', *Journal of Economic Perspectives*, 1990.

Debreu, G., *Theory of Value*, New Haven: Yale University Press, 1959.

Laffont, J.J. and J. Tirole, *A Theory of Incentives in Procurement and Regulation*, Cambridge: MIT Press, 1994.

Lal, Deepak, 'From Planning to Regulation: The New Dirigisme', in *Unfinished Business: India in the World Economy*, New Delhi: Oxford University Press, 1999.

Stiglitz, J., 'Some Theoretical Aspects of Agency Policies', *World Bank Research Observer*, vol. 2, 1987.

11

An Assessment of Public–Private Partnership Opportunities in India*

Vinod B. Annigeri, Lizann Prosser,
Jack Reynolds, and Raghu Roy

INTRODUCTION

Various examples of public–private partnerships (PPPs) exist in India, a number of which have been replicated and expanded. The examples include social marketing of condoms, oral contraceptives, and oral rehydration salts (ORS); community-based distribution of contraceptives through non-governmental organizations; development of workplace projects; and contracting of primary health care services. The United States Agency for International Development (USAID) was interested in identifying, testing, and documenting effective mechanisms that encourage the private and public sectors to work together to expand access to quality Reproductive and Child Health (RCH) services, especially among the urban and rural poor. Toward this end, USAID commissioned an assessment team to identify potential public–private partnership models that could be designed, developed, and tested in Uttar Pradesh under the Innovations in Family Planning Services (IFPS) project.

PPP TRANSLATED IN REALITY

The basic mechanisms of PPP are social marketing, social franchising, and contracting. A brief description of each, including basic strengths and weaknesses, follows.

* Originally published as *An Assessment of Public–Private Partnership Opportunities in India*, New Delhi: USAID-India, 2004.

SOCIAL MARKETING

Although numerous definitions for social marketing exist, they share the same general principles. Social marketing, at its simplest, is the application of commercial marketing techniques to achieve a social objective. Most social marketing programmes include

1. an objective that is beneficial to the consumer and/or society;
2. implementation that is not driven by profit;
3. a goal focused on changing behaviour, not simply increasing awareness;
4. an approach that is tailored to the specific needs of the target audience;
5. the creation of conditions that are conducive to the targeted behaviour change; and
6. reliance on commercial marketing concepts.

For nearly thirty years, social marketing has been applied to expanding the use of and access to contraceptives. Approaches to social marketing vary, and different philosophies are held by different implementers. Traditionally, there have been two broad models for the social marketing of contraceptives: the distribution model and the manufacturers' model. The distribution model focuses on maximizing access and usually relies on donated or subsidized products. The manufacturers' model usually includes an agreement with the contraceptive manufacturer to provide products at a reduced price in return for demand creation that is achieved through an information, education, and communication (IEC) programme or a behaviour change communication (BCC) programme. Currently, there are many variations on these two models.

RCH products that have been socially marketed include male and female condoms, oral contraceptives, intrauterine devices (IUDs), injectable contraceptives, emergency contraception, ORS, micronutrients, mosquito nets, and safe delivery kits.

SOCIAL FRANCHISING[1]

Franchising is an established business model designed to allow growth and replication while retaining certain controls and quality standards. Social franchising applies the principles and structure of franchising to initiatives that are designed to bring about social change.

Three key components need to be in place for social franchising to function:

1. a business format,
2. a brand, and
3. quality assurance.

The franchising format defines the services that are being franchised and how they must be delivered by franchisees. The brand links a particular service delivery point with the franchise in the minds of consumers. The brand is advertised to consumers as an indication of high-quality, affordable services. If marketed properly over time, the brand will build up a great deal of equity. For the franchisees, the primary benefit of association with a high-equity brand is increased business. Thus, two mechanisms—quality assurance and monitoring and evaluation—need to be in place to ensure that the franchisees deliver products and services that are consistent with the brand image.

1. Quality assurance mechanisms include training and support provided by the franchiser to enable franchisees to deliver goods and services in accordance with specified quality standards.
2. Monitoring and evaluation mechanisms ensure that franchisees are, in fact, operating in accordance with the protocols of the franchise.

Two primary models have evolved in social franchising: stand-alone or full franchises, and fractional or partial franchises. In a stand-alone social franchise, the franchiser controls all of the goods and services. An example would be Apollo Family Health clinics. Apollo provides the blueprints for facilities, the equipment, and protocols for services; screens all staff; sets prices; and handles quality assurance and related issues. In a fractional franchise, the franchiser only controls one or a few of the goods and services. The Vanitha clinics, which are limited to IUDs, condoms, and oral contraceptives, illustrate this type of franchise. Another entity controls all other services (such as antenatal care, immunizations, and surgery).

Each model of social franchising has advantages and disadvantages. The principal advantage of stand-alone franchises is that the franchiser has done all the development work. For a fee, the franchisee acquires the business blueprint containing all the information and systems needed to operate a business. The franchiser often provides advertising, discounted products, and training, among other services. A fractional franchise is usually smaller, less expensive, and involves less risk than a full franchise.

CONTRACTING

A contract is a legally binding written agreement between two or more parties that specifies something provided (such as products or services) and something received in return (usually payment for the products or services). In most RCH cases, the government contracts with an individual or an organization to provide certain products (example, contraceptives, posters, test kits) or services (example, training, HIV testing, x-rays) in return for money.

A World Bank report lists five contracting mechanisms; the assessment team focused on the first three:[2]

1. contracting in,
2. contracting out (outsourcing),
3. subsidies,
4. leasing or rentals, and
5. privatization.

Contracting In

The government hires one or more individuals on a temporary basis to provide services. A typical example is a health centre hiring a medical specialist (example, an obstetrician or a pediatrician) to work at the clinic once a week.

Contracting Out

The government pays an outside individual or organization to manage a specific function. Examples include contracting an NGO to train reproductive health (RH) providers, contracting a university to conduct needed research, and contracting a hospital to operate a primary health centre.

Subsidies

The government gives funds or commodities to private groups to provide specific services. The government might, for example, contribute vaccines or a per capita stipend to a private hospital to provide immunization services to the poor.

Leasing or Rental

The government offers the use of its facilities to a private organization. The government might, for example, rent its primary health centre to an NGO to provide services to people in the area.

Privatization

The government gives or sells public health facilities to a private group. The government might, for example, give a primary health centre to a private hospital on the understanding that the hospital would provide RCH services to the local population.

The most common of these options is contracting out. A recent World Bank article summarized the advantages and risks of this mechanism.[3] The advantages are increased competition, focus on outputs rather than inputs, increased responsiveness, increased emphasis on performance, improved coverage of the poor, and improved public sector efficiency. The risks listed are cost overruns, reduced equity, reduced quality, fragmentation of health services, and monopolistic prices.

QUALITY ASSURANCE AND ENABLING ENVIRONMENT

The literature shows that these partnership mechanisms may not work without quality assurance and a positive enabling environment. That is, separate activities may need to be undertaken to ensure that providers are adequately trained and supervised, political commitment has been secured, and government agencies have the capacity to ensure that the private providers are regulated and monitored.

On the quality side, there is a need to ensure that providers are accredited, standards are set and followed, guidelines and protocols for diagnosis and treatment are developed and used, providers are kept up to date through continuing medical education, and systems are in place to monitor and correct such important aspects of quality as infection prevention, client satisfaction, and access to services.

On the enabling side, there is a need for the government, including the district and block levels, to understand the advantages, disadvantages, and requirements of partnerships. They need to understand that partnerships are based on common objectives, shared risk, shared investments, and participatory decision making. They also need to understand the characteristics of different partnership mechanisms (that is, social marketing, social franchising, contracting); the different payment options (example, block grants, capitation, fee for service, third-party insurance); the advantages and disadvantages of bidding (example, open bidding, short lists, sole source bids); the size, scope, and duration of partnerships; and the negotiation, management, sanctions, and termination of partnerships.

One World Bank paper noted that 'what is required...is a gradual change in the mindset of government officials....Government will have to focus on its stewardship of the sector, on policy setting and regulation, and will have to avoid micromanaging the provider's business'.[4]

DESCRIPTION AND ANALYSIS OF MAJOR PPP MODELS

This section elaborates on the descriptions and analyses of major PPP models summarized in the matrices. These models are described as major because they are the most likely to have significant outcomes on coverage and health status if enacted effectively. However, only three of the six seem worth pursuing at this time. The models are listed in approximate order of feasibility.

UTTAR PRADESH: CLINICAL CONTRACEPTION THROUGH PRIVATE PROVIDERS
DESCRIPTION

RCH problem: Need for increases in voluntary sterilizations and IUDs to achieve population stabilization.

Service delivery problem: Inadequate involvement of the private sector in providing sterilization and IUD services.

Public entities: District societies, Uttar Pradesh State Department of Health and Family Welfare.

Private entities: Private hospitals and nursing homes.

Target groups: Rural poor in Uttar Pradesh.

Transactions (public and private): The government will reimburse private hospitals and nursing homes that provide sterilization and IUD services. District societies will implement the programme with funds allocated through the decentralized district action plans.

Implementation: Interested private institutions will sign a memorandum of understanding with the appropriate district societies to cover service protocols, quality standards, roles, and responsibilities. The private hospitals and nursing homes will be selected by the project manager and chief medical officer. The latter will authorize the private hospitals and nursing homes to provide sterilization services. The district societies will assess the need for no-scalpel vasectomy training. The private hospitals and nursing homes will provide free sterilization and IUD services, including preoperative investigations, postoperative medicines, follow-up visits, transportation, management of complications, and reporting to the district society. The district society will set up and pay for verification. Upon verification and within forty-five days, the district society will reimburse the private hospitals and nursing homes Rs 1,000 per sterilization and Rs 100 per IUD insertion as well as an additional Rs 100 for each year the patient does not get pregnant for up to five years.

Coverage: Each private hospital or nursing home will be given a geographic catchment area based on capacity and unmet need.

Assessment

Strengths: The programme is straightforward, would cover the entire state, and would increase sterilizations significantly. Management and monitoring are decentralized to the districts.

Weaknesses: Private hospitals and nursing homes would have to subsidize the programme as costs are likely to exceed government subsidies and the services have to be free. They need to have enough working capital to finance delays of government payments. The district societies may not have the capacity to monitor quality of care. Older women and those who have more than three children are not eligible.

Costs: The government will only reimburse costs on specific line items up to Rs 1,000 per sterilization and Rs 100 per IUD insertion. The actual cost to the private hospital or nursing home is likely to be greater than that, given the services required (especially transportation, community mobilization, follow up, and management of complications). However, state officials in Karnataka believe that if laparoscopy was the standard procedure and the state paid a flat fee of Rs 1,000 per sterilization, then this would be attractive to private hospitals and nursing homes.

Equity: The programme is specifically designed to reach the poor. Reimbursements are limited to women of 'low age and parity, up to a maximum of three children'.

Quality: The district societies will be responsible for monitoring adherence to standards and grievances. Whether they will have the time, resources, and capacity to do this is uncertain.

Sustainability: The programme is not self-sustaining. It requires continued contributions from the government and the participating private hospitals and nursing homes.

Scalability: The State Innovations in Family Planning Services Project Agency (SIFPSA) notes that this strategy 'has been tried out with success in 2003–4 in Allahabad district (and)...hence the practice can be up-scaled for the entire state wherever the accredited private nursing homes/private hospitals are willing'. Whether they are willing and able is a key question.

Coverage: Theoretically, the programme would cover the entire state, including the poor in both urban and rural areas. Whether this would really occur, especially in rural areas, is uncertain.

Health impact: Theoretically, the programme would have a significant impact on health and fertility, if implemented as planned.

Constraints and issues: There are no obvious incentives for private providers to join the programme. It would have to be sold on the basis of social responsibility. The reimbursement is unlikely to cover costs, much less make a profit for participating private hospitals and nursing homes, which would make it unattractive to many institutions and providers. However, if the government paid a flat fee of Rs 1,000, it would be attractive to those who do laparoscopies. The district societies may not have the management or monitoring capacity to fulfil the roles assigned to them. Required approval from the chief medical officers could dissuade some private hospitals and nursing homes from joining the programme. It may be difficult to find private hospitals and nursing homes that reach rural areas.

Experience from other states: In Tamil Nadu, the government has partnerships with accredited private nursing homes that are paid Rs 200 for each case. The client pays the remainder directly to the nursing home (about Rs 2,800). A pilot project in Bommidi and Dharmapuri does not charge the patient anything, but pays the nursing home (Rs 800 for a visit in Bommidi and Rs 1,800 per case in Dharmapuri). The Chhattisgarh government has identified twenty-seven not-for-profit hospitals (with good coverage in tribal areas) and 131 commercial hospitals with which to form partnerships. Under this plan, the government would reimburse its partners for all RCH services offered to clients living below the poverty level, and for family planning, sterilizations, and IUDs provided to all clients. The fee schedule for these services would be fixed, but the facilities would be free to provide other services at their own prices. A monitoring programme of facility visits, client interviews, and annual rate reviews has been designed.

Conclusions and recommendations: The SIFPSA strategy looks attractive from a service perspective but not from an economic one. However, if the Rs 1,000 payment was a flat fee instead of a reimbursement, then it would probably be more attractive to the providers. In addition, it would probably work if it adopted the Bommidi or Dharmapuri financing mechanisms. It will also be important to examine the experience in Allahabad district to identify the advantages and weaknesses of this strategy, especially in rural areas. Finally, it would probably be prudent to try the model out in two or three districts before expanding it statewide.

ANDHRA PRADESH: URBAN SLUM HEALTH CENTRES
DESCRIPTION

RCH problem: Poor health outcomes among urban poor.

Service delivery problem: About six million urban slum dwellers had little access to primary health care services and could not afford private care. The governments of India and Andhra Pradesh received assistance from the World Bank to establish the Andhra Pradesh Urban Slum Health Care Project (2000–2). Afterwards, the state government continued the project with its own funds.

Public entity: Andhra Pradesh Commissioner of Family Welfare (CFW).

Private entity: NGOs (example, Lions, Rotary, Vasavi Clubs, women's organizations).

Target groups: Poor in urban slums.

Transactions (public and private): The Commissioner of Family Welfare, with World Bank support, built 192 urban health centres in 74 municipalities. The urban health centres are similar to a primary-health-centre outpatient clinic in structure, staffing, and services. The CFW contracts with NGOs and provides an annual budget of Rs 310,000 that covers salaries, operational expenses, equipment, furniture, and pharmaceuticals in addition to NGO training. The NGO hires five providers and three support staff. It provides basic RCH preventive care (antenatal care, immunization, vitamin A, birthspacing, reproductive tract infections, and sexually transmitted infections); services for childhood diseases (example, acute respiratory infection, diarrhea, measles); referrals (for high-risk pregnancies, newborns, emergencies); and outreach. It does not provide such inpatient care as deliveries, sterilizations, or abortions. The urban health centres are open six days a week, from 9 am to 12 pm and from 4 pm to 6 pm. The schedules are determined by a local urban health centre advisory committee to fit the needs of local residents.

Implementation: The project has three components: service delivery, community mobilization, and BCC. There are no fees or registration charges. The local urban health centre advisory committee oversees the project. Two auxiliary nurse-midwives alternate between providing services at the urban health centre and community outreach.

Coverage: Services are limited to the poor in the geographic area (population of 15,000–20,000). The objective is to cover all households in the area (about 3,000–4,000). The NGOs claim that the two auxiliary nurse-midwives cover all households every 1–3 months.

ASSESSMENT

Strengths: There was no significant opposition to contracting NGOs to operate these clinics, apparently because they were new facilities and the NGOs are non-profit organizations. Demand has been high and most of the urban health centres have performed well. The structure, service package, staffing pattern, and schedules all seem to be well designed and implemented. Community involvement is strong. The local advisory committee involves local stakeholders in selecting NGOs and oversees management. There is heavy emphasis on performance and achievement of results. The government provides a rigorous training programme for NGOs.

Weaknesses: Staffs complain of low salaries, especially for physicians and auxiliary nurse-midwives, compared with similar government positions. Payments from the government are often late. There is a lack of basic laboratory equipment (example, microscopes) and supplies as well as a shortage of medicines. User fees have been prohibited because of political opposition.

Costs: The funds provided by the CFW cover about two-thirds of the costs. The NGO has to raise the remainder, about Rs 5,000–20,000 per month. Three of the NGOs visited raise these funds from their memberships; another solicits contributions from commercial firms.

Equity: Equity is very high. The urban health centres only service the poor; however, some who can afford to pay have tried to obtain free services, at least in some areas. Some urban health centres have eligibility criteria and others do not.

Quality: Quality appears to be very good but there does not seem to be a quality assurance mechanism, except for client complaints. Everyone seems to equate performance assessment with quality assurance.

Sustainability: As long as NGOs can raise adequate funds to complement the government contribution, the centres will be easy to sustain.

Scalability: The fact that there are urban health centres at seventy-four sites indicates that the model is scalable.

Coverage: The advisory committee oversees performance, which is assessed along seventeen service statistic indicators (example, number of antenatal care cases registered, number of children fully immunized). Over time, the urban health centres seem to reach all of the target population, either through clinic services or outreach.

Health impact: NGOs have seen significant reductions in childhood illnesses, 100 per cent immunization rates, 100 per cent institutional deliveries, improvements in child nutrition, and similar improvements in all other indicators.

Constraints and issues: Physicians are difficult to find because of low salaries. Most physicians who take the jobs are retired government officials. It is difficult to institute user fees for political reasons. However, there is no objection from clients. Government commitment to the scheme has been good so far but permanent support is not certain as yet. New facilities have to be constructed because of the political opposition to handing over existing facilities to private entities.

Experiences from other states: The Mitra Chikitsak Yojana in Chhattisgarh is intended to identify a pool of specialists that would be available and willing to provide services at specific health centres on either a scheduled or as-needed basis. Although this programme is yet to be implemented, interest in participating is reported to be high among specialists.

Conclusions and recommendations: The urban health centre project appears to be a resounding success from most perspectives, including the service package, outreach, costs, staffing patterns, and most importantly, results. This is a legitimate public–private partnership that is both replicable and scalable. As such, it deserves serious consideration. However, the enabling environment needs to be assured beforehand to ensure that there is no community or political opposition to the scheme.

KARNATAKA: CONTRACTING OUT
PRIMARY HEALTH CARE CENTRES
DESCRIPTION

RCH problem: Poor RCH status among rural poor.

Service delivery problem: Lack of reliable and affordable primary health care services, especially RCH.

Public entity: The State Department of Health and Family Welfare.

Private entity: The Karuna Trust is a charitable trust that provides health, education, and other services to the poor. There are other NGOs that have taken over primary health centres in other sites.

Target groups: Primary health care catchment areas.

Transactions (public and private): The basic transaction is turning over the management and operation of some of the worst primary health centres to the trust. The Karuna Trust currently operates seven primary health centres (and their subcentres), two public health units, and three health centres. In return for operating the primary health centres, the government provides the building and all of its equipment, furniture, and supplies. It also pays 75 per cent of staff salaries (the trust is responsible for the remaining 25 per cent) and provides Rs 75,000 annually for medications. The trust receives the facilities and uses its own funds for whatever is needed, including renovation, equipment, furniture, and beds.

Implementation: The Karuna Trust hires all staff, provides training as needed, and handles procurement. The staff consists of one physician, one laboratory technician, one nurse, two auxiliary nurse-midwives, two clerks, and an administrator, all of whom are on one-year contracts. The centre also supervises about 20 community workers. The primary health centre is open seven days a week from 9 am to 1 pm, and from 2 pm to 5 pm. All staff members live nearby and are on call twenty-four hours a day. The centre offers the same primary health care services as government-operated centres, specializing in RCH and outreach. It handles normal deliveries and sterilizations. The trust has added a few new services, including pregnancy, haemoglobin, and HIV tests as well as cataract examinations and treatment.

Coverage: The population in the target area is 14,000. The community workers and auxiliary nurse-midwives reach all of the households. In addition, they carry out an annual household survey to update health status and to set targets for the next year.

Assessment

Strengths: There has been no significant opposition to the government's contracting primary health care services out to a non-profit NGO. The Karuna Trust has enough resources to complement those of the government. Management appears to be supportive but businesslike. The primary health centre is able to provide a full range of primary health care services, in particular RCH. Performance is good and constantly monitored.

Weaknesses: The model may not work where there is mistrust of the private sector on the part of the government and/or the community. The model is highly dependent on the reputation of the NGO and the recruiting of physicians and paramedics, who are willing to live in the community, accept lower wages, and be on call twenty-four hours a day. NGOs that do not have management capability and adequate resources to provide partial subsidies would have difficulty implementing this model.

Costs: The government originally provided 90 per cent of the costs, but the trust requested that the amount be reduced to 75 per cent to avoid attracting unstable NGOs. The government is considering raising its contribution to 90 per cent again to encourage expansion of the model. The trust has made significant investments in the facility, including an ambulance and renovation. Currently, it provides approximately Rs 200,000 (2 lakh) annually to keep the centre operational.

Equity: Almost all the people in the target area are poor. The centre does not require proof; it accepts all who come for services. All basic primary health care services are free except for pregnancy, haemoglobin, and HIV tests; these are provided at cost. The centre makes no profit on any of its services.

Quality: An important element of quality is reliable access to services. This is assured by the centre's policies and the proximity of the staff. They live close by and are on call twenty-four hours a day. The centre assesses service quality by examining its performance indicators to determine, for example, if a pregnant woman received antenatal care and tetanus toxoid shots. There is no mechanism for assessing the quality of service delivery (example, client-doctor interaction, adherence to clinical standards, and infection prevention practices), except for client complaints.

Sustainability: The fact that the trust has been doing this kind of work for nine years without any significant problems indicates that this model is sustainable. However, an interested NGO will have to cover part of the costs with its own funds. If the government adopts a 90 per cent contribution policy, again, that will make sustainability much more certain.

Scalability: The fact that the trust operates twelve centres and expects to have twenty-seven eventually (one in every district) is a good indicator of the scalability of this model. However, scalability is dependent on a large enough pool of capable NGOs that have independent sources of funding. One expert noted that of approximately 1,600 primary health centres in his state, only about 50 could be contracted out to NGOs.

Coverage: Service statistics and the annual household survey show that coverage on all basic indicators (antenatal care, fully immunized children, and contraceptive usage) is very good.

Health impact: Although there are no population-based surveys to assess coverage and improvements in health status, the annual household survey could be used to make such an assessment in some areas. Qualitative data indicate that health status is, indeed, improving.

Constraints and issues: This model has to overcome a number of constraints. One of the most important is the scarcity of physicians. The trust now employs retired government and newly graduated doctors. It is very difficult to attract other physicians as well as auxiliary nurse-midwives. The trust is now hiring general nurse-midwives and training them in outreach and other auxiliary nurse-midwife skills. The model requires an NGO that has the financial resources to complement the government's contributions.

Government officials at state, district, and block levels as well as local leaders have to be educated about PPP. Many are distrustful of private organizations being involved in the delivery of primary health care services. It is also essential that the NGO have full hiring and firing authority over staff. User fees are generally prohibited, but some charges can be made for extra services, and donations are acceptable. The government does not advertise for contracting out primary health centres; NGOs have to submit proposals. Profit-making organizations are not considered.

Experiences from other states: This very popular model has great appeal but also generates great resistance. In Uttar Pradesh, SIFPSA spent almost two years trying to find an appropriate NGO to take over a primary health centre only to be asked by the district to find another site. Apparently, the district thought that it would be embarrassing to admit that it could not provide basic health services. SIFPSA came up with a less ambitious plan but the district has not responded to it. The issue is now 'in cold storage', according to SIFPSA. In Bihar, the government has no plans to introduce this scheme because it is concerned about the quality of care and its ability to monitor the NGOs. In Andhra Pradesh, the government believes that it is not at all possible to implement this scheme for several reasons: the primary health centre is the only facility that can provide a broad range of services—NGOs would not be able to do that; private hospitals would be suspect unless they were non-profit; and the Communist Party would see this as the first step in privatizing health care in India. In most states, the scheme may not be economically viable because primary health care services are supposed to be free. The private entity would not be allowed to charge user fees, even to cover costs, and the government is not willing to provide a large enough subsidy to make up the shortfall in income. Where this idea has been proposed, the trade unions have been upset, seeing it as a way to reduce government jobs. Tamil Nadu is strengthening its primary health centres rather than contracting them out to the private sector. The head of the Karuna Trust in Karnataka believes that only 50 out of 1,600 primary health centres in the state can realistically be contracted out to NGOs because of the lack of qualified NGOs. He believes that the NGOs should work at the *taluka* (a governmental local district) level to build the capacity of district and taluka staff to improve primary health care services, with an NGO-managed primary health centre as a demonstration model in each taluka.

The Society for Education, Welfare, and Action (SEWA) Rural project in Gujarat was 100 per cent funded by the state government for ten years. It was very successful; introduced a number of changes (new management information and accounting systems, team meetings, quality control, and evaluation); and increased contraceptive prevalence (from 37 per cent in 1983 to 71 per cent in 2000). The government made a number of concessions early on and that contributed to the project's improvements, but as time went on the relationship deteriorated and SEWA Rural returned the primary health centre to the government. The official reason was that SEWA Rural wanted to set up a first referral unit but did not have enough human resources to manage both it and the primary health centre. Other respondents reported that SEWA Rural had become too frustrated with the government to continue.[5]

Providing twenty-four hour access to primary health care services is becoming a popular primary health centre feature. In Karnataka, the medical staff members (doctors and paramedics) live close to the centre and are on call twenty-four hours a day, largely to handle deliveries and emergencies after regular hours. This option is only possible if staff members are willing to live in the village. In Tamil Nadu, there is a pilot project to provide the same twenty-four hour service by hiring three staff nurses (one for each eight-hour shift) at the primary health centre. The government believes that it is so successful that it will train 1,000 additional staff nurses to expand the service.

Contracting in specialists is now routine in Tamil Nadu and common in other states. The government pays these specialists (obstetricians, anesthesiologists, surgeons, dentists, and ophthalmologists) to fill gaps in services and to meet local demand. Some of these are hired full time, while others have contracts to provide services two or three times a week.

Conclusions and recommendations: Assuming that the constraints mentioned above can be overcome, this model appears to be a viable PPP. It is a legitimate public–private partnership that is both replicable and scalable. The USAID and SIFPSA should examine it closely and seriously consider testing it in Uttar Pradesh, perhaps starting with defunct centres or subcentres. The USAID and SIFPSA should also consider the suggestion to set up model primary health centres and use them to train district- and block-level officials in how to operate a primary health centre.

BIHAR: JANANI SOCIAL FRANCHISING MODEL
DESCRIPTION

RCH problem: One-third of the deaths in Bihar are due to poor RCH and communicable diseases.

Service delivery problem: Poor RCH coverage of the low- and middle-income segments of the population is a major reason for these deaths. Janani is working with state and district government agencies to address this problem.

Public entity: State and district government agencies.

Private entity: Janani, an affiliate of DKT International.

Target groups: Low- and middle-income segments of the population throughout the state.

Transactions (public and private): This is not a true example of a public–private partnership. The public sector role is limited to providing condoms and oral contraceptives to Janani for a discounted price. However, the value of that transaction is significant— approximately US $1 million annually. Nevertheless, there is no formal or informal agreement between Janani and the state government and no coordinated planning or services. The entire operation is planned, implemented, and monitored by Janani.

Implementation: Janani uses economies of scale and subsidies to lower the costs of RCH and other services, so that those who cannot afford to pay full private sector prices can receive high-quality RCH services. Janani relies on three delivery mechanisms: shops that sell products to clients; Titli Centres, which also sell products and provide basic services and referrals; and Surya Clinics, which provide the entire range of RCH services. Janani helps private providers set up and operate these services through a franchise mechanism. In return for a small fee and adherence to quality standards, Janani provides training, advertising, commodities at bulk prices, referrals, and support services. As a result, prices are 30–40 per cent lower than commercial prices, which attracts the target groups. Providers make money as long as they adhere to Janani's quality standards and prices, and clients are assured of reasonably priced quality services. Janani relies heavily on outsourcing in implementation, which lowers its management burden and costs.

Coverage: Couple year of protection (CYP) data show that the programme accounts for 15 per cent of couples protected in Bihar and Jharkhand, or 1.1 million couples. An estimated 640,000 births were averted last year. The cost to protect a couple per year is Rs 115; the cost to avert one birth is Rs 200. These figures are based on sales, not on population-based surveys, and are unverified.

ASSESSMENT

Strengths: Janani combines social marketing, social franchising, much contracting out, and even some contracting in. Although complex, the model is clearly defined and easy to understand. The project was originally designed to expand contraceptive use, but it has evolved into an RCH and then a general health services programme. By broadening the range of services, the programme is more successful in attracting both providers and clients. In general, the programme is well designed. The three-channel delivery system (shops, Titli Centres, and Surya Clinics) provides an effective referral chain that seems to work very well. Janani has found ways to outsource much of the implementation of the system, which lowers Janani's overhead costs and management burden. The IEC strategy relies on local media, interpersonal communication, and mass media (especially radio, wall paintings, and billboards), which seem to be effective in attracting clients. Television is limited in the area. The scale of the programme is impressive: there are now 32,000 shops, over 25,000 Titli Centres, and 550 Surya Clinics. Janani plans to establish one Super Titli Centre for every 20 villages, and one Super Surya Clinic in each district to take over basic training, supervision, and distribution functions. The creation of Super Surya Clinics will allow for a reduction in the number of Surya Clinics. When fully operational, there will be 40,000 shops, 57,000 Titli Centres, and

360 Surya Clinics. The programme plans to cover the entire states of Bihar and Jharkhand, including all villages.

Weaknesses: The programme takes years to establish. It began in 1996; in 2000, training physicians and setting up clinics began. Probably half the planned shops, Titli Centres, and Surya Clinics will not be completely operational for another two years. Abortion is a key service that is provided by the Surya Clinics. Janani contends that it could still operate effectively without offering that service (and is willing to do so in Uttar Pradesh) but that seems debatable, given that the programme earns so much from this service. The public sector role is limited to the provision of condoms and oral contraceptives to Janani for a discounted price. However, this source is unreliable.

Costs: The programme is very expensive. DKT International estimates that a three-year budget for Uttar Pradesh would be US $19 million. In the fiscal year (FY) 2001–2, total expenditures were $3.7 million (42 per cent for IEC and advertising, 24 per cent for Titli Centres, and 15 per cent for commodities).[6]

Equity: The market has been segmented into the affluent (those who can pay full price), low- and middle-income, and those below poverty level. Janani targets the low- and middle-income segment that cannot afford to pay full private sector prices but that can afford partial payment. This is one of the weaknesses of the programme—that the poorest population is not a target group. This group has to be covered by subsidies or discounted prices, neither of which is built into the model.

Quality: Built-in training, supervision, and infection prevention are keys to maintaining quality, most of which has been contracted out. Although quality appears to be much better than in the public sector, a number of deficiencies were found in the Surya Clinics visited.

Sustainability: To date, the programme is highly subsidized by donors. Although Janani management believes that the programme will be self-sustaining, that is years away at best.

Scalability: The programme is already being scaled up and plans call for it to be operating statewide in the next several years.

Coverage: A deficiency is the lack of evaluation. Janani relies exclusively on CYP data. There is no evaluation of the effect of the programme on contraceptive prevalence or other RCH coverage indicators. Janani states that it would be too expensive. The coverage estimates described above are based on CYP calculations and cannot be verified without population-based data.

Health impact: No data were collected or are available; management believes that this would be too expensive.

Constraints and issues: Infrastructure is often worn down and could require extensive renovation. The principal income-generating service is abortion. Whether the model would work without abortion is uncertain. Costs are very high, perhaps too high for Uttar Pradesh. The time required to set up the various shops, Titli Centres, and Surya Clinics is at least several years. The lack of evaluation means that there is no way to determine whether the programme has any effect on coverage or an impact on health. The programme is not designed to reach the poor.

Experiences in other states: Chhattisgarh has developed a franchise model called Mitan Kendra. It is fashioned after the Janani franchise model except that a project management unit under the State Health Society or the State Health Research Committee (SHRC) would serve as the franchiser. The proposed components of the network are medical clinics providing comprehensive RCH services, including emergency obstetric care; medical clinics providing some RCH care, but not all; and paramedical (largely nurse and midwife) clinics providing some RCH services, but not all. In return for paying a franchise fee, the franchisees will receive a logo/brand name, active promotion of the clinic, paid referral arrangements, management assistance with franchiser staff at each clinic, and training to close skill gaps. The project management unit has developed detailed budgets, proposed fee schedules, and project management protocols.

Conclusions and recommendations: The Janani model is attractive in many ways. Given the experience gained to date in Bihar, the management believes that it would be relatively easy to replicate it in Uttar Pradesh, even without the abortion component. That may or may not be true. However, the programme is very expensive, would take too long to cover the state, does not reach the poorest of the poor, and has not yet been evaluated. If it were tried, it should be limited to one or two districts, then fully evaluated in terms of its RCH coverage and effects on contraceptive prevalence and other RCH indicators. It might be worthwhile for SIFPSA to visit Chhattisgarh to examine its franchising plan.

Notes

[1] Julie McBride and Rehana Ahmed, 'Social Franchising as a Strategy for Expanding Access to Reproductive Health Services', Commercial Strategies Project, September 2001; also 'Franchising for Primary Health Care', Draft Discussion document, the World Bank, March 2004.

[2] James E. Rosen, 'Contracting for Reproductive Health Care: A Guide', discussion paper, The World Bank, December 2000, p. 4.

[3] 'Contracting for Primary Health Care', World Bank, South Asia Region, November 2003, pp. 3–5.

[4] 'Contracting for Primary Health Care', World Bank South Asia Region, November 2003, p. 13.

[5] SEWA, 'Making a Primary Health Centre: The SEWA Rural Experience', 2003.

[6] 'Franchising for Primary Health Care: Draft Discussion', World Bank, March 2004, p. 18.

Annotated Bibliography

During the last decade or so, there has been a remarkable change in the role of government in different societies. The World Bank's report of 1992 and the emergence of a new paradigm in public administration have added a new dimension to the whole issue of governance. Traditionally, governance refers to the forms of political systems and the manner in which power is exercised in utilizing a country's economic and social resources for development. It also deals with the capacity of a government to design, formulate, and implement policies and, in general, to discharge government functions.

This is a selective annotated bibliography that is, basically, a pathfinder for further research in this new genre of governance. Those interested in pursuing further queries will find it useful, though this bibliography is by no means exhaustive. By placing both the articles and books in the field of governance, the primary aim here is to underline the rich literature on this subject. Given the complex unfolding of the processes of governance in both the developed and developing countries, it would be difficult to trace the genealogy of the concept in a straight-jacketed manner. And, also the fact that governance is organically linked with the constantly evolving administrative processes is also suggestive of its complex nature. This annotated bibliography is just a modest attempt to identify the roots of such a complex process as governance is.

CONCEPTUALIZATION

Governance was first problematized in a World Bank document of 1989 on Sub-Saharan Africa, which suggested that the bank's programmes of adjustment and investment in the area were being rendered ineffective by a 'crisis of governance'. An entire volume of the *Indian Journal of Public Administration* (XLIV, no. 3, July–September 1998) has been devoted to deal with this new perspective. For conceptual clarity, the following two articles of the above volume deserve mention. O.P. Dwivedi's 'Common Good and Good Governance' and Mohit Bhattacharya's 'Conceptualizing Good Governance' have ably amplified the intricate dimensions of the perspective. The other useful work dealing with conceptual clarity include UNDP's *Reconceptualising Governance* (New York: UNDP, 1997), T.N.Chaturvedi's (ed.), *Towards Good Governance* (New Delhi: *Indian Institute of Public Administration*, 1999), the World Bank's *Governance and Development* (Washington DC, 1992), Jan Kooiman's (ed.), *Modern Governance: New Government-Society Interactions* (New Delhi: Sage, 1993), James N. Rosenau's 'Governance, Order and Change In World Politics', *Governance Without Government: Order and Change in World Politics,* in James N. Rosenau and Ernst-Otto Czempiel (eds), (Cambridge: Cambridge University Press, 1992), B.Guy Peters' *Models of Governance for the 1990s, The State of Public Management,* in Donald F. Kittl and H. Brinton Milward (eds), Baltimore: the John Hopkins University Press, 1996, O.P. Minocha's (*Good Governance: Concept and Operational Issues, Management in Government*), *Indian Journal of Public Administration* (29, no. 3, October–December, 1997), Ramaswamy Iyer's 'The Meaning of Governance', *Indian Journal of Public Administration* (50 no. 1, Jan–March 2004), Nand C. Bardoville's 'The Transformation of Governance Paradigms and Modalities, *Round Table* (353, January 2000).

GLOBALIZATION AND PUBLIC ADMINISTRATION

The 1992 World Bank Report is one of the most influential documents that radically altered the approaches to public administration. A clear description of 'globalization' and 'liberalization' is available in the report submitted by the UNCTAD's Secretary-General, entitled *Globalization and Liberalization: Development in the Face of Two Powerful Currents* (1996); David Held and A. McGraw (ed.), *The Global Transformation: An Introduction to the Globalization Debate,* Cambridge: Polity Press, 2000); P. Hirst and G. Thompson, *Globalization in Question: The*

International Economy and the Possibilities of Governance, (Oxford: Oxford University Press, 1999). One of the most recent attempts to conceptualize globalization is evident in Paul Streeton's 'Globalisation: Threat or Opportunity' *Public Administration in Development*, in Paul Collins (ed.), (England: John Wiley and Sons, 2000, pp. 59–63). Amit Bhaduri and Deepak Nayyar's *The Intelligent Person's Guide to Liberalization* (New Delhi: Penguin, 1996, is a well-written text raising questions on the feasibility of liberalization as a strategy for the so-called developing countries. Raja J. Chelliah's *Essays in Fiscal and Financial Sector Reforms in India* (Delhi: Oxford University Press, 1999) is a specific study of the impact of liberalization on the Indian economy in the 1990s. The special number on 'Liberalization Policy and Social Concerns' of *The Indian Journal of Public Administration* (XLII, no. 3, July–September, 1996) has relevant articles. Arvind K. Sharma's 'People's Empowerment' in the above volume (pp. 235–44) has brought out the possible adverse impact on the people in the developing countries. Similarly, Mohit Bhattacharya's 'Rolling Back the State: Public Administration in the Age of Market Supremacy' (Above volume, pp. 245–57) defends the utility of state especially in the social sector that will hardly attract private investment for obvious reasons.

Two new expressions—new public management and governance—figure prominently in the lexicon of public administration, underlining its new perspectives. Reflective of the changes in public administration following globalization, new public management throws open those issues which are relevant to understanding the new directions in governmental activities in both developed and developing countries. The governance perspective is another, seeking to articulate governmental activities under the changed environment, where government seems to be a peripheral actor in public administration. The thrust of new public management and governance has been toward a determined effort to implement the three Es–efficiency, economy, and effectiveness.

The theme paper entitled *Government in Transition—a New Paradigm in Public Administration*, circulated during the inaugural conference of the Commonwealth Association for Public Administration in 1995, identifies the distinctive features of new public management. The 1996 and 1997 World Bank reports also provide significant inputs towards conceptualizing changes in public administration. While the 1996 *World Development Report: From Plan to Market* (Oxford: Oxford University Press, 1996) indicates the growing importance of market, the 1997 *World Development Report: The State in a Changing World* (Oxford: Oxford University Press, 1997) articulates the government activities in a new milieu. In *Reinventing Government: How the Entrepreneurial Spirit is Transforming the Public Sector* (Mass: Adison-Wesley, 1992), D. Osborne and T. Gaebler coin a new term 'entrepreneurial government' to describe the new orientation of governments. The counterargument is provided by Paul du Gay, *In Praise of Bureaucracy: Weber, Organization and Ethics,* (London: Sage, 2000). For a very nuanced account of the growth of new public management one of the most impressive studies is in P. Dunleavy and C. Hood 'From Old Public Administration to New Public Management', published in *Public Money and Management,* (14 no. 3, 1994, pp. 9–16). Andrew Gray and Bill Jenkins have articulated their thought in 'From Public Administration to Public Management: Reassessing a Revolution', published in *Public Administration,* (73, Spring, 1995, pp. 78–99). The idea was further elaborated by N. Denkin and K. Walsh in 'The Enabling State: The Role of Markets and Contracts', published in *Public Administration* (14, 1996, pp. 33–48). One of the recently published comprehensive works is *The New Public Management in Action* by Ewan Ferlie and others (Oxford: Oxford University Press, 1996). That market may not always be a panacea is the basic theme, pursued by John B. Goodman and Gary W. Loveman in 'Does Privatization Serve the Public Interest?, published in *Harvard Business Review* (November–December, 1991, pp. 27–38).This is the basic theme in Paul Streeton's 'Markets and States: Against Minimalism and Dichotomy' (*Political Economy Journal of India,* 3, no. 1, 1995). This line of argument is pursued by P. Dunleavy in 'Explaining the Privatization Boom: Public Choice versus Radical Approaches', *Public Administration* (64, no. 1, 1986). Similarly, Martin Minogue in 'Changing the State: Concepts and Practice in the Reform of the Public Sector', published in *Beyond the New Public Management: Changing Ideas and Practices in Governance,* Martin Minogue *et al.* (eds), (Cheltenham: Edward Elgar, 1998, pp. 17–37) has gone beyond what constitutes the fundamental principles of new public management. Ian Scott has shown the impact of new public management in the Asian context in his 'Changing Concepts of Decentralization: Old Public Administration and New Public Management in the Asian Context', published in *The Asian Journal of Public Administration*, (18, no. 1, June 1996, pp. 3–21). A critical assessment of the 'new world order' that emerged in the wake of globalization is made by Manfred Bienefeld in 'New World Order: Echoes of a New Imperialism' (*Third World Quarterly*, 15, no. 1, 1994).

Governance is an equally significant perspective striving to grapple with the changed reality in public administration. An entire volume of *The Indian Journal of Public Administration*, (XLIV, no. 3, July–September, 1998) has been devoted to deal with this new perspective, where the boundary of government has been substantially shrunk. For conceptual clarity, the following two articles of the above volume of The *Indian Journal of Public Administration* deserve mention. O. P. Dwivedi's 'Common Good and Good Governance' (pp. 253–64) and Mohit Bhattacharya's 'Conceptualising Good Governance' (pp. 289–96) have ably amplified the intricate dimensions of the perspective. The other very useful article is by Gerry Stoker entitled 'Governance as Theory: Five Propositions', published in *International Social Science Journal*, (155, March, 1998, pp. 14–28). In the same volume of this journal, Bob Jessop's 'The Rise of Governance and the Risks of Failure: The Case of Economic Development' (pp. 29–47) is a critical assessment of this model. The other useful and serious interventions are (1) R. Rhodes, 'The New Governance : Governing without Governance', *Political Studies*, (44, no. 3, 1996, pp. 652–67); (2) Bob Jessop 'The Regulation Approach and Governance Theory: Alternative Perspectives on Economic and Political Change', *Economy and Society*, (24, no. 3, 1995, pp. 307–33); (3) J. Rosenau, 'Governance, Order and Change in World Politics' in James N. Rosenau and E.O. Czempiel (eds), *Governance without Government: Order and Change in World Politics* (Cambridge: Cambridge University Press, 1992, pp. 1–30); (4) B. Guy Peters, 'Models of Governance for the 1990s' in *The State of Public Management*, Donald F. Kettl, and H. Brinton Milward (eds), (Baltimore: The Johns Hopkins University, 1996, pp.15–43); and also, Jan Kooiman, *Modern Governance: New Governance-Society Interaction*, (New Delhi: Sage, 1993); Paul du Gay, 'Against Enterprise', *Organization* (2, no. 1, January 2004); J. Pierre and

B. Guy Peters, *Governance: Politics and the State* (New York: Macmillan, 2000).

Public choice theory provides the most significant input to understand the changing nature of bureaucracy or civil service in response to the process of globalization. V. Ostrom's *The Intellectual Crisis in American Public Administration* (Alabama: University of Alabama Press, 1974) is one of the first serious attempts to understand non-economic activity using the language and analytical tools of economics. The other major theoretical works are William A. Niskanen, *Bureaucracy and Representative Government*, (Chicago: Aldine, 1971); Mancur Olson Jr., *The Rise and Decline of Nations*, (New Haven: Yale University Press, 1982); Anne O. Krueger, *Political Economy of Policy Reform in Developing Countries*, (Cambridge: MIT Press, 1993); J.E. Lane (ed), *Bureaucracy and Public Choice*, (London: Sage, 1987); Rober Bates, *Markets and States in Tropical Africa*, (Berkeley: University of California Press, 1981); James M. Buchanan and Gordon Tullock, *The Calculus of Consent: Logical Foundations of Constitutional Democracy* (Ann Arbor: University of Michigan Press, 1962); Clifford S. Russell and Norman Nicholson (eds), *Public Choice and Rural Development*, (Washington DC: Resources for the Future, 1981); Gordon Tullock, *The Politics of Bureaucracy*, (Washington DC: Public Affairs Press, 1965); P. Dunleavy, *Democracy, Bureaucracy and Public Choice: Economic Explanations in Political Science* (Hemel Hempstead: Harvester Wheatsheaf, 1991).

Drawing upon the 'rational choice' theory, Israel Arturo provides a theoretical basis of these obvious changes in public administration in his *Institutional Development: Incentives to Performance* (Baltimore: Johns Hopkins University, 1987). In his World Bank Working Paper, 'The Changing Role of the State: Institutional Dimension, Policy Research and External Affairs' (Country Economic Department, World Bank, August 1990), Arturo comments on the growing importance of globalization in radically altering the boundaries of the state in the so-called Third World context. For a clear description of the limits of globalization, the volume edited by Robert Boyer and Daniel Drache is a useful collection. In fact, the title *States against Markets: The Limits of Globalization* (London: Routledge, 1996) unambiguously suggests the direction of the volume. Gerald Caiden's 'Globalizing the Theory and Practice of Public Administration' in *Public Administration in the Global Village*, Jean-Claude Gracia-Zamor and Renu Khator (eds), (Westport, CT: Praeger, 1994, pp. 45–59) provides a clear glimpse of the changes in public administration in response to globalization. Milton Esman's 'The State, Government Bureaucracies and their Alternatives' in Farazmand, *Handbook of Comparative and Development Public Administration*, Ali Farazmand (ed.), (New York: Marcel Dekker, 2000) is both an elaboration of changes in civil service and also a search for alternatives within the prevalent socio-political international framework. Ali Farazmand's 'The New World Order and Global Public Administration' in *Public Administration in the Global Village*, Jean-Claude Gracia-Zamor and Renu Khator (eds), (Westpost, CT: Praeger, 1994, pp. 62–81) is an endeavour to explore the new dimensions of public administration, linking its articulation with the forces of globalization. This argument was developed further in his 'From Civil to Non-Civil Administration' (paper, presented at the 1997 American Society for Public Administration). That globalization is a unifying tendency is elaborated by Eric Welch and Wilson Wong in their 'Public Administration in a Global Context: Bridging the Gaps of Theory and Practice between Western and Non-Western Nations', published in *Public Administration Review* (58, no. 1, 1998, pp. 40–9).

GLOBAL PERSPECTIVE OF GOVERNANCE

Globalization and the resultant pressures for reforms towards good governance have recently become the central theme of the development discourse of the scholars, the media, the policy makers and implementers as well as the politicians all over the world. The following books and articles deal with the global perspective of governance. *Commission on Global Governance*, Our Global Neighborhood (Oxford: Oxford University Press, 1995), P.L. Sanjeev Reddy, Jaideep Singh, and R.K. Tiwari's (ed.), *Democracy; Governance and Globalization: Essays in Honour of Paul H. Appleby* (Indian Institute of Public Administration, New Delhi, 2004), Esref Aksu and Joseph A. Cailleri's (ed.), *Democratizing Global Governance*, (New York: Palgrave Macmillan, 2002), Aseem Prakash and Jeffrey A. Hart's (ed.), *Globalization and Governance*, (London: Routledge, 1999),

Surendra Munshi and Biju Paul Abraham (ed.), *Good Governance, Democratic Societies and Globalization*, (New Delhi: Sage Publications, 2004) discusses good governance in democratic societies in the context of globalization from a cross-cultural perspective. Diana Leat, Kimberly Seltzer and Gerry Stoker's *Towards Holistic Governance; The New Reform Agenda*, (New York: Palgrave, 2002) presents an authoritative assessment of successes and failures to date as well as a new framework for analysis and implementation. This book is the first major study of holistic governance. The book by Joseph S. Nye and John D. Donahue (eds), *Governance in a Globalizing World* (Washington D.C.: Brookings Institution Press, 2000) deals with: How are patterns of globalization evolving? How do these patterns affect governance within nation-states? And, how might globalism itself be governed?

The other significant books on the theme include the one by Davesh Kapur and Richard Webb, *Governance-Related Conditionalities of the International Financial Institution* (Geneva: UNCTAD, 2000), Mike Moore's *A World without Walls: Freedom, Development, Free Trade and Global Governance*, (Cambridge: Cambridge University Press, 2003), B. Guy Peters's *The Future of Governing; Four Emerging Models* (Lawrence: University Press of Kansas, 1996), James N. Rosenau's, 'Governance in a Globalizing World', in *The Global Transformation Reader*, David Held and Anthony MC Grew (eds), (Cambridge: Polity Press, 2000), Tarneem Ahmad Siddiqui's *Towards Good Governance* (Oxford: Oxford University Press, 2001), David Held's *Democracy and the Global Order; From the Modern State to Cosmopolitan Governance*, (Cambridge: Polity Press, 1995), Paul Hirst and Grahame Thompson's *Globalization in Question: The International Economy and the Possibilities of Governance* (Cambridge: Polity Press, 1996).

David Osborne and Ted Gaebler's *Reinventing Government: How the Entrepreneurial Spirit is Transforming the Public Sector*, (New Delhi: Prentice Hall, 1992) suggest a ten-point programme for what they call entrepreneurial governments. The following articles deal with the same theme: Leftwich Adrian's 'Governance, the State and the Politics of Development, *Development and Change* (25, 1994), Madhu Dandavate's 'Global Governance', (*Mainstream*, 34 no. 40, 7 September 1996)', Niraja Gopal Jayal's 'The Governance

Agenda: Making Democratic Development Dispensable', (*Economic and Political Weekly*, 32, no. 8, 22–8 February 1997).

GOVERNANCE IN INDIA

Amrit Lal's *Governance in India: A Theatre of the Absurd* (Delhi: Shipra, 2004) reflects on almost all major national ailments including poor governance, corruption, inefficiency, and lack of accountability and suggests systematic attention and effective cure without further delay. The book by Surendra Munshi and Biju Paul Abraham, (eds), *Good Governance* (New Delhi: Sage Publications, 2004) discusses good governance in democratic societies in the context of globalization from a cross-cultural perspective. The book by E. Vayunandan and Dolly Mathew (eds), *Good Governance: Initiatives in India* (New Delhi: Prentice Hall of India, 2003) focuses on the issues and strategies of good governance. The following books and articles deal with the same theme: C.P. Barthwal (ed.), *Good Governance in India*, (New Delhi: Deep and Deep, 2003), R.B. Jain, *Public Administration in India: 21st Century Challenges for Good Governance*, (New Delhi: Deep and Deep, 2001), Jayanta Kumar Ray, *India in Search for Good Governance*, (Maulana Abul Kalam Azad Institute of Asian Studies, Calcutta, 2001), Joginder Singh, *Good Governance* (Delhi: Indian Publishers, 2002), Atul Kohli *Democracy and Discontent: India's Growing Crisis of Governance*, (Cambridge: Cambridge University Press, 1991), John P. Lewis, *India's Political Economy: Governance and Reform* (Delhi: Oxford University Press, 1995), Nawnihal Singh, *A System of Governance: Parliamentary or Presidential*, (New Delhi: Anmol, 1998), B.Sivaraman, *Bitter Sweet: Governance of India in Transition*, (New Delhi: Ashish, 1991), V.A. Pai Panandiker and Ajay K. Mehra, *The Indian Cabinet: A Study in Governance*, (New Delhi: Konark, 1996), S.R.S.Rao (ed.), *Accountability of Public Institutions: Emerging Issues in the Indian Context* (Rajaji International Institute of Public Affairs and Administration, Hyderabad, 1991), Shriram Maheshwari, *Administrative Reform in India* (New Delhi: Jawahar 1993), Administrative Reforms Commission's report of the study team on machinery of the Government of India and its procedures of work (Administrative Reforms Commission, New Delhi, 1968), Government of India, Committee on Prevention of Corruption

Report, Chairman, K. Santhanam, (Controller of Publication, Delhi, 1964), U.C.Agarwal's case for a national level ombudsman, (*Indian Journal of Public Administration,* 34, no. 2, April–June, 1988), and 'Administration Reforms: No Panacea for Good Governance' (*Politics India,* 3,no. 2, August 1998), G.R.Bhattacharjee, 'Judicial Activism; Its Message for Administration (*Administrator,* 42, no. 3, April–June, 1997), Vinay Dharmadhikari, 'Elections and Governance: A Systems-Engineered Design', *(Politics India,* 2, no. 4, October 1997), Kamla Prasad 'India's Leadership and Governance', (*Mainstream,* 34, no. 42, 21 September 1996), V.K.Mehrotra 'India's Governance: An Agenda for Change, *(Politics India,* 11, no.7, January 1998), Asok Mukhopadhyay 'Ethics in Governance: The Indian Perspective' (*Indian Journal of Public Administration,* 41, no. 3, July–September 1995), and Ch. Bala Ramulu, 'Development Policies and Governance in India: From 1947 to 2003' (*Indian Journal of Public Administration;* 50, no. 1, January–March 2004).

For a critical study of Indian bureaucracy in recent times, 'Evolving Trends in the Bureaucracy' by B. P. R. Vithal in *State and Politics in India,* Partha Chatterjee (ed.), (Delhi: Oxford University Press, 1997), is a useful introduction to bureaucracy in its contemporary manifestation in India. Similarly, Anil Bhat's 'Colonial Bureaucratic Culture and Development Administration: Portrait of an Old-Fashioned Indian Bureaucrat' (*Journal of Commonwealth and Comparative Politics,* 17, no. 3, 1979), is a well-argued article showing the extent to which the colonial bureaucratic culture continues to remain a significant influence in Indian bureaucracy. A sharply critical account of the intimate linkage between bureaucracy and local political power is the essay by Jan Breman, 'I Am the Government Labour Officer .... State Protection for Rural Proletariat of South Gujrat' *(Economic and Political Weekly,* 15 June 1985, pp. 1043–55). Though slightly dated, R. B. Jain dealt with the growing politicization of Indian bureaucracy in 'Politicization of Bureaucracy: A Framework for Comparative Assessment', (*The Indian Journal of Public Administration* 20 no. 4, October–December 1974). Based on field data, Kuldeep Mathur identifies the historical roots of 'over-bureaucratization' that flourished in India in the aftermath of independence in his 'Bureaucracy in India: Development and Pursuit of Self-Interest' (*Indian Journal of Public administration,* 36, no. 4, 1991). The experience of a bureaucrat has been recorded by N.N. Vohra in 'The Rusting Steel Frame', published in *India at 50s: Bliss of Hope and Burden of Reality,* V.N. Narayanan and Jyoti Sabharwal (eds), (New Delhi: Sterling Publishers, 1997, pp. 154–71) For a detailed description of India's bureaucracy in its contemporary manifestation *Annual Reports,* (published by the Ministry of Personnel, Public Grievances and Pensions, Government of India) provide exhaustive data for further research in this area. Sudipta Kaviraj's essay entitled 'On the Crisis of Political Institutions in India' (*Contributions to Indian Sociology,* 18, no. 2, pp. 223–43) is a balanced commentary on the growth of crucial political institutions, including bureaucracy, in India. Similarly, Ashis Nandy's 'The Political Culture of the Indian State' (*Daedalus,* 118, no. 4, fall 1989, pp. 1–26) is a thought-provoking article seeking to link the emergence of a peculiar state structure with an equally peculiar political culture. Articulating the changes in public administration, *The Fifth Pay Commission Report* (Ministry of Finance, Government of India, 1997) provides clear directions to civil service reform. S.K. Das's *Civil Service Reform and Structural Adjustment* (Delhi: Oxford University Press, 1998) is one of the first full-length studies of this phenomenon in the context of India.

GOVERNANCE AND ADMINISTRATIVE REFORMS

Bibek Debroy's (ed.), *Agenda for Improving Governance* (New Delhi: Academic foundations, 2004) sets out the reform agenda for governance or, alternatively, for the role of the state. Other sources on the same theme include the work by Ann Seidman, Robert B. Seidman, and Thomas W. Walde, *Making Development Work: Legislative Reform for Institutional Transformation and Good Governance* (Boston: Kluwer Law International, 1999), Mamadou Dia's *A Governance Approach to Civil Service Reform in Sub-Saharan Africa,* (Washington, DC: the World Bank, 1993), S.K. Das's *Civil Services Reform and Structural Adjustment* (Oxford: Oxford University Press, 1998), Julio Faundez (ed.), *Good Governance and Law: Legal and Institutional Reform in Developing Countries* (London: Macmillan, 1997), Leila L. Frischtak's, *Governance Capacity and Economic Reform in Developing Countries,* (Washington DC: the World Bank, 1994), Birkenshaw's *When Citizen's Complain: Reforming Justice and Administration,*

(Buckingham: Open University Press, 1993), Jan Kooiman, *Modern Governance: New Governance-State Interaction* (New Delhi: Sage Publications, 1993). J. Pierre and B. Guy Peters, *Governance: Politics and the State* (New York: Macmillan, 2000). S.R. Sen's 'Reforming our System of Government' (*Economic and Political Weekly*, 26 no. 9410, 2–9 March, 1991).

CROSS-CULTURAL PERSPECTIVE ON GOVERNANCE

A number of good works have appeared on the cross-cultural perspective on governance. The important among them include Jude Howell (ed.), *Governance in China*, (New York: Rowman and Littlefield Publishers, 2004) explores the key dimensions of governance in China, Cheryl W. Gary and Rebecca J. Hanson *Corporate Governance in Central and Eastern Europe*, (Washington DC: World Bank, 1993), J.S. Furnivall, *The Governance of Modern Burma* (Institute of Public Relations, New York, 1958), Mamodou Dia, *A Governance Approach to Civil Service Reform in Sub-Saharan Africa*, (Washington, DC: World Bank, 1993), Harold Wilson *The Governance of Britain*, (London: Weidenfeld and Nicolsan, 1976), Harald Fuhr, *Public Sector Modernization and Improving Governance in Latin America—Lessons from a Decade of World Bank Assistance* (Washington, DC: World Bank, 2001), Herman W. Hoen's (ed.), *Good Governance in Central and Eastern Europe: Puzzle of Capitalism*, (Cheltenham: Edward Elgar, 2001), John E. Bardill's *Towards a Culture of Good Governance:* 'The Presidential Review Commission and Public Reform in South Africa', (*Public Administration and Development*) 20, no. 2, May 2000), Christopher Benninger's 'Urban Governance in Asia: Conference Report', (*Cities*, 12, no. 3, June 1995). John P. Burns's 'Administrative Reform in China: Issues and Prospects', (*International Journal of Public Administration*, 16, no. 9, September 1993), Chong-Hyum Ro's 'Reforms to Improve Performance: Korea's Experience' (*Asian Review of Public Administration*, 7, no. 2, July–December 1995), Marc Dubois's 'The Governance of the Third World: A Foucauldian Perspective on Power Relations in Development', (*Alternatives*, 16, no.1, winter 1991), Sir William Reid's 'Public Accountability and Open Government in United Kingdom' (*Indian Journal of Pubic Administration*, 41, no. 3,

July–September 1995), Rainer Rohdewohld's 'Government Reforms in Developing Countries: The Case of Indonesia' (*Indian Journal of Public Administration*, 43, no. 2, April–June 1997) and S. Akbar Zaid's 'Pakistan: Crisis of Governance' (*Economic and Political Weekly*, 33, no. 11, 14 March 1998).

The other significant literature on governance include, J.N.Rosehau and Ernstotto Czempiel (eds), *Governance without Government: Order and Change in World Politics*, (Cambridge: Cambridge University Press, 1992), Judith Gruber, *Controlling Bureaucracies: Dilemmas in Democratic Governance*, (Berkeley: University of California Press, 1987), Paul Hirst, *Associative Democracy: New Forms of Economic and Social Governance*, (Cambridge: Polity Press, 1994), Arvind K. Sharma, 'Reorienting Governance for Speedy Service Delivery', (*Indian Journal of Public Administration*, 40, no. 3, July–September 1994), Sandeep Shastri, 'Towards More Effective Governance' (*Mainstream*, 36, no. 5, 24 January 1998), D. Bandyopadhyay, 'Administration, Decentralization and Good Governance' (*Economic and Political Weekly*, 31, no. 48, 30 November 1996), Bhabani Sen Gupta, *India: Problems of Governance*, (Delhi: Konark, 1996), Richard Rose (ed.), *Challenge to Governance: Studies in Overloaded Politics*, (Beverly Hills: Sage, 1980), Tony Cutcher, *Delivering Welfare: The Governance of the Social Services in the 1990s* (Buckingham: Open University Press, 1995), Norman Lewis, 'The Citizen's Charter and Next Steps: New Way of Governing? (*Political Quarterly*, 64, no. 3, July–Sept 1993) and A. Leftwich, 'Governance, the State and the Politics of Development' (*Development and Change*, 25, 1994).

Contributors

Vinod B. Annigeri is Project Officer, USAID-India, New Delhi.

Subhash C. Bhatnagar is Professor, Department of Information Technology, Indian Institute of Management, Ahmedabad.

Mohit Bhattacharya is former Vice Chancellor, University of Burdwan, West Bengal.

Saugata Bhattacharya is Vice President, Business and Economic Research, Axis Bank, Mumbai.

Sven Bislev is Associate Professor, Department of Intercultural Communication and Management, Copenhagen Business School, Denmark.

Gerald E. Caiden is Professor in Public Policy, University of Southern California, Los Angeles.

Bidyut Chakrabarty is Professor of Political Science, University of Delhi, Delhi.

H. George Fredrickson is Distinguished Professor of Public Administration, University of Kansas; President Emeritus of Eastern Washington University; and President of the American Society for Public Administration.

Hans Krause Hansen is Associate Professor, Department of Intercultural Communication and Management, Copenhagen Business School, Denmark.

Kuldeep Mathur is former Professor, Centre for the Study of Law and Governance, Jawaharlal Nehru University, New Delhi.

Urjit R. Patel is with Reliance Industries Limited, Mumbai.

SAMUEL PAUL is former Professor and Director, Indian Institute of Management, Ahmedabad.

LIZANN PROSSER is Project Officer, USAID-India, New Delhi.

JACK REYNOLDS is Project Officer, USAID-India, New Delhi.

RAGHU ROY is Project Officer, USAID-India, New Delhi.

DORTE SALSKOV-IVERSEN is Associate Professor, Department of Intercultural Communication and Management, Copenhagen Business School, Denmark.

Index